T0309947

The Second Spring of the Church in America

The Second Spring of the Church in America

George A. Kelly

Preface by Ralph McInerny

ST. AUGUSTINE'S PRESS
South Bend, Indiana
2001

1 2 3 4 5 6   07 06 05 04 03 02 01

Library of Congress Cataloging in Publication Data
Kelly, George Anthony, 1916–
    The second spring of the Church in America / George A. Kelly ;
    preface by Ralph McInerny.
      p. cm.
    Includes bibliographical references and index.
    ISBN 1-890318-79-5
    1. Catholic Church – United States. I. Title.
  BX1403.2 .K45 2000
  282'.73'09045 – dc21   00-010788

Contents

Preface

When the history of the post-conciliar Church in the United States is written, Monsignor George Kelly will loom large as one who kept a clear head while all around him something approaching madness seemed to reign. Kelly has been close to the center of ecclesiastical power as right-hand man to Cardinal Spellman. He has been pastor of a major Manhattan parish. He has been a university professor. He has served on Vatican commissions and been the confidant of high prelates. No one was better equipped to recognize where the battle for the American church would be fought. It would be in the academy. It would be in the ever-growing diocesan bureaucracies. It would be in the Catholic knowledge class.

Theological dissent went noisily public in 1968 in reaction to *Humanae Vitae* and captured the fancy of the secular media. Air time could always be found for a priest, wearing a Roman collar for the occasion, explaining to the camera how misguided the Holy Father was on this or that. Magisterial documents were graded – and degraded – to amused secular interviewers. Brash theologians set themselves up as rival authorities of the Pope and bishops. One fateful day a Vatican cardinal asked Monsignor Kelly whether there was anyone left in the United States who was receptive to Church teaching. Kelly's response was to found the Fellowship of Catholic Scholars, now approaching its silver anniversary.

The Fellowship would gather and amplify the voices of loyal Catholics and offer moral and intellectual support to the bishops. A fundamental premise of the Fellowship was that bishops seemed muted by dissent because they were unaware of the existence of large numbers of Catholic intellectuals who welcomed and defended the teachings of the Magisterium. That assumption has been sorely tested during the history of the Fellowship. Many bishops seemed edgier around orthodox Catholics than they did in the company of dissenters. It is interesting to speculate how different the past twenty-five years in this country would have been if the bishops in number had found Monsignor Kelly's courage contagious. There have been exceptions, of course. The Fellowship and its founder have had the support of many bishops who recognized that a war was under way for the soul of the Church in this country. But there were others who, like Nicodemus, sought Kelly out in the dead of night to state their support but were nowhere to be found when daylight came. And there was powerful opposition. But nothing could stop this tireless defender of the faith.

His landmark book, *The Battle for the American Church*, has been followed by a steady stream of books addressing the situation the Church confronts in this country today. The *Battle* gave a frank account of the bizarre interpretations given Vatican II's call for *aggiornamento*. Subsequent books have addressed specific areas where straight talk was needed, for example, biblical scholarship. Nor has he hesitated to give the bishops detailed advice as to what their duty is and the courses they might take in fulfilling it. In the present book, he provides a survey and suggestions for action. It is quintessential Kelly. And it can speak for itself.

I would speak for the hundreds of men and women, college and university professors, who have found in Monsignor Kelly the clear voice the times required. He has rallied the troops again and again and led them like a happy warrior against the foes of orthodoxy. Here was a man who through the years of his priesthood had never wavered from the demands of his vocation, he did not shirk from bringing to light what others chose to ignore, nor did he, through good times and bad, ever lose the ebullient confidence that all would come out right in the end. Well, things are brighter now than they were when Monsignor Kelly threw himself into the battle, and they are brighter in good part because of him. The ranks now swell with young men and women for whom the old battles predate their mature lives. They are conscious that battles have been won and that they are the beneficiaries, but their faces are turned to the future. These fresh young loyal Catholics represent Monsignor Kelly's best gift to the Church he has served so long and so well.

Ralph McInerny

Introduction

On June 30, 1988, John Paul II definitively reaffirmed what Catholics must believe and do to remain "in full communion with the Catholic Church," and he warned those who dissent from this "obedience of faith" (Rom. 1, 5) that they are subject to "just punishments" for either culpable denials of faith or disobedience to Church law. This action provides hope for a second spring of a vibrant Catholicity at some time in the twenty-first century. If this policy becomes the rule for every diocesan bishop, and for institutional leaders who claim the name "Catholic," the hope for a renewed Church promised by the Second Vatican Council may be realized. For thirty years the American Church, a paragon for Catholics throughout the world, has lived in purgatory, suffering with priests who know not how to obey and laity who live by the godless norms of secularist society. The Church's flowering will begin only when most Catholics – especially its priests and religious – keep their word to Christ and his Church (Jn. 8, 31).

That is the thesis of the present book, *The Second Spring of the Church in America*, will happen only when large segments of the clergy and laity reconvert to the teaching, norm, and laws of the Church's faith. Only the pope and the bishops in union with him are the guarantors of the faith that is still embodied in Catholics and their communities at every level. And hierarchy, above all, has been bound by Christ to see to it that Catholics "observe all those things that I have commanded you" (Mt. 27, 20). A quarter century ago Bishop Fulton J. Sheen was saddened by the loss of faith among young Catholics, "stolen from them," he said, in Catholic schools. Christ told his apostles that this can happen whenever the caretaker of the house is tied up and robbers loot the owner's property (Mt.

12, 29). Something like this has indeed happened, and John Paul II now says the thievery must stop.

Recovery can come about only after we make a proper assessment of the damage. The Church cannot have true faith without discipleship. "A house divided against itself cannot stand" (Mt. 12, 25). But this unity must be grounded in the faith as given, not on the favor of those who do not believe in it.

The American state is now well entrenched in its secularism. Its courts, its think tanks, and its media reinforce secularist tenets, even if this means rewriting the country's Protestant foundations and the Constitution itself. Judeo-Christians, if they remain professedly orthodox in their religious convictions, are quarantined from influence on public law, not unlike the socialists of an earlier era. A fully believing Catholic, Protestant, or Orthodox Jew in the White House is politically unthinkable, if he or she refuses to disavow the Ten Commandments or continues to insist that the family holds primacy in the body politic within the state.

Is the Catholic Church prepared to defend the integrity of Christ's mission against this *kulturkampf*?

Catholic bishops, following the lead of their academic elites, have gone a long way toward making the condition of the secular world their guide and being politically correct in their priorities and modes of operation. Ironically, in the process, the Catholic Church has lost a large amount of its political influence in this country. Many of her constituents have come to believe that the secularists are right and that many Church doctrines may not be God-given after all.

This much is true about the present state of Catholicity: Without her unique integrity properly argued for and defended in an unfriendly world, the Catholic Church becomes just another religious sect, no longer recognized even by Catholics as Christ's instrument for the redemption of mankind. The Church may continue to attract attention because of its dramatic presence and social utility, but it will have lost its credibility as the *vox Dei*.

"The battle" no longer can be categorized with any plausibility as a tug of war between conservative and liberal Catholics over styles and procedures of Church business. The question is much more critical, one asked by Christ at the end of his life when he confronted his Apostles: "Do you believe?" (Jn. 16, 21). John Paul II's question might be: "Are you a believing Catholic?"

Many bishops turn out to be less effective than their office demands.

Once such assessments were left to historians, but now when religious upheavals take place more often before television cameras than in archives, examination of how Church overseers handle the disturbance within their ranks cannot be left to chroniclers of the future. Today's faithful deserve ready answers, since it is their faith that is being weakened by the de-Catholicized learning centers and religious they come across at every turn. Many bishops search for roads out of the battlefield conditions under which they presently live, praying that revolutionaries seize no more "ecclesial" territory. But the better ones realize how high the cost has been to the Church for misjudging the intentions of "secularized" Catholic educators, including theologians and major superiors.

The Second Spring of the Church in America attempts to review in detail the various obstacles standing in the way of a real Catholic moment in the history of the United States, and to outline the road to recovery.

The Second Spring of the Church in America represents one priest's view – developed over half a century – of where the Catholic Church is, what is wrong with its present state, where it must go if its future is to equal its condition when this priest was born in 1916, and how it might fulfill the dreams of the aging John Paul II.

This book, however, is not mine alone. It owes a great deal to unnamed members of the Fellowship of Catholic Scholars, to the editors of magazines like *The Fellowship Quarterly, Catholic Dossier, Catholic World Report,* and *New Oxford Review,* where some of these ideas were first tried out. The devotion of William and Bernadette Kimmig, who for the better part of three years transcribed and word-processed the text, duplicated and edited it, transmitted it to appropriate readers, and followed every line to its ultimate resting place, is publicly acknowledged and received with profound gratitude.

George A. Kelly

ONE

The Catholic Crisis
Its Nature and Scope

If the Vatican were to hire me as a management consultant, the first question I would ask is whether there is consistency of rhetoric throughout the organization. The Roman Catholic Church is at heart a service organization, and service organizations' primary contact with its customers is through its first-line staff. If those staff are not reflecting the objectives and philosophy of the management, or if those objectives and philosophy aren't clear, I would expect to find a good deal of organizational pathology. Were I to construct an index on which lay parish staff, parish priests, bishops (in private and in public) professional theologians and the Vatican are talking at rhetorical cross-purposes, I suspect the results would be alarming.
Charles R. Morris, author of *American Catholic*

Crisis

Until recently, the Catholic Church in the United States was a model for its counterparts in Europe and the Third World. Today, however, it gives evidence of the same divisions and controversy that have, for several centuries, debilitated Christendom's ancient sees.Indeed, by all the quantitative measurements contemporary social scientists use to assay progress or depression, the American Church is in crisis. Her major vital statistics are down – Mass attendance, religious vocations, public influence, school attendance, Catholic fertility. Her signs of disarray are up – public scandals, broken marriages, leakage, financial problems, family breakdown, illegitimacy, intramural disputes, and so forth. The facts are indisputable.[1] The deeper questions have to do with the quality of pre-Vatican II Catholicity compared to that which has taken its place, and with the justification of the supposedly remedial strategies since adopted which have in fact debilitated the Church even more, particularly in the United States. Debilitated her to the point that some now doubt whether the Catholic Church can anymore maintain a claim to unique authority over God's word.

In some respects the Second Vatican Council has failed to reform or renew the Catholic Church according to plan. Many changes were properly designed, some long overdue because popes were talking of them well back in the nineteenth century. Others which arose, as if by spontaneous combustion, have led to a "runaway Church.[2] John XXIII, whose field of expertise was Catholic Europe, no doubt had hopes of invigorating the Continental Church, where nominal Catholics abounded. *Post-factum,* however, those Churches, with their glorious Cathedrals, are today worse off than before. One renowned French theologian, when asked in 1995 about regular Mass attendance in France, responded without hesitation: "Less than ten percent!" The Church of Holland, a model for Europe before World War II, has been substantially Protestantized. The Church of Belgium is said to be no better.

We do not speak here of the leakage that not uncommonly follows vast cultural change outside the Church. On the contrary, the 1960s were revolutionary within the Church. Leading Catholic opinion-molders, using Vatican II as the excuse, undertook to undermine the historical tradition – liturgical, doctrinal, moral – of the Church.

The one reliable means of testing the nature and extent of the crisis in the United States is, not by consulting elite writers, but at the parish level, and by evaluating the experience of faithful Catholics in the pews. Journalists and other professionals, in their estimate of Church well-being, often quote each other or rely on what they perceive to be optimistic numerical correlations and flow charts. Such elite structures rarely measure the spirituality and Catholic morale of those who have gone to Mass every Sunday all their lives. Footnoted reports are often intended to assure audiences, even during problematic and dangerous times, that "prosperity is always just around the corner," while the parochial roof falls in on ordinary people who least deserve more suffering. When the American bishops were called to Rome in 1962 for the Second Vatican Council, they hardly understood its purpose, since their Church was at the peak of her piety and development. Some of their successors, like the country's baby boomers, are too young to evaluate whether the revolution that has since occurred really helped or hurt Catholic religious life. Some might not even know that overnight revolutions usually do more harm than good, because those who are talented at tearing down old walls frequently prove inept at rebuilding the house.

During the crisis, the younger laity, and religious too, creatures of an intrusive secularist culture, never acquired a developed sense of Catholic community. If formative Catholic neighborhoods are hardly to be found anymore in large metropolitan areas, similarly scarce is the unified family-based parish as the source of internalized Catholic identity. During the present period, during which the Church seems to be muddling through a refashioning of its own priorities, young Catholics have come to associate religion with what they perceive to be the noblest aspirations of the secular American mores – free choice, autonomy, human rights, good works, brotherhood, fun, tolerance, and self-fulfillment. The chances are slim that they, unaided by a unified Church, have internalized a world view which accentuates the religious demands of a universal order of creation to which they are subject. In a divided Church, it is hard to see how they could recognize, with the surety of convinced faith, the Lordship of God the Father, and of Christ, absolute moral norms, or the destructive nature of human sinfulness and its peril to human unhappiness, here and hereafter. Elusive, too, might be their understanding of the redemptive significance of suffering and sacrifice with Christ as a model, and the place of merito-rious atonement in their lives. If they have any value at all, statistics indicate that the young do not consider regular worship and the worthy reception of the sacraments as prerequisites for identifying themselves as Catholic.

Veteran Catholics, on the other hand, when they sit around the fireplace with the priests and religious who trained them, always acknowledge that among their number are those who say they are happy to have been liberated by Vatican II from the constraints of the Catholic system. Most of the talkers, however, hardly remember having lived in a Catholic ghetto or under the oppression of bossy pastors or rigid nuns, nor do they remember needing liberation at all. Instead, they bemoan the fact that they now seem only to live under temporary pastors and no nuns. Reaching a priest at the rectory, even to administer the Last Rites, seems to many of them all but impossible, now that telephone answering services are everywhere. Some veterans laugh sheepishly about the Church law seriously demanding Mass on a Holy Day one year but not in the next; yet they take more seriously the lack of choice of confessors when they want absolution. Nor are they amused when a confessor sounds more like a psychic comforter than a moral guide, or tells them they may receive communion without confessing, when they know that some of what they have confessed are in fact mortal sins. They remember lazy priests, and an occasional friend of John Barleycorn, but a pederast?

An old hand in the priesthood can also attend a bishop's birthday party and find himself fascinated by the conversation at table with lay Catholics: There is no more Original Sin; babies need not be baptized; a Catholic can receive communion in a Protestant Church; a Methodist can take Catholic communion; you need not get an annulment it a priest thinks you are in a good faith relationship; the important thing is to be a good Christian, not necessarily to do all that the Church expects. Where did these Catholics acquire this new learning? Some priest or nun told them so. One pastor in attendance reported how his diocesan office of religious education instructed him that first graders were henceforth to be told that God is their Mother as well as their Father, and added that the diocese in its directive made no mention of Original Sin or of grace.

The same pastor fell upon a book called *Grace Under Pressure: What Gives Life to American Priests,*[3] an anthropological study of priestly opinion, which devotes serious space to the growing gap between hierarchy and parish clergy (with their laity). Fr. Eric from the South does not pay attention to Church controversies, the bigger social issues like racism and violence preoccupy him. Fr. Joe in the West resents having to "mouth the party line," "we are afraid to question," "bishops are afraid of the Vatican." Fr. Fred tells people Church teaching is not a judgment; training people to make their own consciences "and not be bothered by it" is. Fr. George from the East would be comfortable with women priests and a married clergy. Fr. Gary thinks the Church may look unsettled and dark but his "happiness and peace has to come from within." Fr. Don thinks that to have the Church is a good thing but to let go of the goofiness and the monkey business is a gift. According to the authors, all these priests are "effective" and "respected" by diocesan officials, including bishops. It is equally clear, however, that the focus of their complaints is their inability to solve personal or social problems because the Church gets in the way. From reading the commentary it is clear that faith in the Revealed Word of God or Christ is hardly the framework within which they think. Training Catholics, especially those with real or imaginary problems, to rise to the demands of the faith does not appear to enter their minds, content as they are to serve within but in spite of the Church.

Stranger, still, is their sense of superiority over conformists, a snobbery for which they cannot be blamed because this is how they were trained. For a certain kind of new priest the Church is "not a club of people who think alike or who are united in a common cause," but a *sacramentum mundi*.[4]

Old-timers shake their heads at the breakdown of Catholic discipline. They understand, better than most, that a Christian does not live by dogmas alone, nor by moral norms either. They realize from their family experience that unless action or example follow words, the household is in trouble. Ideas, good or bad, have a disciplinary effect on those who take ideas seriously. Shift the emphasis in religion from the worship of God to the celebration of peoples' worship of God, from Christ Son of God to Christ the Jewish reformer, from a Church instituted by Christ to one invented by his followers, from priests as Vicars of Christ to priests as representatives of the worshiping community, from sacraments as instruments of God's grace to meaningful symbols of religious bonding, from Real Presence in the Eucharist to search for the Real Presence, from God's Revealed Word as objectively given and binding to interpretative understandings of the ineffable, however contradictory, from a department of theology which studies God to a department of religious studies, which studies mankind's experience with notions of God, and you have eviscerated Christianity of its historic meaning. Applauding a priest at a Mass, as if he were an actor, may seem harmless, but it does make the Church less of a holy place.

In earlier days, the heresies of the Church moved in an entirely opposite direction – denying that Christ had a human body, affirming that flesh, of itself, was evil, or that Original Sin was lust, that life on earth was of no account, that death was better than life, that only very holy people could receive the Eucharist, that trusting faith needed no reason, that suffering in itself was good, that freedom was a vice, and so forth.

Aggiornamento was supposed to remedy the vocal discontent of the "knowledge class," who by the 1950s resented the power bishops exercised in the Church. Since they lived with an anti-Church-authority fixation, they assumed that change, any change, equaled betterment and became angry when they discovered that the Church is not going their way. Their mistake was underestimating or downgrading the very authority that explains her durability. They rationalized their dissatisfaction as a reaction to the authoritarianism of the pre-Vatican II Church, but this argument was overworked. Catholics experienced ample freedom in the American Church, more likely to complain about how slow bishops were in taking papal advice on liturgy, inter-credal cooperation, and socioeconomic reform, than about their oppressiveness. Pius XII, however, recognized the budding signs of serious doctrinal dissent when he chastised the Jesuits for some of it the year before he died.[5] As later events demonstrated, they turned out to be "the underground" apprenticeship for the leaders of what John Paul it now calls counter-magisterium.[6] What these theoreticians began to do privately eventually spread (as discontent and skepticism) to parish levels via journals, seminars and cloisters. The rebellious spirit fell upon superiors, as well as bishops, like a tidal wave from the outside world.

The Church Bishops Made

Let us scan momentarily the Church of fifty years ago which Catholic university professors wanted to change.

Little did I know at my priestly ordination in 1942 that I was entering one of the most impressive periods in the history of the Church of the United States, or anywhere. Three quarters of the married Catholics made their Easter Duty and attended Mass every Sunday. These couples had larger families than non-Catholics. The better educated were the practicing Catholics, and also had larger families than the less educated. More than 85 percent of single Catholics attended Sunday Mass. The Catholic population was to double from 20 million in 1940 to 40 million by the opening of the Second Vatican Council, mostly practicing Catholics, priests doubling from 25,000 to 50,000, religious tripling from 50,000 to 150,000, and a Catholic school enrollment that grew to 5 million and more. This system was already turning out upwardly mobile Americans and practicing Catholics in record numbers. Up until the Council, the most stable and fruitful Catholic families, the most religiously observant, the most zealous lay apostles in the Church, were the graduates of Catholic colleges. Revisionists speak today about how the Church was too institutional, insufficiently charismatic, and had failed to penetrate the American culture.

These complaints to the contrary, the piety of the faithful then, and their "sensus fidei," cannot be gainsaid, and in those respects it would have been difficult to find the equal of the American Church anywhere.

As for educational upgrading, Fordham professor Fr. George Bull, S.J., writing just six years before Vatican II, attributed the success of our American Catholic college system to the Church's ability to improve the intelligence level of its faithful in all fields of secular knowledge and to send forth into secular society young men and women well-informed about the Catholic creeds and worship. Fr. Bull took for granted the educational excellence of the Fordhams of the United States, but was not shy to add: "If the Catholic college in this country has neglected even partially either of its two functions, it has not neglected the first. It has, thank God, sent forth from its halls generations of men and women who know the Catholic faith.[7]

The "Catholic moment" might also have arrived in America had the American Church retained its clear convictions and clerical discipline, for by World War II she was not only a way of life, but a way of thinking.

The Church's Secularist World

Lord Acton it was who said: "Ideas move history," and it is secularist ideas and the secular state which are driving Catholicity toward credal bankruptcy.

Every Catholic historian worth his doctorate, and his faith, takes for granted that a built-in rivalry exists between Christ's Church and the world of secular states.[8] From their study of church-state relations beginning with Emperor Constantine through that of King Louis XIV to President John F. Kennedy, this has been obvious. Secular thinkers, observing how absolute monarchs and strong popes invaded each others' domains century after century, invented the "neutral state" as a blessed relief from the religious wars of yesteryear. Catholics, too, look upon the American experiment as laudable, with benefits to both religion and to civility. However, practice has not always followed theory. Why should any state be neutral to a Church which is never neutral to her? Catholics survived well in Protestant America because the Founding Fathers allowed Catholic bishops maneuvering room. Nineteenth-century divines may not have liked Catholic immigrants, and the upper-class American Catholics were often embarrassed by the behavior of their new co-religionists.

Yet Catholic bishops were free to establish schools and agencies which, although Catholic in purpose and identity, were American in sentiment and enthusiasm, free to manage these infrastructures without interference. Furthermore, the mores of the nation, especially as they pertained to family life, character formation for citizenship, and restraint of social deviance, were based on the Ten Commandments of God, which were Jewish before they were Christian.

This is past history. Protestant culture is no more. The benign welfare state, conceived with Christian inspiration, has grown up to be secularist.

Not secular in the adjectival sense, viz., "worldly" or "of the times." (The Church sympathizes with that.) But secularists, who reject religion "from on high," even the Protestantism of the Founding Fathers. Their "age of man" believes only in the evolutionary betterment of the human condition, without help "from above." They search for wisdom by analyzing human experience scientifically, not by listening to prophets, rabbis, or popes.

Although profit obviously comes to humankind from such studies, it was Christ who reminded his contemporaries: "One does not live by bread alone but by every word that comes from the mouth of God." (Mt. 4, 4).

The secular state remains the Church's chief tempter today. Entanglement with Deity, as represented by orthodox Judeo-Christianity, is now inimical to the state's secularist pursuits. Furthermore, its partisans are determined not to encourage, support, or underwrite any such contentious rival to their secular hegemony over the American mind.

Secular humanism, as a cultural norm, became dominant in 1947 when the Supreme Court used extreme rhetoric in the Everson case to reinterpret the U.S. Constitution as demanding a high wall of separation between government and religion "from on high." By 1961, however, the Supreme Court took one politically correct step further with the declaration (*Torcaso v. Watkins*) that secular humanism was a real religion, constitutionally on a civic par with Judaism and Christianity, and protected by the First Amendment. (Several Humanist Manifestoes[9] have publicly rejected notions of God, of Christ as Son of God, the baptism of infants, the confirmation of the young, and any Christian indoctrination aimed at children.) The country's Protestant forefathers might be surprised to discover, were they alive, that their grand experiment with a neutral state, which favored Protestantism, would two centuries later be an American government legally entangled only with secular humanism. The first American Catholic intellectual, a convert, perceptively understood, as early as 1844, that if democracy was to work it needed "a religion which is above the people." His fear, then, was that, despite the promise of democracy, a secular aristocracy of one kind or another would rise in America, which would arrogate to itself "the voice of God." Orestes Brownson foresaw, too, that the inevitable consequence of a populist Protestantism was secularism.[10] Constitutional lawyer William Bentley Ball calls the recent jurisprudence of the modern Supreme Court as "No popery in new garb.[11]

Secularism grew even more troublesome to orthodox Judeo-Christianity once its disciples gained a foothold within the households of transcendental faith. They called themselves "reformers" and turned the amelioration of the human condition itself into a religious faith. It was no small step for them to substitute the worship of good works on mankind's behalf for the worship of God and his holiness. Nor was it surprising that secularist Christians became addicted to the welfare state and to government uplift programs, even when these proved to be inimical to family life and to religion "from on high." Such a secular state becomes selective about the human rights it will protect. Not necessarily the unborn, nor nonpublic school children, nor the dying, certainly not the rights of the Church. The secular state also denies any church's right to set parameters for the behavior of its public officials, while claiming its own right to regulate the external conduct of any Church which defines itself as "above the people.[12]

At the turn of the twentieth century, Pius X called this ideology "Modernism," a school of thought which considered Christianity to be merely another human religious enterprise. Christianity may claim to be the credible witness of Christ (Mt. 5, 21–22; Jn. 5, 36–37), whose testimony is validated throughout history by the authentic witness of the Apostles and their successors. Modern historians, however, allege that such judgments are unscientific. Furthermore, they aver, the creeds formulated by early Church Fathers are neither divinely inspired, nor timeless, nor irrevocable, merely a body of non-quantitative verbalizations about people's secular experience.

Lest this identification of contemporary secularization with turn-of-the-century Modernism be seen as a flight of unsubstantiated fancy, permit me to single out one area of human experience about which the Church traditionally and secularized Catholics today have had a great deal to say, viz., sexuality. Dr. John Marshall, a British member of the Papal Birth Control Commission, reasserted his opinion of the Church's teaching on contraception in 1996, more than a quarter century after *Humanae Vitae.* Notice the direction of his argument: "Scripture and tradition do not provide knowledge of the nature of sexual intercourse, its biological function, which can only come from living experience and scientific study.[13]

Reword that sentence to substitute for "sexuality" other words like racism, atomic warfare, sweatshops, experimentation on human fetuses, "lusting in the heart" and sundry conduct that has long been declared immoral by informed and enlightened Christians. Then ask: Where does Dr. Marshall's analysis leave the Ten Commandments?

Shortly after the Second Vatican Council, Professor Bernard G. Reardon summarized the present plight of the Catholic Church vis-à-vis Modernism:

> Catholicism, thanks to the modern media of communication, is exposed to world opinion as never before. Argument and protest will not be silenced by imperious gestures, and heresy is no longer a word to scare away any but the most timid. Nor can the non-Catholic Christian stand aside from the anguished discussion, for the crisis of Catholicism is the crisis of Christianity itself. And whatever its outcome will be cannot be foretold. But, "we may be sure" – to quote [George] Tyrell's words – that "religion, the deepest and most universal exigency of human nature, will survive." We cannot be so sure that any particular expression of the religious idea will survive.[14]

He was anticipated in this judgment by Alfred Loisy, the most prominent Modernist of the twentieth century, after his excommunication in 1907 by Pius X. "The Catholicism of the pope being neither reformable nor acceptable, another Catholicism will have to come into being, a humane Catholicism, in no way conditioned by the pontifical institution or the traditional forms of Roman Catholicism.[15]

Much of what was called Modernism then is now known as Secularism. It involves a rejection of what Christ claimed to be, and the truth also of the Church which bears his name. In the Modernist or Secularist world, Christian creeds are man-made concoctions and no moral absolutes exist. Men create their own historically conditioned postulates for human happiness, and these are true only to the extent that they are useful to those who control the Secular City.[16] Here is the nub of the present crisis in Christianity.

Jesus Christ Is the Problem

Priest Martin Luther in the sixteenth century divided Christianity by denying the Church's claim to be the voice of Christ; priest Alfred Loisy in the nineteenth century eviscerated Christianity of all "divine" content by denying Christ's claim to be the Son of God.

The transition from pious Protestantism to a world-centered Christianity was slow in coming. Evangelical Lutheran pastors in the Germany of Otto von Bismarck (d. 1898), an anti-papalist, proved to be helpless against him when their own university professors, under his domination, reinterpreted Lutheran beliefs in a Modernist mode: The faithful could keep their religious identity without the necessity of accepting their church doctrines as true; God and Christ could remain as expressions of their yearnings for the transcendental; and pastors would become the certifiers of the new scientific Christian belief. The notion that "a revealed Word of God" ever existed died with this discovery.

Pius IX (1846–1878) began the Catholic counterattack with his *Syllabus of Errors*. The more diplomatic Leo XI (1878–1903) countered the growing tendency in theology towards similar theological relativism with the revival of Thomistic Theology. His *Aeterni Patris* (1879) had the effect he intended for a time, especially on the training of priests. But as Secularism and Modernism moved through elite Catholic circles, even in Italy, it fell to Pius X (1903–1914) to take steps every good government takes against revolution within its own structures. His *Pascendi Dominici Gregis* (1907), described by Josephine Ward as "reading the riot act" to the Catholic historicists for the mischief they were causing "in her very bosom," deplored their activity because they assailed "the most sacred work of Christ . . . whom with sacrilegious audacity they degrade to the condition of a simple and ordinary man." Developing enough rhetorical steam to blow them to kingdom come, the saintly Pontiff accused Modernists of piously bowing their head in the face of the Church's reproof "only to lift it more arrogantly than before." According to Pius X, "The security of the Catholic name is at stake." To bring orderly discipline to his worldwide Church, this pope initiated the first *Code of Canon Law* in Christian history, although its promulgation was deferred until the close of the First World War. By then Giusseppe Sarto (Pius X) was four years dead.

The nature and scope of the controversy that plagues the Catholic Church a century later causes one to attend to the content of Pius X's forgotten *Lamentabili*. The Holy See recapitulated there the theories about the origins of Christianity, which, in more sophisticated form, continue to make their way through the Catholic system of John Paul II.

The Bible is mythological; exegetes are its best readers. Catholic faith in our time has little, if anything, to do with Christ. He was a man of history, no doubt, but the message the Church teaches is not. The Church cannot determine the genuine sense of the Scriptures, nor can it demand internal assent to its judgments because God is not really their author.

Gospels like John are pure meditations, not a record of historical fact. Revelation, whatever else it is, grows out of evolving human consciousness, and continued to grow after the death of the Apostles. Biblical studies tell us that Jesus saw himself as a Messiah of the Jews – a Son of God only in that sense.

The Church's Councils distorted Jesus' idea of himself.

He did not even or always understand himself as a Messiah. His Resurrection is not a historical fact. Paul, not Christ, created the idea that his death had an expiatory quality. The Sacraments are creations of the Church, rites of identity with a certain symbolic meaning, not effective instruments of holiness. Penance, as we know it, did not exist in the early Church. The Eucharist and the Priesthood merely emerged from the early gatherings, not from an Apostolic Commission. Even the idea of a Church "for the ages" was not on Christ's mind. It is merely one more human society. Peter did not have the least idea that he was a Primate, or that the Roman Church, by Divine Law, was the head of all Churches. Nor did Christ teach a body of doctrine, certainly not the propositions of the Apostles' Creed as Catholics understand them. Modern Catholicity can be reconciled with Modernity, therefore, only if it gives up its dogmas.

The Church has never been without its heresies. Modernism is merely a more empirical Gnosticism, the offspring, too, of Protestantism with its stress on private interpretation. To escape the stigma of heresy – which is usually a distortion of truth, rather than an outright denial – later dissenters claim only to "nuance" the content of the Catholic faith. However, "nuance" when pursued vigorously enough within Catholic structures leads to weakened faith or disbelief, as surely as bold-faced heresy.

Modernists were very artful in their evasions of confrontation with Church authority. The major difficulty often was not what they said but how Church authority evaluated their threat to faith, and how pope and/or bishops reacted to the danger, once they recognized it as such. Historically, hierarchy has responded to heresy and schism rather slowly, charges of authoritarianism to the contrary notwithstanding.

Reappearance a Century Later

Revolution in Catholic belief and practice was not in the minds of American bishops on their way home from the Second Vatican Council in December 1965. By and large, the Catholic college campuses, the mother houses of religious communities, and the chancery offices were about their Father's business faithfully. And pride in the Church was evident in all three places.

Then, unexpectedly, parents of children in Catholic schools and catechism classes began to raise voices of concern about their children's religious education. Early in 1966, for example, Cardinal Spellman's Office of Education began to hear complaints about what "the nuns" were teaching, not the least of which was the advisory to pupils that they need not go to Sunday Mass "if they got nothing out of it." One Italian mother was bold enough to tell the School Principal at a public meeting, called to reorient parents to the "New Catechetics": "It's all right if you sisters tell my kids that God doesn't get mad if they miss Sunday Mass; but if my kids don't go to Mass, I'll break their necks!"

The Charles Curran debacle was still a year away (1967), and so was the declaration of independence from bishops by Land o' Lakes colleges. But once parents' anxiety surfaced over the effect of the "new catechetics" on their children's lives, the first post-Vatican II "battle" among Catholics was underway. One expert explained the tension as "a struggle between those who want to think in today's terms and those who understand loyalty as clinging to traditional ways." The issues in contest would prove to be more serious than that. No one in high Church office at the time saw in this squabble a threat to Catholic well-being, When Lyman Stebbins came to Cardinal Cooke, after Spellman's death, to announce the creation of Catholics United for the Faith, largely made up of school parents, he received a friendly ear but no official encouragement beyond the recommendation that dialogue with the school principal might alleviate their concerns about the disturbing catechesis going on.

During this immediate post-Vatican II period, authority figures had no empirical reason to believe that the "oneness" of the Church's faith was already under siege or that "division" in Catholic education would become the instrument for fashioning a redefined and watered-down Catholicity. In hindsight, the heavy resistance during the Council to a "Catechism of Vatican II" (in the mode of the Roman Catechism of Trent) was an inkling, but at the time no one gave that omission a second thought. A universal catechism would be promulgated in 1992 by John Paul II, and American bishops now are using its text to correct the faulty teaching in religion books currently used in their school systems. But, in 1962, treason to the faith by priests or religious was never seen as a possibility.

Indeed, harmony of thought and discipline in Catholic religious life, in Catholic catechetics and in the most successful system of Catholic education ever devised in the history of Christianity, was the identifying mark of that American Church. Religious teachers taught what they learned in their communities or in colleges owned by religious orders. The supervising role of the pope, bishop, and pastor was respected. In given situations differences of opinions about priorities, clashes of personalities, or political infighting did occur. Still, Church law and the directives of hierarchy prevailed. Rugged individualists might go their own way, even into apostasy, and selected priests or religious were frequently unhappy with their lot. But the unity of the American Church was firm, praised by Pius X, Pius XI, and Pius XII.

Unity prevailed, not exclusively around an abstraction called "Catholic truth," but around a pastor, after the fashion of the solidarity felt by the Apostles around Christ on the Mount of Ascension. In 1941 when Archbishop Spellman opened his first high school, named after his predecessor Cardinal Hayes, he assembled a teaching faculty of ninety – forty-five priests and forty-five Christian Brothers – who turned out extraordinarily pious Catholic young men. It was unthinkable then that Catholic education could exist autonomously of pope or bishop.

Then in 1967 this harmony came to a violent end with three major explosions within the teaching/governance lifelines of the Church: in April, when the faculty of the Catholic University of America in so many words told the hierarchy that bishops could no longer "fire" a professor; in July, when twenty-six Catholic college officials (mostly Jesuit) met at Land o' Lakes, Wisconsin, to tell bishops that henceforth they would conduct their institutions without interference from hierarchy; and in October, when the main teaching religious for Los Angeles Archdiocese – the Immaculate Heart of Mary Community – became (for the secular press) "the nuns who turned their back on the pope." The torch of IHM's rebellion against Church authority was passed to mother houses all across the country, fanned in part by the new president of the National Conference of Catholic Bishops, Archbishop John Dearden, working at cross-purposes against McIntyre, at times against the Holy See.

During those heady days of "renewal," little of Catholic faith was explicitly denied, but new ways of understanding the faith were being explored, so parents heard. "Salvation history," for example, became a popular instruction device, with its stress on God's love for mankind manifested over time in human events. Catholicity was to be understood and lived, not out of learned abstract formulas and rules, but through worshipping together meaningfully, and working with each other in concert to improve the human condition of their fellows. The handbook of Christianity was Scripture, not the catechism, certainly not Church law.

Children, and everyone else, should be taught to experience gospel meaning personally, and so believe intensely. They should recognize good and evil when they saw them in the concrete, not from a book. During the 1970s Brother Gabriel Moran popularized the "continuing revelation theory": God continues to reveal himself everywhere every day; search for him. There are no absolute answers to life's problems, no "deposit of faith," either from Jerusalem or Rome, to be handed down, or binding on everyone at all times.

"Indoctrination" in catechism was looked upon as bad education. "Seek and You shall find" was the objective of learning. Authority and tradition of the Church were guideposts, nothing more. Obedience, especially of the mind, was enslavement.

One of the silent shifts in catechesis was hardly noticed, viz the movement away from "the Word of God" to the concerns of men. "Sin," especially original sin, became an unmentionable, even though the central belief of Christianity was that God became man in Jesus Christ to redeem his sinful people. Fasting and abstinence as exercises in spiritual discipline or as penance for sin disappeared overnight.. The sacrament of Penance was wiped out. Making it into heaven or not took second place to making it here on earth.

Suddenly, the entire drama of post-Vatican II experimentation with Catholicity began to unfold. Religious communities, men as well as women, underwent re-education by university professors, who tilted their thinking toward change and freedom in the Church and away from what was handed down or from obligation. The IHMs of Los Angeles, for example, engaged in sensitivity training for its nuns before, during, and after the Council, which revolutionized their thinking about the Church and her creeds, about religious life and catechesis. One of those instructors, psychologist William Coulson, a Notre Dame graduate, recently reviewed the effect of his work on the IHMs: "When we freed them from Catholic doctrine, Catholic religion, there were no more certitudes available to them, and it allowed their impulses to bubble to the surface."

Looking back over those years, why should anyone be surprised at the negative effects of such "re-formation" on the teaching of the young. While hierarchy was arguing about convent life, Catholic children were being infected with a new but unhealthy attitude toward Church authority and its teaching. The critical issue was not religious habits, but the religious attitudes of vowed religious. Parents, the first to notice the changes in their children, were discredited as authentic teachers of the faith, but so were the popes and their curial officials.

If ever the much-abused domino theory acquired relevance in Church events, the Catholic deconstruction after 1965 is proof of it. At first the revolution seemed to be over management procedures, but in time the very truth of Catholic claims became the victim. This is evident in the cool reception given today by reformers to John Paul II's *Catechism of the Catholic Church,* accusing it of ignoring Vatican II, or at best of being only one view of the Church's faith. The facts, however, must be faced now as they were not thirty years ago. What do the words "Catholic faith" mean? One of the founding fathers of the post-Vatican II Church's new catechetics, Gabriel Moran, from his current teaching post at New York University, tells how the situation really is: "[Revelation] consisting of truths beyond human experience but directly made known by God has proved indefensible. 'Revealed truth' (or an even stranger phrase 'revealed religion') was relentlessly squeezed out of the picture by science. Hence the nearly total silence about revelation in liberal Christian and Jewish discussions."[17]

In simple truth, the die of organized disbelief within American Catholic ranks has been cast before bishops, and denial remains the order of the day. When a relatively young bishop rises at the Synod for America to tell his peers that Catholics, especially the young, now think that they are the final judges of faith and morals, it is an admission that, in a serious way, the bishops have lost their eminent catechetical influence. The vaunted Catholic school system has been cut in half by the flight of religious as "mothers" of the classroom, and what remains is becoming too expensive for the Church's emerging middle-class constituency. In a formidable work, *American Catholic* (1997), Charles Morris predicts that for all practical purposes by the year 2012, "there will be no working nuns." Even the Leadership Conference of Women Religious still denies that "sisters are in crisis," or that the Church is for that matter. Yet if teachers do not believe as the Church believes, then the faith of the otherwise faithful is surely in peril.

This is the crisis.

T W O

The Catholic Bishop
Vicar of Christ or No?

Where the bishop appears
There let the people be,
Just as where Jesus Christ is,
There is the Catholic Church.
St. Ignatius of Antioch (d. 107)

The revival of the Church as a potent force in the lives of the baptized depends especially on bishops re-establishing credibility among their own and, like Christ, refashioning unity among their disciples, especially those who appear to choose to walk no more in their company.

In our time, the second episcopal predicament is the large number of Catholics who no longer believe that their bishop is a vicar of Christ or Christ's voice to the faithful. The first is, of course, the doubt whether Christ himself is the "vox Dei," or whether he intended a Church at all, especially one with "successors to the Apostles."

No one in his right mind holds that every episcopal utterance has supernatural significance. In the course of everyone's life span, many silly or disordered things are said or done by prelates, sins included. One does not need a doctrinal degree to know how often throughout history this or that bishop has been unworthy of his trust. And only an irresponsible theologian would insist that every word that came from the mouth of Christ had equal value, or that all of his directions bound his disciples in the same way. At the Last Supper, he washed feet and instituted the Eucharist, one a pious act, the other a sacrament.

From the earliest days debates over what Christ really meant or commanded – and whether the religion he symbolizes has modern relevance – have been deep, heated, and seemingly everlasting. Out of the acrimony has come development in understanding what Christ is all about and why God became man. From the days of Eden, God's march through history has been perilous, and his creatures' actual sins replaced original sin as interference with God gaining his way with creatures whom he made free.

Still, within the Catholic framework, God became man in Christ to save his creatures from their sins, who founded a Church that is his alone, and who till the end of time is represented by a bishop led by a pope. What is the reason for the Church's existence? To embody the ever-living Christ and to reconcile mankind to God's directed way of human life. The fact that the Catholic Church has endured so long is due to Christ's continued presence through the pope and bishops, their oft-reported failures and sinfulness to the contrary notwithstanding. St. Ignatius of Antioch, the bishop who gave the Catholic Church its name, and who was the first major post-apostolic witness to the pope's primacy had it right: "The Roman Church is the head."

Icons or Idols?

The harm done to the bishops' status since Vatican II is not the result of anything a heavyweight scholar has published, but from the cynicism, skepticism, and impudence of lecturers at the parish or classroom level, often before an audience ill-equipped to deal with the content, let alone the sarcasm. Some of these "funny men," are hard to indict for wrongdoing because what they say is offhanded and unprinted. Calling a bishop an "idiot" or describing the hierarchy as "semiliterate incompetents" may be laugh-worthy, but it is also disrespectful. The mockery of Voltaire, not his learning, brought down the Church of France.

Still, scholars can do a lot of damage, if they are also iconoclasts or covert unbelievers. A Jesuit priest once took umbrage at the use of the title "vicar of Christ" to describe the pope because some of them, like Innocent VIII (1484–1492) or Alexander VI (1492–1603), were public sinners. He might have cited the fact, too, that only 77 of the 262 popes on official lists are canonized saints, two since the fourteenth century. (Pius V [the Tridentine pope] in 1712 and Pius X [the bane of twentieth-century Modernism] in 1954.)

The Jesuit gentleman had more serious problems, however, than his dislike of nomenclature. He disliked authority figures personally. He thought that popes were a development of history more than they were a specific creation of Christ. Such a view, of course, is Protestant, not Catholic, and it nullifies Catholicity of its credentials, although the priest in question remained in good standing all his life, however unhappily.

Until recently, the sacredness of the office impelled the Catholic faithful to treat their bishops as sacred persons. Not all pastors were worthy, and some replayed the Judas role. But many were endowed with greatness and were venerated during their lifetime, with the respect and awe due to vicars of Christ.

A number of these come to mind. On July 13, 1863, Archbishop John Hughes appeared on the balcony of his home on Madison Avenue to address New Yorkers. The Civil War Riots were in process, 1,000 of his fellow citizens had already been killed, and the Governor of New York, in desperation, called on him, "Do something!" Hughes was dying, but sent out the word to his congregation: "Pay me a visit." The following day 5,000 of his fellow citizens came, and Hughes, almost too weak to stand, leaned on his balustrade and talked for more than an hour, as it turned out for the last time. A biographer summarized the event: "Hughes went inside. The crowd cheered until, at length, he came out again. Someone asked for his blessing. He gave it. The entire gathering made the sign of the cross in unison. He told them to go to their homes. Like school children, they obediently answered, 'We will,' and began to disperse." A few months later he died. The New York Herald took note of the respect paid to the archbishop which has never been recorded to any other ecclesiastic in the country since the Declaration of Independence.[1]

Thirty years later on a rainy day in London (1893), Henry Edward Cardinal Manning descended from his carriage on his way into a Westminster Church. Gilbert Keith Chesterton, thirty years away from being a Catholic, was a witness, startled to see ordinary folk go down to kneel on wet cobblestones to pay their homage.

In 1953, the year Joseph Stalin died, Stefan Cardinal Wyszynski was "deposed" as archbishop of Warsaw by the Russian masters of Poland, because he stood tall against their Communist domination of his Catholic people. His gift to Poland was the solidarity of a nation; his gift to the Church is his protégé Karol Wojtyla, to be known throughout history as John Paul II. His funeral in 1981 was an outpouring of national love. James Cardinal Gibbons, primate of the American hierarchy for almost half a century, author of the famous apologetic *Faith of Our Fathers*, organizer of the 1884 Baltimore Council which brought discipline to priests and a catechism for the laity, maintained the respect of his fellow bishops until the day he died (1921), including that of those who disagreed with him on ecclesial policies. An English prelate once said of this maker of bishops: "He reigned in Baltimore like a King, but he met every man like a comrade."

Why were these bishops paid such homage? They generated a "do not touch me" image, the kind Christ conveyed to Mary Magdalen (Jn. 20, 17), personifying "sacredness," as befitting their episcopal office. If they became icons within the Church or outside, it was because they stood apart, above the crowds, and in some respect were godlike. They were uncommon men and were treated with special respect because they uniquely represented Christ himself.

One of the unintended Catholic fallouts of Vatican II – one which Pius XII anticipated at the end of his life – was the de-emphasis of the sacred within the Catholic community, especially of Church authority. These put-downs are not found in the Church's official documents, to be sure, but at lower levels of preaching and catechesis. The Second Vatican Council was hardly over when Dietrich von Hildebrand reported an almost unbelievable account of a 1949 conversation with Teilhard de Chardin at Fordham University. The German philosopher, taken back by the French scientist's "crass naturalism," brought up St. Augustine, as if in rebuttal. To which Chardin replied: "Don't mention that unfortunate man; he spoiled everything by introducing the supernatural!"[2] John Cardinal O'Connor, in the foreward to the re-edition of Hildebrand's 1967 book, deems the author's equation of secularization with the loss of sensus supernaturalis to be correct. Disrespect of other Christs is the natural outcome of secularization.

The Doubting Thomases

The jibes of malevolent pranksters were one element in the debasement of the episcopacy. The uncritical interpolation into Catholic think-tanks of non-Catholic theories about Christianity and its creed depreciated the bishop's role within the Church, while aggrandizing the role of research scholars over bishops in determining who Christ was, what he said or meant, or how binding were his words on the human race. Vatican II might proclaim that the Christian sources of faith – scripture, tradition, and the Church's teaching office – any one of them – cannot stand without the others,[3] but Catholic book-men divided those same fonts of Church faith and proposed views which were condemned more than once by Pius IX, X, XI, and XII. Since most bishops were not professional theologians, the hierarchy's response was at best timid, certainly uncritical.

No field of religious study was more theoretical and more ominous to the Catholic faith than biblical exegesis. We listed some of its principal aberrations in the previous chapter. *The Catholic Theological Society and the Canon Law Society* also broadened their criticism of the Church: the institutional Church with someone in charge was hardly the ideal form of a Christian community; pope and bishops stand not at the top but in the middle of their people, sharing experiences and working out Christian solutions together; there is at least a second teaching office in the Church, beside that of hierarchy; not all the articles of the creed are equally true; all moral judgments are relative, including the indissolubility of a valid consummated sacramental marriage; and so forth.

The reader must realize that historicist studies of the Church's claims usually begin with an investigation of their alleged biblical base. But the Church was at least three decades old, into Greece, North Africa, the Mediterranean Islands and into Rome, by the time St. Paul's writings began to appear – prior to the Gospels.

Peter's and Paul's execution by the Romans (ca. 64–65) signaled how Christianity's expansion had already fascinated, or repelled, the imperial elites. By then, growing numbers of New Testament books were becoming what they still are, the "baby records" of a Church already on the move. They might be inchoative, but they do represent authentically, if incompletely, the Church-in-being, as much as a naked baby on a bear rug of yesteryear images the bulging 6' 4" hulk of a lad presently quarterbacking the San Francisco '49ers. If his mother was around we might know about the athlete's boyhood. However, Mother Church is still around to deal with speculative research about her beginnings. Without the living witness of Mother Church, those "baby records" are susceptible to all kinds of guesswork. Especially from those, like Herod, who did not, or others today who do not, want the baby to continue growing up in the image of the Christ who still lives.

It is not possible, at least for Catholics, to do a scientific study of the Church's baby records without referring to the Church Fathers or the magisterium as their judges. In any case, a pure science of early Christianity does not exist. Every detached inquirer works out of his personal philosophy. Even when he makes what he calls a breakthrough, his mind has as his evidence what he sees – or wants to see. If he is a crass evolutionist, for example, he will presume that the Church, like the universe, was uncertainly born and has been mechanistically determined ever since.

Catholic theologians have become circumspect since 1907 in their use of the study techniques associated with excommunicated exegetes like Alfred Firmin Loisy. They do not challenge dogmas directly as having no base in primitive Christianity, although a book did appear in 1975 entitled *The Case against Dogma.*[4] Progressive Catholics now simply opine that the structures and doctrines of the Church, alleged to derive from Christ, really developed "under the guidance of the Holy Spirit." They assure audiences that the old formulas may remain in vogue, if suitably "nuanced." Traditional moral norms may continue as ideals, but are not obligatory under trying circumstances.

What has all this to do with what Jesus Christ said about bishops? A great deal. Many modern Catholics have been reeducated to examine fundamental truths of their faith in terms more compatible with unprovable theories of academics, than with the firm teaching of magisterium. The Christian mind, unless it clears itself of the clutter with which soft-scientists confound it, will never appreciate how important bishops in union with the pope are to the preservation of Christ's Gospel. Considering the damage already done, it is not going to be easy for bishops to regain their doctrinal credibility with badly catechized Catholics, including priests.

The Catholic Tradition

Catholic tradition has been contradicting critics of the hierarchical Church from the very beginning. The third bishop of Rome, Clement I, writing to Corinthians (96 AD) and Ignatius, the third bishop of Antioch (before 107 AD) writing to the Churches of Asia Minor, testify to the existence and authority of bishops in the infant Church. The first great schism in Christianity – between East and West almost a thousand years later – did not in any way deny either priesthood or episcopacy, only Peter's (and popes') universal jurisdiction. Not until the middle of the Second Christian Millennium, did Protestant Reformers reject, for the first time, both priesthood and apostolic succession as creations of Christ. The Council of Trent (1545–1563), in three canons, anathematized (1) those who denied that a visible priesthood existed in the New Testament, (2) those who denied that the priesthood was instituted by Christ, and (3) those who denied that the hierarchy came about by any force but divine ordinance. The First Vatican Council (1871) reaffirmed the same doctrine.

The Second Vatican Council (1964, *Lumen Gentium*, No. 18) clearly taught that "Jesus Christ, the eternal pastor, set up the Holy Church by entrusting the Apostles with their mission as he himself had been sent by the Father (Jn. 20, 21). He willed that their successors, the bishops namely, should be shepherds of the Church until the end of time."

The Council's Dogmatic Constitution called "The Word of God" (*Dei Verbum*) specifies this birthright as follows:

1. "In order that the full and living gospel might always be preserved in the Church, the Apostles left bishops as their successors. They gave them their own position of authority . . . until such time as she [the Church] is brought to see him face to face as he really is. (Cf. Jn. 3, 2)." (No. 7)

2. "The task of giving an authentic interpretation of the Word of God, whether in its written form [Scripture] or in the form of tradition, has been entrusted to the living teaching office of the Church alone." (No. 10)

3. "We must acknowledge that the books of Scripture, firmly, faithfully and without error, teach the truth which God, for the sake of our salvation, wished to see confided to the Sacred Scriptures. Thus all Scripture is inspired of God, and profitable for teaching, for reproof, for correction and for training in righteousness, so that the Law of God may be complete, equipped for every good work." (2 Tim. 3, 16–17, Greek text). (No. 11)

4. "After the Ascension of the Lord, the Apostles handed on to their hearers what he had said and done, but with that fuller understanding which they were instructed by the glorious events of Christ and enlightened by the Spirit of Truth." (No. 19)

After Vatican II, when certain scholars continued to attack these basic doctrines (the U.S. bishops sponsored a theological study which did no less), Pope Paul VI convoked the Second Synod of Bishops, devoted to the priesthood. The Church's thinking on this subject was summarized in this one line: "Only the priestly ministry of the New Testament. . . . perpetuates the essential work of the Apostles." Three years later (1974) the International Theological Commission collated the arguments underlying Catholic doctrine in a paper entitled "Apostolic Succession." John Paul II carried those arguments all over the Catholic world.

Empiricists are troubled by mysteries they cannot fully unravel. They are unlikely to understand or adequately explain either God or Christ or the Church or the universe, including those created in God's image and likeness. The faithful, therefore, must remain confident in certain essential truths: God exists, Christ made a credible case for his Sonship, and the Catholic Church uniquely speaks for Christ. Tertullian (fourth century) made this claim in reverse: "The Church from the Apostles, the Apostles from Christ, Christ from God." The greatest mystery of all – after why God so loves his creatures – is why God entrusted Christ's ongoing work to creatures called bishops. Catholics can empathize with the mundane temptations which face bishops and realize that bishops have sometimes represented Christ badly or have debilitated his mission by their unfitness or their unworthiness. Who, in the beginning, did this more than the remarkable, if sometimes bumbling, Peter?

"The power of the keys" goes hand in hand with the infallibility of the Church, with the bishops in counsel with the pope, or with the pope alone. It is their responsibility and right to propose without error those truths which God intends to be known and held for the sake of our salvation. Cardinal Newman once assured Christians that revealed truth could not possibly exist without an instrument by which this truth is to be truly transmitted. Vatican II, in the famous No. 25 of *Lumen Gentium,* proclaimed this essential truth of Catholicity: "The infallibility promised to the Church is also present in the Body of Bishops when, together with Peter's successor, they exercise the supreme teaching office. Now, the assent of the Church can never be lacking to such definitions on account of the same Holy Spirit's influence, through which Christ's whole flock is maintained in the unity of faith and makes progress in it."

Christianity would hardly have survived all the aberrations that have been proposed for it through the centuries, unless the Church taught with the surety of Christ. This does not mean that pope of bishops united with him, when they teach definitively, begin their proclamation with a self-serving statement: "This is an infallible statement," Ordinarily, when popes with bishops teach what pertains to the deposit of faith, Catholics know from the subject matter, and from the binding nature of the way they teach it, that this pertains to their eternal salvation. The hierarchy may teach solemnly – as the Council of Trent did (1545–1563), or as Pius IX did (1854) when he declared Mary immaculately conceived – or they may do it simply by teaching ordinarily what is contained in the key sections of the Creeds and of the Ten Commandments. Certainly the perpetual virginity of Mary or the sinfulness of adultery are infallibly taught by the ordinary magisterium of the Church. John Paul II in his recent encyclical *Evangelium Vitae* (1995), after consulting all the cardinals and hierarchies of the Church, goes on at length to explain how he wishes to reaffirm what the Church has always taught, viz., that innocent human life is inviolable, i.e., no human authority may licitly destroy it, and that this Church teaching on the immorality of direct abortion and euthanasia is true. In *Ad Tuendum Fidem* (1998) he added the ordination of men only as also definitively taught. The pope is now wrapping up what is constant Church teaching, but covering it also with the aura of his infallibility. These unique pronouncements do not make the teachings more true than they were, but from now on Catholics must accept them as especially taught for the world to hear, at a time when these beliefs or moral norms are denied by Catholic theologians.

The nature of Catholicity requires that a bishop must teach with authority, and that believing Catholics accept that teaching as a given of Christian faith. Rhetoric may differ in various cultures and places, but the Church's effective witness to Christ loses its significance and authority, if it is voiced unclearly or equivocally. Christ spoke as a man of authority: "You have heard it said of old, but I say to you." St. Paul went to the marketplace to tell Greeks that he noticed their altar dedicated "to the unknown God" (Acts 17, 23 ff.). Then he added, "Now I proclaim to you," proceeding to enlighten them about the one true God. Paul, talking to Stoics and Epicureans, did not object to their belief that divinity was in mankind. He wanted them to recognize, however, the unique dominion of the God whom Christ (and he) represented.

The Fallacy of the Naysayers

Modern skeptics are no more comfortable with this notion than the Stoics were. Ever since Vatican II, "experiential" religious educators preferred bishops to adopt a new pedagogy, the essential theory of which can be synopsized as follows:

> Bishops must dialogue, not dictate. They must present the gospel in a way which appreciates the context of modernity. We live in a multi-faith, multi-cultural society. Bishops must seek to persuade, not seem to impose. In the past preaching and teaching began with what the Church taught. Today, catechesis must begin with an appreciation of human dignity and with the prevailing state of people's development. No longer must bishops make daunting pronouncements about the Catholic faith based on traditional documents; instead we must discuss what Christ said with present life situations in mind, not in abstractions. If bishops teach, they must learn first from the people.

While great teachers perfect their rhetoric through practice, what they hope to impart effectively transcends their method, especially if an authoritative content "from on high" *must* be transmitted. Bishops are teachers, not teaching aides. The experiential revolution in catechesis or apologetics, as practiced since 1965, subordinates what is taught to the students' enjoyment of its hearing. Religious illiteracy, the substratum of agnosticism and immorality, has been the result. More serious, however, is the evisceration of the bishop's role as teacher of God's Word.

Toward the end of its deliberations in 1965, the Second Vatican Council issued a decree entitled "The Pastoral Office of Bishops in the Church," wherein bishops are held responsible for the unity of the Catholic faith. Teaching is listed as one of their principal duties. They are to be modern, use relevant techniques, and seek to make their priests holy, remind the faithful of their obligations, and give special care to those in need. Bishops are also independent of civil authorities, must encourage respect for legitimate civil law, encourage obedience within the religious institutions of their diocese, and cooperation among the clergy. Everything in this decree on bishops reinforces what American Catholics have come to understand as the rights and obligations of their chief pastors.

The phrase "successors to the Apostles" annoys biblical theorists, who consider "apostleship" to have been a personal charism of the Twelve. So serious was this charge raised during Vatican II that Cardinal Franz Koenig of Vienna introduced a section on apostolic succession for inclusion in *Lumen Gentium*. The council fathers were reminded that such a question is debated, "not indeed among Catholics, but among non-Catholic historians and exegetes." The Pontifical Biblical Commission endorsed *Lumen Gentium* as finally approved. Yet, in spite of the Council, Catholic theorists continue to doubt apostolic succession. Some critics quibble further, arguing that the designation "the Twelve" is not a true number, merely an oversimplification invented by the early Church. On this, however, Karl Rahner, in his commentary on *The Documents of Vatican II*, asserted to the contrary: "The concrete content of what is laid down in Scripture as of divine right meets us in the form of historical fact, and we have no right to separate the two things." Lawrence Cardinal Shehan, a council father, answering the charges of exegetes that the episcopacy descended not from Christ, but as a development of the Holy Spirit, raised a serious question for the skeptics: "Where was the influence of the Holy Spirit when the original traditions were being formed among the early Christians? When the gospels and other works of the New

Testament were being written? When the Canon of the New Testament was being formed? When the general Councils, including Trent, Vatican I and Vatican II were making their decision for the Church?"[5]

The Last Word

In summary, faith in Catholic bishops united with the pope, as the only authentic bearers of God's Revealed Word till the end of time, is second in importance for Catholics to their faith in Christ, that he is truly God's Son, and that what he revealed for our salvation, here and hereafter, is true. Not faith in their private judgments or their prudential decisions, but in their "ministry of governance" of the Catholic Church in Christ's name.

The disgruntled Jesuit, who opened this essay, had part of his complaint right. The Church was not born full-grown. She grew like everything human grows – but with what she was given first, a deposit of faith – and with a pope and bishops guaranteed to harvest its meaning infallibly until there is no more need of the Church. Catholicity is the longest lived faith system with a universal outreach. Christ's greatest miracle may be this Church, whose divinity defies her human limitations. These shortcomings are offset by the charism which belongs to the Catholic hierarchy alone, when they function in unison with the successor of Peter on whom – after Christ – the Church is built. Catholics will find all they want to know about this living 2,000-year-old Church, not in ancient documents, but in the manner in which she functions according to law, God's and her own.

THREE

Catholic Bishops and the Church's Law

"Bishops have a sacred right and duty before the ord of
legislating for and of passing judgment on their subjects, as well
as of regulating everything that concerns the good order of divine
worship and the apostolate."

Lumen Gentium, No. 27

Christ – The End of Law

Although there are saints in every parish of the country, statistics tell us
that the American Church AD 2000 has become a lawless community
compared to what it was a half-century ago. In 1950, Catholics took
Church law almost as seriously as they did God's law. By the nature of
their faith, they saw one as enforcing the other. But if the Second Vatican
Council was convoked to reinvigorate this linkage for the nominally
Catholic countries of Europe, it has failed. Worse still, the word "law" has
been turned to mean "rule," not "norm"; and cognitive elites have made it
fashionable to look upon "law abiders" as narrow-minded "legalists." Not
only that, breaking the first commandment, or the sixth, has become as
commonplace for many Catholics as jaywalking.

No second spring for the American Church is possible without the
recovery of the virtue of obedience, an old virtue which in contemporary
society is looked upon as a negotiable item in a human relationship.
Consequently, if Catholics today in large numbers do not obey John Paul
II, they are unlikely to submit themselves to the Lordship of Christ (Lk.
16, 31). Reinstalling obedience, therefore, will call not only for bishops
who are geniuses at evangelization, but for a Lazarus returned from the
dead.

Today's parishioners have been largely secularized. They have not the faintest idea of canon law's place in their spiritual life. Further, they have been persuaded that the most acceptable lawmakers, including bishops, are those who give them what they want, and the worst are those who restrain their freedom to do what they want. The laity also know little, if anything, about the juridic demands imposed on the successors of the Apostles by Christ himself. It is this ignorance which makes it easy for enemies of hierarchy to befuddle the canonical responsibility of bishops.

The Second Vatican Council restated the Church's understanding from Christ that bishops with the pope govern the teaching, discipline, and worship of the Catholic community. Their authority is to preach Christianity, to fashion saints, to reconcile sinners, and to lead mankind to eternal life with God. If they are good at doing what they were consecrated to do, their ministry should have salvific results.

Bishops are mysterious figures, however, whether they are looked upon with reverence as they used to be, or are enjoyed as "hail fellows well met" as so many are today. Yet, beyond the visibility that comes with public appearances, and from occasional sermons people hear from one of their numbers, many of their modern audiences are inclined to ask: "But what do they do?"

Part of the answer to this question could come from history books or from Church Fathers, but these old documents have a limited readership. Few priests, either, are privy to the details of what makes a bishop critically important to the Church. One source of information about bishops is hardly read by anyone, including priests. This is the *Code of Canon Law,* promulgated in 1983, which specifies the rights and duties of ordinary bishops through the twenty-first century at least.

One of the best kept secrets of Vatican II is that John XXIII, on the day of its announcement (January 25, 1959), declared that the writing of a new *Code of Canon Law* was his first objective. Some later insisted that the Council got away from him, others claim it was hijacked, but few can argue against John XXIII's hope that Vatican II would produce a more law-abiding Catholic community. Indeed, the last act of his life (1963) was to create a pontifical commission to write a new code. His immediate successor, Paul VI, wanted the framers of the new *Code of Canon Law* (1983) to develop the juridical structures without which, he said, the Church cannot function. Many years later, John Paul II warned canon lawyers to "avoid any undue accommodation of ecclesial norms and structures to the prevailing ethos of civil society.[1]

John XXIII's patrimony to the Church of the twenty-first century, therefore, is the 1983 *Code of Canon Law* and the 81 canons which deal with the nature of the episcopacy and the duties of bishops in the Church.[2]

Canon law does not a good bishop make, especially a casuist looking to excuse his failures. Christ had trouble with legalists who, to accommodate Caesar, had a way of gutting the best law of its meaning. He scolded the Scribes and Pharisees for turning God's law into a mess of human traditions opposed to that very law (Mt. 15, 1–9); on several occasions he criticized his own disciples and Moses for distorting God's will. (Mt. 19, 10). Law, of itself, therefore, does not make civilized or religious order. It merely creates the conditions under which a community with divergent interest groups can live together without strife, if society's officials implement it correctly. St. Paul laid out the case for Timothy: "Law is not laid down for the just but for the lawless and the disobedient, for the ungodly and the sinners, for the unholy and profane, for murderers of fathers and mothers, for man slayers, immoral persons, sodomites, kidnappers, liars, perjurers, etc." (1, 1:18).

Following Vatican II, a heresy of sorts emerged which argued that an enlightened Catholic community would be more Christ-like if the faithful enjoyed more freedom from binding precepts handed down by Rome. The Canadian Bishops' Conference hoped that any new *Code* "takes adequately into account the need for a greater freedom and flexibility, so that priests and bishops will be under few restrictions about how best to meet the pastoral needs of their people in a society that is constantly changing.[3] Three years earlier those same bishops equivalently dispensed their congregations from the moral demands of *Humanae Vitae*. Interpreting almost any law against its very meaning became the new form of casuistry . . even against the mission of him who came to fulfill God's law (Mt. 5, 17) and who gave authority to his Apostles to bind and loose believers for the sake of their salvation (Mt. 16, 19). Christ understood that God's laws were to be obeyed. Why else did St. Paul insist that Christians acquire "the mind of Jesus Christ" (Phil. 2, 5), and that they exemplify "the obedience of faith" (Rom. 1, 5)? Why else would Christ himself rebuke Peter for thinking like a Jewish casuist rather than a man with the mind of God. (Mt. 8, 33)? The Psalmist constantly reminded the Jews (e.g., 81, 119, etc.) to rejoice in God's precepts by using their freedom responsibly.

These reflections are germane to the proper understanding of what Church law and its language say bishops are or are expected to be and do.

Bishops Are Successors of the Apostles

The new *Code of Canon Law* reaffirms the Catholic belief that the bishop's office comes directly from Christ, and that, as apostolic successors, they have the power of the keys to the kingdom of heaven.[4]

Other Christians do not believe this to be true, holding that Christian worship and teaching derives from the congregation of believers, and by whatever name the "overseer" is called, he or she is the delegate of the community. A similar notion surfaced in Catholic circles during Vatican II in the interest of better ecumenical relations but, quite rightly, went nowhere. Congregational-minded Catholics, who like to think themselves "on the cutting edge" of the Church, sought to "cut away" episcopal dominance of things Catholic. But since the Greek root of the word "episcopos" means "to cut," the better argument is that Christ conferred the "cutting edge" role on bishops, to cut into disbelief, into immorality, into worldliness, especially into the arrogance of God's enemies. New Church law reaffirms the sense of "bishop" which the faithful have always understood the office to be.

By naming bishops as "teachers of doctrine," "priests of sacred worship," and "ministers of governance," that same law notifies the Catholic public that "apostolic succession" is no mere figure of speech. Bishops are the Church's chief teachers, rulers, sanctifiers.

No single bishop, however, all by himself, is a successor of the Apostles. No individual Catholic bishop is autonomous of the pope. His freedom is exercised "only in hierarchical communion with the head of the [episcopal]) college and its members." Just as Christ came to do the will of his Father (Jn. 5, 30), so the bishop must conduct himself out of "the wholeness" of a revelation known and certified by the College of Bishops in union with the pope. Although maverick bishops were commonplace during periods of Church history when heresy was rampant, an autonomous bishop in the Catholic Church is a contradiction in terms. Even the saints of the Church, mostly heroic personalities, sometimes critics of episcopal conduct, were obedient to the faith community which gave them life. Without obedience in faith, the result of conscience formation under law, even for bishops, the Church is deformed.

What Are Bishops Made Of?[5]

The Church, with her long memory of unworthy popes who gave apostolic sees away to incompetent and corrupt nephews or to royal court clowns, is fussy about who becomes a bishop. American Catholics have had reason to appreciate the Church law that demands he be "outstanding for his solid faith, good morals, piety, zeal for souls, wisdom, prudence and human virtues and endowed with other talents which make him fit to fulfill the office."

The practical problem, however, of finding men of faith, wisdom, or prudence is more difficult than defining the words, especially since virtue can become vice in the wrong circumstance. The bishop of a serene diocese who does nothing to upset the *status quo,* may well be a prudent prelate; if suddenly he witnesses outrageous heresy, scandal, or bankruptcy in his household and does nothing, he will likely end his days as a mediocrity or in disgrace. Virtues anywhere are not a collection of abstract principles but forms for doing, or having done, what is necessary for piety, peace, justice, and charity to prevail in a person's life or in a community. The pope and his congregation for bishops can only pray, at times, that they make few mistakes in filling Catholic sees according to their own law.

Normally, the Church prefers "safe" bishops, an understandable predilection in times of ecclesial peace. Discerning safety, however, is dangerous business. The barque of Peter does well at times with bishops who know how to row; in other situations the Church needs men who know how to walk on water. Great bishops, like great presidents, only seem to rise in time of war. They leave something behind to treasure only because they handle danger effectively and defeat enemies. The Neville Chamberlain-types, usually good men, are not good at war. The public figure who looks good, and appears to be sensitive to people's needs, may appeal to the contemporary image-makers who think like pop-psychologists, but it is the Charles de Gaulles, the Harry Trumans, and the Cardinal Spellmans who make history.

The pope makes all episcopal appointments but, unless he has a personal favorite, he usually rubber-stamps the names that are given to him by the congregation for bishops and/or the apostolic nuncios/ delegates. Those recommendations, in turn, are heavily influenced by the wants and wishes of powerful prelates in Rome and elsewhere, although it would be unjust to exaggerate the pitfalls of "cronyism," out of which certain fine bishops have emerged. Still, whomever the top of the ecclesiastical ladder likes best is the likely one to receive the miter. Having made this concession to reality, it must also be added that the risks in bishop-making multiplied after Vatican II because Catholic discipline broke down, even over matters of faith, and something more than "liking" was required. How does the pope find the equivalent of an ecclesial Churchill or Roosevelt in this time of trouble?

Consider, for example, Rome's standard intellectual qualifications for an episcopal candidate. He must have theological expertise, the law says, symbolized ordinarily by an advanced degree in some field of ecclesiastical study. That a diocesan shepherd should be better educated than the average priest who works under him is a capital idea. Even so, this requirement, unless interpreted carefully, does not reflect present-day reality.

First, advanced degrees are not of themselves proof of a superior grasp of the Catholic issues, nor of how to deal with doctrinal problems in the private or public forum. Familiarity with theological literature is no guarantee of perspicacity in debates about the faith, nor an index of ability to deal with anti-religious movements close at hand. While anti-intellectualism is undesirable in episcopal candidates, high marks in seminaries or graduate schools do not, of themselves, procreate outstanding bishops. Present Church law relies on traditional norms for guessing who future episcopal worthies might be, but doctorates do not help decide where the James Gibbons, the John Hugheses, and the John Irelands are to be found. At one time it was important to have a Charles Borremeo in the See of Milan, and a St. Augustine in Hippo. But it is also unlikely that John Henry Newman, a superior scholar, would have made a better archbishop of Westminster than Henry Edward Manning.

In elite circles of pre-Vatican II days, a view was commonly hold in Europe that the American hierarchy was inferior because its bishops came out of chancery offices. Few of those fortune-tellers could argue successfully, however, that their bishops were more effective pastors than the Americans. If pre-Vatican II European bishops were better degreed than their American counterparts, it is also true that their churches were also in decline.

Another old assumption dictated that the really good bishops were graduates of Roman universities. Cardinal Spellman, himself Roman trained, became so annoyed with this allegation that he went out of his way, after 1939, to see that within his area of influence only American trained priests were so elevated. Degrees from institutes "approved by the Apostolic See" are no longer guarantors of episcopal authenticity.

Leading academic lights at places like Louvain, the Gregorian, or the Alphonsianum do not necessarily illuminate the Catholic minds of their publics with the vision of John Paul II, or even of John XXIII. In essence, Church law dealing with bishops – apart from sections dealing with their relationship to the pope and certain technical issues such as their appointment, retirement, etc. – specifies three matters of interest to all Catholics: (1) their divine authority from Christ; (2) their fitness for the office; and (3) their responsibility for the diocese which they govern.

Selecting men capable of exercising apostolic authority involves complex practical judgments, as much as declarations of principle. New media interest in the nomination of bishops simply complicates the process. Years ago, when a media favorite for New York, Chicago, or Los Angeles was passed over by Rome in favor of an unknown prelate, the priests and the laity accepted the surprise announcement, almost as if they cared little about the subject. Today priest-activists gain notoriety by letting the world know in advance of their unhappiness with the rumored appointment or his anticipated behavior. Church law may call for the bishop to be a "minister of governance," but elite Catholics no longer want to be governed, except on their terms. They agitate for a "chairman-of-the-board" type who reigns but does not rule. This, in spite of the fact that Canon 392 directs the bishop to "protect the unity of the universal Church," "promote the common discipline of the whole Church," "urge the observation of all ecclesiastical laws," and to be vigilant "lest abuses creep into ecclesiastical discipline," in teaching, worship and the sacraments, and administration.

The office of the bishop itself, as the Code defines it, becomes difficult to fill or to manage when there are prelates who publicly disagree with Rome or who dispense from Roman requirements or forestall Vatican policy decisions or appointments which they do not like. Dissenters want bishops to be elected, arguing that the early Church practiced a "democracy." However, today's 1-billion-member Church is hardly the "little folk" community of Pentecostal Jerusalem, and the virtues required for bishoping in 2000 AD are hardly measurable by the size of a vote. Indeed, the clergy of a given diocese may not be capable of judging the faith, morals, or talents of any *episcopabilis.* In any case, the scandal inherent in a public brawl over whether one candidate is a better or more up-to-date Catholic than his rivals would be, to say the least, a poor episcopal beginning for the winner. That winner, who must make a profession of Catholic faith and an oath of fidelity to the pope, would have large difficulty with the very opinion-molders of his diocese who refuse to make such a profession, or to take such an oath.

Every Bishop a Little Pope

The word "pope" in several European languages merely means "papa." By Church law the bishop is "Father" to all the people in his diocese. The pope in Rome names him, and he remains always subject to universal Catholic demands, but once in office, the diocese is his to govern alone. His authority over that portion of God's people is like that of the pope's over the universal Church – personal, direct, ordinary. He is not a delegate of the pope, nor does the pope micro-manage his diocese, unless somehow its mismanagement impinges on the well-being of the larger Church. The Catholic Church remains one of the most decentralized institutions in history, and relies for its effectiveness on the virtue of her office holders first, and only secondly on her canon law.

In practice, the bishop is a man of authority, like Christ, with the power to command obedience. A commandment is not a suggestion. Some of his commands bind in conscience, others bind to the extent that violators are subject to punishment. When the diocesan bishop is very good, the Church exemplifies "free enterprise" at its best; in other situations *laissez faire* does serious damage to faith and discipline.

A bishop's authority these days annoys those who would rather live without it, especially without his "power" to command obedience. Nonetheless, the Church boldly proclaims episcopal authority as necessary, legitimate, and divinely conferred.[6] Lawfully exercised, authority rewards the good and punishes evildoers. Virtue may be its own reward for ascetics and for the well-behaved, but the enforcement of law is necessary for civic pride, for public morale, and to ensure social harmony. Disestablishmentarians are present everywhere, living in their own worlds, but they, above all, are subject to law. Entire nations have been lost to the faith, for example, when hierarchy failed to create or maintain a high pride of membership in the Church or stood idly by in the face of contumacious violence against faith and morals by heretics and schismatics.

Power in use, even by legitimate officeholders, involves politics, an art form about as natural to human beings as religion. Religion regulates man's relationship with God, politics the relations among diverse members of society. Good politics, like good medicine, aims to cure disorders, but it works only when directed by good practitioners. The successful politician is not necessarily the glad-hander, the crowd-pleaser, the vote-getter or the fund-raiser, but the one who knows when and how to intervene in the body politic with persuasion first, and with lawful force as necessary. All the more reason, then, for Church law to spell out in detail what is the range of a bishop's obligations to the laity, to his priests, and religious.[7]

According to law, he is to have his hands personally on the care of his faithful, of "those who no longer practice their religion," of the poor and the weak, and of non-Catholics. He is commissioned to organize his diocese with great skill. He may be a great preacher, a poet, a social personality, a fund-raiser of no mean achievement; he may have a beautiful voice for sung Masses, look very good on television, but, above all, he is overseer of all activity that calls itself Catholic. If he walks into a situation where pederast priests are being sued, where the local college is anti-Catholic, where the diocesan debt is five times the income, where his inherited chancellor is a drunk, his governing ability will be put to the test immediately. Governing involves decision-making, not merely overlooking bureaucracies. Archbishop Spellman arrived in New York May 23, 1939 to be notified by bankers that they held mortgages of $28 million on various Catholic institutions at 6 percent interest, which required his immediate intervention, they said. When his offer to assume the total debt himself, if they gave him a 3 percent interest rate, was rejected, he journeyed to Boston where he found more agreeable bankers. Many years later, another archbishop, newly installed, found himself with a bad seminary on his hands. He facilitated its closure in short order.

The bishop's most important collaborators are priests, and these above all he must cultivate and govern personally. The *Code* says so. One archbishop began his administration with a smashing convocation for his laity, leaving his priests waiting on the sidelines for attention. That prelate has not regained the respect of his clergy to this moment. Pastors, particularly, are to bishops what cabinet officers are to presidents. One can hardly do without the other. Yet, the priestly state is in trouble today, especially among those priests who see nothing sacred about their bishop. Recently a priest, ordained little more than ten years, writing in *Salesianum* (Fall/Winter 1994), reveled in the fact that priests his age have no memory of the pre-Vatican II Church and that, as a result of the Council, they are now satisfied with "a more secular approach to the secular priesthood." The *sine qua non* of the modern episcopacy, therefore, is the ability to command respect for the office. A disrespectful "father" is a poor "head" of a family.

Teacher and Guardian of the Faith

Church law binds every bishop to this double obligation – teaching and catechetical formation – "so that the whole of Christian doctrine is imparted to all.[8]

This demand on hierarchy is treated as a joke in many quarters of the Church. In 1996 a young theologian arose at a priests' assembly in Massachusetts to tell the story of a bishop who informed three scripture professors privately that he had no great education in matters biblical. But on introducing the three to his own clergy proclaimed: "In this diocese, I am the authentic interpreter of scriptures." Not surprisingly his audience roared with laughter. A quarter century earlier (1971), Gabriel Moran wrote: "The supposition that the bishop is the teacher of the diocese and that religion teachers in the schools are an extension of the bishop is a fallacy that must be laid to rest."

Presuming that Rome, in naming bishops, is realistic about the low estate to which their predecessors have fallen as theologians and catechists, Church law remains clear nonetheless: Bishops are the chief teachers and guardians of the faith. The ability to preach well may not be an absolute requirement for elevation to the episcopacy, but St. Alphonsus Liguori placed it first among his list of qualifications. The failure of metropolitan media any longer to feature the bishop's Sunday sermon on Monday is no great loss, if the same man effectively supervises the educational machinery in his diocese.

The most serious difficulty for a teaching bishop today is his own catechetical household. A handful of examples will illustrate the problem:

*In 1976 the president of St. John's University in New York, who also taught 300 college students weekly, informed the president of the National Conference of Catholic Bishops that his own incoming students, after twelve years of Catholic schooling, did not know the number and meaning of the seven Sacraments.

*Almost ten years later, a Pennsylvania bishop, in the presence of a Roman cardinal, told an audience of catechetical leaders that he personally examined every text that went into his classrooms. A theologian challenged him with the question: "Why don't bishops get together and do that consistently?" At which point the cardinal interjected to say: "The cardinals in Rome need to get together first!"

*A woman religious from diocesan headquarters walked into a new pastor suggesting that his parishioners be told that the parochial director of religious education is now the chief catechist in the parish. She was taken aback, as if the idea was news to her, when the pastor rejoined: "Sister, I am the chief catechist!" The nun was flabbergasted!

*A preacher returned from theological training in Germany speaking only of the humanist God, the humanist Christ, the divine world. He sounded like a pantheist.

After Vatican II theologians and other academics, including catechists, asked the bishops to trust them to be responsible exponents of Catholic doctrine. Eliminated from the 1983 *Code* was the 1918 canon 2317, which decreed: "All who obstinately teach either publicly or in private defend a doctrine that has been condemned by the Apostolic See or by an Ecumenical Council, but not as a formal heresy, are to be excluded from the ministry of preaching the Word of God, or hearing confessions, and from the Office of Teaching." Before World War II that decree was rarely implemented because Catholic preachers and teachers were fully Catholic, aware that they would be held to account for aberrations. That can no longer be said. As the present situation stands, the problem for bishops is not the teaching of the Church, but its governance.

Present Church law reasserts the bishop's obligation to safeguard the faith, adding "strongly," as if to make the point clear. The law also cautions that the safeguarding be done "through suitable means" and "acknowledging a rightful freedom in the further investigation of its truths." What are "suitable means" of restraint? At the very least it means that a dissident teacher will be "chewed out" by a bishop, a common experience at times of everyone who works for a living. There is no reason why a bishop cannot criticize someone for a dangerous opinion, as he would for a sacrilegious or immoral act. The dangerous opinion, depending on the circumstances of the delivery, can be immoral, too. In the present climate, controls of thinking and behavior do go on, usually by academics against academics, academics against bishops. One "distinguished professor" at a secular university, known for his admiration of John Paul II, recently announced that the last place he would be welcome is on the faculty of his order's institutions of learning.

Bishops, no less than academics, are immersed in the blandishments of freedom to individuals, pluralism of truths, worldly salvation, relativist morality, and popular will. But whether they like it or not, professionals are subject to judgment by bishops, singly or collectively, if they are Catholic or work in a Catholic setting. Church teachers may no longer like to look upon bishops as patristic Fathers, and Church Fathers need be prudent and flexible in dealing with everybody. But a knowledgeable bishop need not hesitate to remonstrate with an errant theologian, privately or publicly, when he is certain that the academic is doing harm to the faith of his people.

Something less than *bona fide* intellectualism is operating, therefore, when the Catholic Theological Society of America felt free to proclaim resentment against any intrusion by a prelate into its affairs "exacted on the basis of fear, a sheer sense of duty, enforced obedience." Or, when another president of that same society blithely asserted in a diocesan newspaper that "the *magisterium* carries very little weight with a Catholic majority, that no thinking person can achieve honest certitude by accepting every Church document, and that the faithful are nowhere admonished to live by official doctrine alone."

Contemporary Catholics are creatures of a culture which has canonized everyone's right to choose how to think or speak or act, without interference from anyone in authority. This notion of freedom is not even classically pagan, let alone Christian. The concept of human rights grew out of a study of higher law – natural law for Aristotle, out of God's Commandments for the Christian. Notice how the Ten Commandments spell out duties, not rights. If we have rights against other people, it is because of that higher law. When the Church defended the right of private property against the socialists, it understood that property would be held "for common use." In classic and Christian law, justice required that freedom be used to benefit others and for the common good most of all. Rights exist, but they must be asserted responsibly.

Due process for individuals, therefore, is not intended, by law at least, to be undue process for bishops. Good governance requires that Catholics be held to account for the proper exercise of their freedom in faith. Unrequited evil in the household does not spell virtue. A bishop who guards the faith fulfills the law better than the one who simply talks about it.

The Minister of Governance

The bishop ordinary bishop has legislative, executive, and judicial power over his entire diocese. Secular states tend today to separate these powers. The Church unites them, as they were in Christ.[9] Modern political thinkers abhor whatever appears to be "oneness." Monotheism, monogamy, monologue, monolith, monarchy are out; polytheism, polygamy, pluralism are in. (Even the monocle is out, for almost everyone.) They are so distrustful of politicians that their "best" government keeps legislators, executives, and judges at war with each other, leaving "idea men" in control.

The Church places her confidence for good government of the Catholic community more in virtuous men than in political mechanisms. Conformity to God's laws, the virtues, and proper procedures listed in her canons are the founding principles for the governance of Christ's mystical body. Church affairs are assigned to the oversight of one bishop. He "rules" the local Church. The chosen Latin word for the bishop's role is *regere,* which means "to regulate," not "to reign" or "to guide." (In popular English "reign" has come to mean "to preside over," not "to rule." Queen Elizabeth II reigns over, but does not rule, England.) "Ruling" has little popular currency in a culture which pays small heed to what Greek or Roman classics called the natural order of things or to the Christian concept of "revealed" religion. Most civilized people accept legitimated authority as a necessary component of their civility, not because it represents "power," but because it stands for decision-making by someone with the title of "author" or "creator" or "Father." The Jewish priests had it right when they demanded of Christ: "By what authority do you do these things?" (Mt. 21, 23). Legitimate authority is natural to all societies. In the Catholic scheme of things, the bishop represents Christ authoritatively. Efforts have been made, in Vatican II's name, to create new models or new paradigms which would water down even the authority of Christ. Words like "patriarchy," "patrimony," or just plain "father," even when applied to God, are not in favor in some circles. This revisionism has no basis in what Vatican II actually said about the bishop as shepherd of the people of God.

Church authority cannot function properly without the virtues mentioned in Scripture and the canons. In 1997 the Congregation of the Doctrine of the Faith reaffirmed and revised its regulation of possible abuses by the Holy See or by local bishops. Even so, authority, properly used in the Church, is the right of bishops and of others under his jurisdiction. The longest section of Vatican II's *Constitution on the Church (Lumen Gentium)* defines the meaning, rights, and duties of hierarchy. Crises in the Church arise more from the non-use of timely and proper authority by bishops than from episcopal abuse. It is then that "hirelings" shepherd Christ's flock to its harm. The real traitors to Christianity are not its sinners, but its scoundrels. Shakespeare's account of how Cardinal Wolsey regretted his treachery to the Church in favor of Henry VIII's lust, is on the mark: "Would that I had served my God as I served my King!"

Bishops in the World

Bishops have always been concerned about state matters, if only to protect the Church and her people. Church law now directs them to be involved in the care of the poor, and in world matters such as war and peace.[10] In other words, bishops have more than a "sacristy" mission on behalf of life to come, they have a public ministry to secular society as well. The direct priestly mission is "to save souls," i.e., to form a faith community for purposes of sanctification and eternal life; its other is to save the world" so that mankind's quest for God's kingdom is enabled. The City of Man and the City of God share the same Lord and the same people. Both are objects of a bishop's concern. As early as 1931, Pius XI addressed two critical human problems in *Quadragesimo Anno* – moral v. immoral men, moral v. immoral institutions. The time was overdue for reform in both quarters, he argued. The radical reform of social institutions, which he proposed, would be of little significance, however, if it only meant that a new kind of rascals replaced veterans in the game of institutional chicanery. Shaping the morals of people is primarily priest business, he added, while uplifting the quality of the world's institutions is primarily the laity's, because they live at its center. This distinction was recalled in John Paul II's warning against a post-Vatican II tendency, viz. the laicization of the clergy and the clericalization of the laity, oversupplying picket lines and political clubhouses with clergy, and overcrowding the Church's altars with working people. Theologian Brian Benestad is only one of the many contemporary theologians who see a reversal of roles in the making. In olden days Catholic bishops devoted their time at national meetings to outlining ways and means for perfecting the Christian character of their faithful so that their ministry might help laity to recon-struct a decent social/world order. Since 1966, episcopal energy has been devoted more to providing blueprints for the solution of social problems and supporting governmental social remedies, while the discipline related to piety collapsed.

This worldly apostolate, beyond works of charity, is modern, of course. But what bishops do best is old-time, viz. to create and develop pious families at the parish level. Without practicing Catholics respectful of bishops, the Church's claim to a civic role and the episcopal voice on earthly matters falls on deaf ears. The masters of government, business, labor, cultural corporations and media, pay little attention to the *vox populorum,* unless the spokesman carries one of Teddy Roosevelt's big sticks. Power centers respect real power brokers, i.e., those who can deliver votes against them. Who pays attention anymore to clergy as clergy, unless they demonstrably represent a ruling power bloc?

When the Catholic community grew between 1940 and 1960 from 20 to 40 million, the Church and its clergy were highly regarded in the marketplace, even if they were unloved by Americanized elites. Anti-Catholics were fearful that a Catholic moment had arrived, that Alfred E. Smith and his kind were propagating in such alarming numbers as to shape the future ethos of the nation. That moment was lost with John Fitzgerald Kennedy's ambivalent Catholicity and so, too, the opportunity to improve what Protestant Christianity had created.

A Church which expects to influence the body politic through its laity must be sufficiently disciplined internally to appear as a credible voice for its causes. The support it enjoys within the voting constituency tells the story. A Church with contradictory trumpets blaring messages to a public historically suspicious of papists anyway is doomed to be dismissed as politically insignificant. Anytime the AFL-CIO, NAACP, NAM, or similar pressure groups appear divided, they lose political clout. Richard John Neuhaus hit the nail on the head years ago, when he said that the American public square, patently naked of revealed religious insights about human nature or the nature of human society, was ready for "a Catholic moment." The time had arrived, he thought, for the Church to provide the nation the kind of guidance it needed to fulfill its original experimental vision. That moment obviously has not yet arrived.

During political infighting episcopal choices are never easy to make. By the terms of the Church's recent self-understanding, the reform of secular social institutions is still primarily the laity's business. Priests are not excluded absolutely from political interventions, e.g., in the absence of property informed or available laity, but only by way of exception. When the life or freedom of the Church itself, or of its schools and agencies, is threatened by enemies outside, the Church, led by bishops, has as much right to political self-defense as anyone else. By and large, civic, industrial, racial, class, international or other secular conflicts – qua politics – are none of the clergy's business. But bishops are commanded by Church law to form consciences correctly. Unfortunately, those laity who are used to priestly dominance in the pursuit of holiness often take a back seat in the area which is their secular sanctuary. During the days of *laissez-faire* economics, bishops were frequently *laissez faire* themselves. In 1924, for example, they opposed the Child Labor Act largely because it brought federal interference into family life. After 1934 those old prelates embraced federal intervention in many aspects of American life. They were America First in 1941, one-worlders by 1961. Riding a popular political tide is a dangerous game for Catholic bishops at any time, largely because clerics are not very good at politics. Bishops and/or Rome usually consider the partisan conduct of their priests unseemly, whether he be an Edward McGlynn, Charles E. Coughlin, or Robert Drinan. (FDR once threatened the hierarchy over the behavior of Fr. Coughlin.) After Vatican II, episcopal pastorals tilted *away* from American security interests in matters of war and peace, and *toward* the welfare state in social matters, feminism, and ethnic nationalism, *away* from motherhood and family unity. The political independence of bishops was also compromised during the rabid continent-wide controversies over abortion in the 1970s. First, bishops favored a constitutional amendment protecting the right to life from conception; then they were against it; finally they floated a "consistent ethic strategy" to make it appear they did not intend the Catholic community to be a single-issue voting bloc. This turned out to be a strange strategy since Jewish voters unabashedly supported candidates favorable to Israel, blacks voted for those who enforced affirmative action, unionists whatever political banner the AFL-CIO held high at a given moment, feminists resisted anti-abortionist legislation, homosexuals vowed to punish so-called homophobic Congressmen. Although first positions of the national hierarchy were later modified by the negative reactions of bishops-in-the-field or by Rome, those controversies raised questions about the political competency of hierarchy.

The failure of the Catholic Church in recent years to enhance its political clout demonstrates anew the lack of an American lay apostolate. Bishops are sometimes blamed unfairly for this lack, as if they preferred to keep the laity subordinate. In truth, it is often priests, including those within bishops' bureaucracies, who cannot abide independent lay political opinion, especially if it is conservative. In earlier days practicing Catholics emerged from the melting pot to head important public institutions, and Catholic influence, such as it was, was due to those lay Catholics. Priests then usually remained in the background.

The Catholic Church, the only voluntary institution with a "clubhouse" in every nook and cranny of the country, owns more potentially apostolic units than any other cultural conglomerate. Protestants and Other Americans for Separation of Church and State was organized specifically to combat growing "Catholic power," e.g., by the Legion of Decency.

The Church's apostolates presently in existence – in education, in welfare, in medicine, in law, in social-uplift politics, in cultural affairs, etc.

– have the potential of becoming a movement toward the Catholic moment in American history. Church law says that the bishop is "to coordinate" these apostolates, without specifying what this means. It certainly does not mean that he is to manage civic reform, nor to substitute his judgment for the creativity of fully believing and practicing lay Catholics. One thing is clear, however: American culture would not likely accept a Catholic political alliance, as it does other pressure groups, and Catholic bishops would likely be embarrassed by it.

Bishops and the Pope

Catholic bishops govern their dioceses in union with the pope. This is the law. The pope expects every bishop to report to him on the condition of his diocese at least once every five years.[11]

Once upon a time, especially during the Middle Ages, the Catholic faithful hardly ever saw their bishop; today the laity are likely to see their bishop everywhere but never get to know him. In their turn, bishops have come to feel they must listen to everyone, fearful usually of those who can inflict harm on their diocese or on them. At the turn of the century – in the horse-and-buggy age – bishops on parochial visitations were free to stay overnight, have a meal with the priests and/or the teaching staff, answer friendly questions about policy matters, preside at liturgies, and find time for those laity who wished to speak with the bishop privately. They likely obtained a better sense of their diocese this way. Examining parish records himself – the adult baptisms, the conversions, the convalidations, the sick calls – gave him a good idea of who was doing what in the parish, the kind of parochial visitations John Neumann used to make. When the modern bishop gets to Rome on his so-called *ad limina* visit (on "the pope's doorstep," literally), his five-year report (called *quinquennial)* usually is loaded more with summaries of reports than of personal experience. No pope would read these in detail, but the recaps he receives enables him, if he chooses, to raise questions with a local bishop during any face-to-face meeting.

John Paul II is reported to have twitted bishops on some of the oddities he finds, e.g., an extraordinary number of eucharistic ministers in a small diocese.

These reports do help the pope estimate the conditions of the Church in various parts of the world, and they do contribute to his comments to different hierarchies when he lands on their shores. Back in 1977, for example, Terence Cardinal Cooke laid great stress on the harmful impact of chaotic American mores on recent Catholic immigrants to New York. What bothered Cooke was the equation in the modern American mind of morality with legality. Abortion, pornography, and homosexuality were his three examples.

In that same report, the New York archbishop complained about biblical scholars who compromised the reliability of the scriptures as a source of God's revealed Word. He asked Rome "to reaffirm and clarify authentic teaching on the doctrine of inspiration and the place and function of sacred tradition." He was also critical of the "mis-emphasis on Christ's humanity alone by some theologians" and the deleterious effect of this on religious education. He further blamed "misunderstood ecumenism" for the lost or lessened appreciation of the Church as the vehicle of salvation. Cooke decried the "lack of proper formation of a correct Catholic conscience," "the distortions about the Church as the *locus theologicum* in that formation," "the undue and uncritical attention given to sociological surveys," the disparagement of the magisterium as mere "official teaching," and the detrimental effect on the practice of the faith by theological personalities who fostered "an alleged right to dissent." He saw the greatest sin of his time to be the loss of the sense of sin. In later years, the Holy See addressed all these issues in various forums – through congregations, the International Theological Commissions, and in the voluminous addresses of John Paul II. When the pope reinforces the judgments of the local hierarchy, in whose jurisdiction the difficulties first appeared, corrections can follow.

An archbishop is a middleman between a pope and the local ordinary, overseeing a number of bishops within his area or province. He normally governs only his own diocese, each diocese within a province having its own bishop. Church law, however, gives the archbishop oversight of another bishop in clearly defined circumstances: (1) He is "to be vigilant that the faith and ecclesial discipline are carefully preserved and to inform the Roman Pontiff of abuses if there are any"; (2) "to perform the canonical visitation if the suffragan bishop has neglected it, after the reason for doing so has first been approved by the Apostolic See"; (3) to appoint a diocesan administrator in accord with the norms of canon law; and (4) may receive special duties and powers thereto, whenever circumstances demand it.[12]

Chains of command are commonplace in every institution the size of the Church, which explains why archbishops came into existence. On his own initiative or at the urging of the pope, the archbishop is expected to forge unity among his suffragans, which may not be easy for some personalities, or when one or more of his suffragans disagrees with the pope. The feat in 1995 of seventeen Pennsylvania bishops, under the leadership of their cardinal archbishop, publicly declaring that invalidly married Catholics are not eligible to receive the Eucharist as a matter of their own conscientious decision, was a demonstration of remarkable unity, especially since their letter was a direct contradiction of the widely publicized letter of three German bishops which said they might so approach the altar under specified circumstances.

Church law specifies the responsibility of archbishops to be a "watchdog" (a free translation of the word "vigilance") over the faith and discipline of their entire province. Not many years ago an archbishop sat with a group of priests evaluating a situation in his province which affected the larger Church. At one point the archbishop excused himself and was gone for half an hour. Only later did it appear that he left to take one of his suffragans to task on the telephone. The bishop in question was annoyed, but he did not dispute the metropolitan's authority in that case. Authority unclaimed, or unasserted, tends to breed disrespect for lawful supervision and for the law.

Bishops and their National Conference

Since Vatican II, a new structure has been inserted in the Church's chain of command, called the National Conference of Catholic Bishops, and Church law specifies the nature and membership of this new instrument of ecclesial government.[13]

1. The Conference of Bishops is to be a "permanent institution" whose function is to form programs for the Church's apostolates suitable to the circumstances of their situation.

2. Diocesan bishops are its ordinary members.

3. Only the Holy See can erect, suppress, or change these conferences, but once erected, they have a "juridic personality" of their own.

4. Other bishops – auxiliaries, coadjutors, and specified titulars – are by law members of the conference.

5. Each Conference shall determine its own statutes (to be approved by the Holy See), hold meetings, select officers, and establish its own administrative machinery headed by a general secretary.

6. The conference will select its own president.

7. The conference shall meet at least annually.

8. Legitimate members shall have a deliberative, i.e., decisive vote on ters, except drawing up or modifying the conference statutes. Only diocesan ordinaries can do this.

9. The conference can issue decree, but only in matters covered by the Church's common law or when otherwise mandated by the Holy See. These decrees have effect when they are passed by two-thirds of the bishops with a deliberative vote, and after they have been approved by the Holy See. When, however, neither the Holy See's mandate nor the Church's universal law empowers a conference to legislate, "the competence of individual bishops remains intact; and neither the conference nor its President may act in the name of all bishops unless each and every bishop has given his consent."

10. Reports of annual meetings and decrees must be sent to the Holy See for review.

11. The conference's "permanent council," viz. its elected officers and staff, are to prepare the agenda for national meetings and see to that the approved decrees are implemented.

12. The general secretary is the chief staff officer to the permanent council, in charge of the secretariat and communication with bishop members and other conferences.

13. When contemplated actions take on an international tone, other conferences and the Holy See must be consulted.

Recovery through Law

The "common discipline of the whole Church" involves the restraint of scandalous evildoers. This is the function of good governance. Catholic opinion once took this for granted.

When Cardinal Edward Mooney directed Fr. Charles E. Coughlin in 1942 to remove himself from public life and confine himself to his parish, the priest obeyed, When New Orleans's Archbishop Rummel excommunicated three Catholic racists in 1963, the Catholic community applauded. When in 1986 the Holy See insisted that the bishops fire Charles Curran from the Catholic University of America, a federal court said they had every right to do so.

Disobedience, a measurable cause of today's Catholic crisis, is everywhere. Recently, a report of the 34th general congregation of the Society of Jesus equivocated over St. Ignatius's "Rules for Thinking with the Church," gave them a new meaning "that transcends the particularities of its [*sic*] historical origins in the sixteenth century Church." Though not exactly what the Jesuit Founder had in mind, the report maintained that disobedience of law can be discernment:

> Ignatian obedience, in accord with the tradition of Catholic theology, *has always recognized that our first fidelity is to God*, to the truth and to a well formed conscience. Obedience, then, cannot exclude our prayerful discernment of the course of action to be followed, one that may in some circumstances differ from the one suggested by our religious and Church superiors.[14]

Unless the pope discerns that a disobedient Society of Jesus is responsible, as much as anyone, for the present state of the Church, and restores authentic Ignatian obedience to its ranks, it is difficult to foresee bishops successfully restoring "discipleship" to their dioceses.

F O U R

The Present Episcopal Dilemma

> In some places matters have reached such a point that it is no
> longer a question of sound and fruitful investigation, or
> legitimate efforts to adapt the expression of traditional new
> doctrine to new needs and to ways of modern human culture, but
> rather of unwarranted innovations, false opinions, and even errors
> of faith. . . . Those who are rash or impudent should be warned
> in all charity; those who are pertinacious should be removed
> from office.
>
> First Synod of Bishops, October 28, 1967

> The emerging question for the Catholic community may well be
> whether in the future, as in the past, it derives its fundamental
> beliefs and attitudes from the traditional value system of Catholic
> Christianity, or whether its beliefs and attitudes will be drawn
> more and more from the secularistic, humanistic value system
> around it.
>
> National Conference of Catholic Bishops, 1974

The National Conference of Catholic Bishops stated the dilemma in 1974.
Is the Catholic Church God's work or man's creation? Is it "founded as
necessary by God through Christ" to proclaim His Word (*Lumen Gentium,*
14) or invented by men to satisfy arcane and mysterious needs? Does the
Church have a divine revelation and an eternal dimension or is it the voice
of the people seeking answers to life's insoluble problems? Thinkers have
divided over the answers to questions like these from the days of Moses,
and culture wars have been waged in their honor ever since. If the God-
man Jesus had difficulty with Jews, why should his God-man Church
encounter less with Catholics?

From a modern perspective, the dilemma can be variously phrased:

Will the pope and the bishops continue to suffer the present, ongoing drift of the Church toward ambiguity of Catholic faith and conditions of discipleship or will they use their authority to reclaim Catholicity's "obedience of faith."

> * Whether the pope will establish directives for episcopal conferences so that the unity and discipline of one Church prevails, or permits the rise of national Catholic communities at odds with Rome and Catholic churches elsewhere.

> * Whether bishops will remain content with institutions or bureaucracies which call themselves Catholic but are not, or firmly clarify the terms under which that name can be used. Is the American Church abandoning its hard-earned body of pious churchgoers in favor of the nominal Catholicity – in which only the name counts – that has characterized the ancients sees of Europe for centuries? Will the secularists – the godless – succeed in doing what the Gnostics, Arians, Albigensians, and Jansenists never did – make the Church irrelevant to the people of God?

The fate of the Catholic Church depends on the choices pope and bishops make in the next quarter century. With Christ, they alone govern the Catholic community.

To Ignore History

Catholic defeats throughout Church history were often the result of a conspiracy by Catholic monarchs against Church influence, or their lust for its properties. Still, in many contests with these enemies, the loss of Catholic faith never occurred without bishops squandering their high ground as vicars of Christ, or their freedom, in exchange for state favors. Sometimes the unholiness of their lives was a factor. In such circumstances, the laws of Christ and of the Church became ineffective norms for people because their primary witnesses, the clergy, were insincere or incredible.

Within the past century and more, the Church has come face to face with a new enemy. Not a royal house, but the secularist state whose hostility to "revealed" religion is constitutional and virulent. (A Catholic emperor had to face a confessor for his sins against religion, at least on his deathbed.) Catholic bishops now find themselves in the fight of the Church's life, often with secularists within their own fold. The debate, it is said by enemies, is about modernity v. mythology, rationality v.

irrationality. Factually, the confrontation is a battle over sanity – whether God has a role in governing the universe and humankind, as he did in its creation, or whether the world is as mysterious and autonomous of any god as its unverifiable beginnings. The fight between theism v. atheism or agnosticism is one argument that cannot be debated out of existence – at least for those who believe in Christ and the Catholic Church.

This is a first of a kind for the American hierarchy. By the end of the nineteenth century, Catholic bishops had triumphed on behalf of the faith of their people against other Christians, who believed in Christ, but not in the pope. How are they doing today against those who do not believe that Christ is the Son of God? If Rome's repeated warnings to bishops about the contemporary faith crisis mean what the papal words say, the answer to this question must be: They are not doing well.

As one of the few modern institutions whose fate rests with a single bishop somewhere, the Church is accustomed to having her strong leadership compared unfavorably to the likes of Napoleon or Bismarck or Stalin. The best Church Fathers think instead of Abraham and Moses, Christ and Peter taking comfort in a Catholicity that has outlived all the monarchs and a large number of republicans.

The hierarchic structure of the Church gives the bishop, if he is good in his role, the hardest job in the Catholic community. Hard because he is a ruler at a time in history when the secular culture depicts authority figures as untrustworthy. Harder because so many Catholic divines now believe that the episcopal office has been mis-defined by the Church. A bishop is not the vicar of Christ, they say, but merely an agent of the Catholic community. Not surprisingly, therefore, disobedience of bishops by priests and. religious, based on disrespect for the office itself, has become commonplace. Contesting a bishop's prudential judgment on a liturgical translation or his political decisions, is respectable Catholic practice, especially when it is undertaken by people who are not bound to the bishop by vows or priestly promises. Questioning a bishop's Catholic teaching or his authority over Church discipline was unthinkable in the early twentieth century, by religious above all until now.

Historically, the Catholic Church is whatever a bishop, a group of bishops, or a pope make it, for good or for ill. The good ones leave behind an edified Church body; the incompetents squander the strengths they inherited, while those whom Scripture calls "hirelings" allow "sheep stealers" to divide and demoralize the flock. Whatever the results, theories about Church-building, even those based on New Testament readings, never built a Church. Only good bishops did that. Miracles carried the

Church through many crises, as Christ assured the Twelve they would. Nonetheless, his mission, till the end of time, remains at the mercy of bishops.

Exercising Authority

At the peak of its Catholic influence during the World War II period, the following prelates were in command of the major archdioceses: William O'Connell (Boston), Francis Spellman (New York), Dennis Dougherty (Philadelphia), Michael Curley (Baltimore), Joseph Rummel (New Orleans), Robert Lucey (San Antonio), J. Francis A. McIntyre (Los Angeles), John Mitty (San Francisco), Samuel Stritch (Chicago), Edward Mooney (Detroit), John McNicholas (Cincinnati). These prelates, each and every one, were men of authority, and the fruit of their decisiveness was a Church unique in its piety and social works. Revisionists have, since then, made them out to be "authoritarian" or "autocratic," but even those designated as "liberal," such as Mooney, Stritch, or Lucey, governed their dioceses with single-minded awareness of their sole responsibility for the faith of their flock. Each of them, as a diocesan shepherd, also recognized his independence of the national conference. Cardinal Spellman took a certain pleasure in his freedom to ignore the NCWC, once he paid New York's dues to that organization. A successor to one of the eleven archbishops, mentioned above, complained after Vatican II, "There was more freedom for bishops at the national level when Stritch and Spellman ran things." He was referring to the strictures imposed on national discussions and on local bishops by the NCCB, of which John Dearden and Joseph Bernardin, successors to Mooney and Stritch, were the chief architects. Central to the present Catholic crisis is the loss of status for the diocesan bishop as a man with unique responsibility and authority.

The Second Vatican Council did not authorize or legitimate many of the decisions done in its name, but it did reaffirm that bishops are the Church's vicars for Christ. *Lumen Gentium* (No. 26) decreed that bishops "regulate" Church worship and the sacraments, "govern" the local churches, and "have a sacred right and duty before the Lord of legislating for and of passing judgment on their subjects, as well as regulating everything that concerns the good order of divine worship and of the apostolate." No statement of Vatican II could be clearer. Search for explanations of the Catholic crisis, therefore, must go beyond the episcopal office to examine the way authority has been used or misused in recent years on behalf of the Church's "reformation" or "deformation." The

Catholic bishop is an anomaly in a contemporary society which would make all authority relations a matter of dialogue, not hierarchical.

The effort after Vatican II to enlarge input into episcopal decision-making was not intended to compromise the bishop's solitary authority. "Shared responsibility," however, did become a device for delaying or obstructing episcopal decisions. The technique of saber-rattling against Church authority by protesters became unsettling to bishops. Fr. Charles Curran, Fr. Theodore Hesburgh, and the Immaculate Heart of Mary nuns in Los Angeles used "shared responsibility" as an art form on behalf of disobedience and dissent. They opposed what the Church believed about Catholic theology, a Catholic school, and Catholic religious life.

A dramatic example of how the process worked was the confrontation which occurred in 1968 between the IHM nuns and the Holy See over the "essentials of religious life." Cardinal J. Francis A. McIntyre of Los Angeles, who at first was not directly involved, expected the IHM nuns to accept the Roman directives or jeopardize their role in his archdiocesan school system. The community president, Anita Caspary, simply said, "No." After much bickering over many months between the IHMs and Rome, with McIntyre in the middle, the matter was referred for mediation to an NCCB April meeting in St. Louis. There Cardinal John Dearden announced that he had written personally to Paul VI, expressing alarm at the Roman decision. Not only did McIntyre object strenuously to the NCCB president's intervention, but several West Coast bishops also challenged Detroit's right to interfere in a matter involving the Holy See and the Los Angeles archbishop.[1] Once this controversy was nationalized the die was cast against local episcopal authority in union with Rome. The IHMs seized this moment to rebel against Church authority at all three levels.

Time would prove Rome and McIntyre right, and Dearden wrong. Temporizing at the national level, followed by uncertainty in Rome, turned defiance into revolution. A Vatican spokesman, in response to a reporter's question, gave a further ominous signal when he said: "The case is not closed as long as there is agitation." The IHMs, as a major force in Catholic piety, would wither away – by then the vast majority of their nuns were no longer interested in anyone's ecclesiastical approval. Yet they passed the torch of autonomy across the convent life of America and made intimidation of hierarchy a way-station to a bicameral Church. Thereafter, bishops were expected to use their authority only to ratify mutually satis-factory agreements with the Church's antagonists. A few years later (1972) the Conference of Major Superiors of Women, when they reorganized into The Leadership Conference of Women Religious, dropped words like "authority," "obedience" or "Superior" from their lexicon.

In due course, the bishops themselves were divided into the "orthodox" and the "pastoral," the one whose starting point of governance was belief and practice, ready to cope with violations, the other who accepted the condition of people as the reality, hoping to gain conversion. One leader would be classified as "conservative," the other as "liberal," one judged to be closed-minded, the other broad-minded. The pastoral bishop was seen as developing a sheepfold around his flock; the orthodox bishop as one who concentrated on leading his flock into the sheepfold through the narrow gate of God's Word. Jesuit Thomas Reese, who has written a great deal on this subject, distinguishes Paul VI's pastoral bishops, from John Paul II's orthodox types.

This commonly used distinction was rejected by Paul VI himself on many occasions. In his exhortation *On Evangelization (Evangelii Nuntiandi,* 1975*)*, for example, he warned "bishops, clergy, and the faithful of the entire world" that "the deposit of faith must be transmitted exactly as the ecclesial *magisterium* has received it," "without the slightest betrayal of its essential truth," faith which disappears "if one empties or adulterates its content under the pretext of translating it."

This temptation of latitudinarian Catholicity is an old one. Tendered anew under the rubric of modernity, this seductive nomenclature legit-imizes three types of Catholics – high, middle, low. Church members are no longer "good" or "bad," practicing or non-practicing, merely different. "Truth" and "right" recede in consciousness, and bishops wonder how to regain the "assent" or "obedience" from Catholics who no longer think Catholic. If bishops accommodate antagonists, they may gain "détente," but in the process lose the aura of being vicars of Christ.They also appear as pleaders to those they are called upon to govern.

Power over Church affairs then tips toward "veto groups," whose role exclusively is to frustrate bishops in the proper exercise of apostolic authority.

What Must Bishops Do?

The contemporary episcopal predicament is twofold: (1) how to exercise Church authority in a culture suspicious of authority figures; and (2) how to reclaim authority over those priests and religious who have become agents of virulent dissent. The composition of the episcopal body, its unity and fidelity to the pope, is a critical factor in determining the Church's future. Business-as-usual bishops are not major problem-solvers; rebel-type bishops make matters worse.

A large amount of animosity has been directed at John Paul II for allegedly trying to stack the hierarchy with conservatives. Apostolic Delegate Jean Jadot's recall from Washington to Rome in 1980, and the Belgian's subsequent exile to oblivion, was supposedly the new pope's signal that orthodoxy would be a prime qualification for bishops to come. Conservatives, however, are not too sure that this has really occurred because the ongoing priorities and enactments of the American hierarchy are little different from what they were under Paul VI, though unrest among bishops-in-the-fold is more noticeable today than it used to be.[2]

However, in any war, like the one going on now between Catholicity and secularism, the first priority is a sound "battle plan," the second is the right general staff. The Council of Trent had one such plan. Pius IX had another for Ireland, once he realized the sorry state of the faith on that pitiful island during and after the potato famine. He plucked Paul Cullen out of the Irish College in Rome and sent him to Armagh as archbishop and apostolic delegate. Cullen's mission – to do something about the warring Irish bishops and the low state of piety there. Here is how Emmet Larkin describes the turnabout that Cullen engineered:

> Cullen determined the opposition to him by having only those who agreed with his reform principles succeed to bishoprics in that province, and gradually, but relentlessly, those bishops who were reluctant to change their ways in the rest of Ireland were replaced by Cullen's more energetic and aggressive nominees. By 1875, therefore, there was hardly a bishop in Ireland, except McHale [Tuam], who did not zealously promote pastoral reform in his diocese, whatever his educational and political views were. Actually this resolution of the distribution of power in the Irish Church in favor of Cullen was not nearly so smooth or inevitable as it may appear from this oversimplified account, but what is most important to understand is that this resolution of power was absolutely necessary to the making and consolidation of the devotional revolution that did take place.[3]

Cardinal Cullen's ministry, which lasted thirty years (1851–1880), worked because he and the pope knew what they wanted and found the right bishops to help bring 96 percent of the Irish people to Mass on a Sunday morning.

How does John Paul II or a pope of the twenty-first century hope to correct the present malaise in the American Church?

Never in Church history have so many declarations of faith, instruments of catechesis, directives for worshiping and discipline, critiques of aberrations, and *monita* to disturbers of Catholic peace come from Rome with so little impact on Church piety. The crisis is wider and deeper in 1998 than it was in 1968.

When the United States was plunged into a two-ocean war in 1941, a plan of counterattack went into effect almost overnight – from a declaration of war to invigorating the country's internal strengths, to surveillance and quarantining of potential enemies, to determining priorities (Europe first), plotting the recovery steps, island by island, beachhead by beachhead, and selecting generals good at waging war. (It is interesting in hindsight how General Pershing gave FDR George Marshall, who brought Dwight Eisenhower to the fore, while George Patton emerged on his own, and the President immediately brought Douglas MacArthur from retirement.)

The Church does not seem to have such a battle plan, even if its war – far more worldwide – has nothing to do with aerial bombs or tanks. But even if there were a plan, where does the pope find the equivalents of Paul Cullen, Charles Borremeo, or Stanislaus Hosius?

Bishop-making looks complicated, at least as it reads on paper, if the "Norms for the Selection of Candidates for the Episcopacy in the Latin Church" are taken at their word. Proposing names in a provincial meeting of bishops, having those names processed through the office of the apostolic delegate or nuncio for investigation and evaluation, forwarding the results eventually to the congregation for bishops in Rome for final selection by the pope is a thorough process designed to eliminate the misfits. It may also bury the naturals. The theory says that the candidate ought to be a good pastor with a good reputation and an irreproachable moral life, be even-tempered, orthodox, faithful to the Holy See, theologically informed, pious, zealous, with an aptitude for good government. He should also possess the spirit of dialogue, openness to the signs of the times, have the right family background, and so forth. Jesuit Thomas Reese singles out, as desirable, "a spirit of ecumenism," "the promotion of human rights," and "a fatherly spirit," qualities which Reese interprets as indicating that "an authoritarian pastor is not wanted" in the Vatican II Church. When all is said and done, however, it is bishops who make other bishops, and the more powerful the prelate, the greater the influence he has on the final choices, if he decides to make his presence known, The examples are numerous. Cardinal Spellman is reported as having given coadjutor archbishop McIntyre his choice of Los Angeles or Washington, D.C.'s Patrick A. O'Boyle, confirming the report, said: "I was to get what was left over." Another American cardinal used his red hat to force the appointment of several bishops whom Roman authorities considered unfit.

The process includes politicking, of course. The unmeasurable factor is providence. Christ remains the model: a believable personality; an uplifting and inspiring preacher with a good message; an unusual public demeanor, which made him seem godlike; ability to gather faithful followers and train them; a willingness to confront criticism by arguing his case against enemies, and against disciples, if need be; special regard for the holiness of God's temple; and remarkable courage to stand up for his cause, even if it means death.

Presuming all the Christ-like qualities are present, what else does a modern pope want in a bishop? And how does he know, in advance, that the favored candidates are competent in the art of governing? These are not easy questions to answer. During the 1830s, the Holy See elevated Francis Kenrick and John Hughes, one to Philadelphia, the other to New York. The former, a pacific personality, enjoyed a better reputation with bishops than the fiery Hughes. The Nativists, however, never burned the New York churches down the way they did Kenrick's. They did not dare! Unless the pope, by experience, is a good hands-on manager of the Universal Church, his choice of appointing the right man for the right See depends on "the system," and this means on sponsoring bishops.

In 1921 Cardinal Hayes received as auxiliary bishop a chancery official who, two years earlier, had written to him as follows: "It has always been and, please God, always be my keenest happiness to serve you. It may sound like hero worship, but there are some things one cannot explain, or define. Your approval is all I want." In 1943 Cardinal Mooney finessed the appointment of Msgr. Francis Haas, a disciple of John A. Ryan, to the bishopric of Grand Rapids. Haas made clear to the apostolic delegate that he did not want the promotion, but made a fine bishop nonetheless. In 1968 New York's Coadjutor Archbishop John J. Maguire was asked to take a major see. He turned it down, saying afterward, "I'm a Good No. 2 man; I do not know that I'd be good as No. 1."

A pope never knows, for sure, who will work out and who will not, nor how providence sometimes intervenes to upset "the system." Dennis Dougherty, as bishop of Buffalo during the pontificate of Benedict XV, was touted to succeed to New York. That See did not come open on time, so in 1918 he was sent to Philadelphia instead, where he reigned for thirty-three years. Dougherty never stayed in his office after high noon on a given day, but to this moment, as his three successors readily confessed, when the word "cardinal" is mentioned in the City of Brotherly Love, it is understood to mean Dougherty – over forty years dead!

The strange thing about the governance of the Church is that the pope does not have the least idea, when he chooses a bishop ordinary, whether he will work out in practice. They say that any worthy priest can be a good auxiliary bishop, but this is no longer true. An Ordinary, however, must be a master of human relations, a wise and resolute decision-maker, a whiz at finance, a deputizer of detail while remaining "the boss" of his bureau-cracies, and an exemplar of what the Church incarnates. And he is rarely supervised any more, even though the pope's curia, sometimes *il Papa* himself, receive all kinds of complaints about his shortcomings. Unless financial disaster or scandal emerges, every diocese has its Ordinary for a relatively long time.

Even if the pope has at his disposal an approved registry of potentially superior diocesan overseers, how can he be sure, as his critics fear, that all – future appointments will go only to the so-called "orthodox" or "conser-vative" *episcopabili?* Here we have a question which never surfaced in this century during the pontificates of the last three Piuses. The eventual appointee in those days might prove to be an ineffective diocesan shepherd, but all bishops then recognized their responsibility to be the protectors and defenders of One Lord, One Creed, One Pope, One Worship, without fear of contradiction from anyone at or below their station.

Two posers lurk in one new question: How does a nuncio decide that a candidate accepts the orthodoxy of John Paul II's Catholicity if, unlike the pope, he has accumulated no public record in the defense of any of its controverted parts? Who is the candidate likely to move through the process successfully – the priest with no record or the one labeled "contro-versial" because he is well-identified as a John Paul II protagonist?

John Paul II presides over a strange household, viz., one in which a certain pluralism of belief and practice has become the established orthodoxy in Catholic education, even in the seminaries from which most of the forthcoming episcopal candidates will emerge. Adjectives like "orthodox" and "conservative" are well-discredited terms in the best Catholic circles. No one seemed upset when a young college alumna wrote blithely for an *America* audience: "In college we were forever being admonished not to tie our faith to any particular dogma or precept.[4] Although *Humanae Vitae* touches on the nature of Christian marriage and sexual morality far more than on a contraceptive act, Avery Dulles is placidly received by an assembly of bishops in 1993, and is later published in *Origins,*[5] with his remedial advice that adherence to Paul VI's encyclical teaching should not be used as a litmus test in the appointment of bishops. William Byron, S.J., former president of the Catholic University of America, responding to a statement that a Catholic college should be a source of pure Catholic teaching, retorted, "Baloney![6] The reigning pluralists extend their reach to the Church's discipline and moral code. In 1994 Crossroads Publishers produced *Bending the Rules: What American Priests Tell American Catholics,* written by an ex-Jesuit. This account of twenty-nine veteran parish priests "bending the rules" is not a story of reconciliation and forgiveness, not even of social support for struggling habit-formed sinners, but of indulgence, of doctrinal skepticism, of sexual sinfulness, free and easy Catholic divorce, violation of liturgical norms, pope-bashing, and hypocrisy. This is the atmosphere under which many priests and future *episcopabiles* are being trained.

More than twenty years ago, sociologist Daniel Bell, speaking of what he saw as a revolution going on within the Church, opined that the weaker Church authority seemed to be, the greater would be the attacks on it, on its power first, on its teaching eventually, prompting more of her people to look to other religious sources for faith. Jesuit Francis Canavan in his *Pins in the Liberal Balloon* (1995) attaches the word "hypocrisy" to the present Catholic situation. Faced with the choice of practicing what the Church teaches or leaving the Church, the orthodox pluralists elected instead to remain in the Church and undermine its standards. And they expect bishops to sanction this hypocrisy by leaving it be, counseling shepherds not to interfere: "You cannot undo the reform." "Law will not work." "You cannot mandate." "You'll sound un-ecumenical." "You must be compassionate." "Don't be taken in by fundamentalists." "Things will die down." "Be pastoral, not dogmatic." "The media will kill you." "Rome doesn't have all the answers." "The NCCB President will not like it." "The nuncio will be upset." Or, as Richard McBrien remarked on the pope's apostolic letter, "To Defend the Faith" (May 19, 1998): "They'll have World War III on their hands if they suddenly decide to declare war on theologians!" Since good Catholics usually recognize good bishops by what they do (e.g., building a Church) more than for what they say, does it not seem that in tendering these admonitions, "the pluralists" want and expect "pluralist" shepherds? The situation is worse than it was in the cynical days of Alfred Loisy, when he proclaimed in his *The Gospel and the Church:* "Jesus preached the Kingdom, and, behold, it is the Church that is come." The post-Vatican II cynics say: "The Church is here, and it is ours."

Is the Holy See thinking of potential bishops in terms of this kind of Church, and of their ability to bring such cynicism under control?

The Bishop and Liturgical Abuses

A bishop told the story many years later of how he never had a problem with a priest of his diocese. Shortly after his installation he presided over a Sunday Mass at which the pastor introduced his own homemade eucharistic prayer. Later, when he was alone with the priest, the prelate remembered saying: "Father, if I ever catch you or any priest of this diocese tampering with the liturgy, I'll wipe Main Street with your body! Do I make myself clear?"

Not every bishop is capable of that form of Catholic action, but the incident illustrates what has been a serious problem for parishioners – even for those who think that the liturgical abuses are an improvement, or even fun. The same bishop, later at another parish, found himself watching what he called "the dance of Salome" to a Caribbean drumbeat around the main altar prior to the offertory. When the pastor leaned over to ask how the bishop liked it, his lordship replied: "If she asks for your head, she'll get it!" Changing the words of the Mass, eliminating the Creed, celebrating without liturgical attire, turning the liturgy into theater, celebrating the homosexual lifestyle, preaching false doctrine, using profane music, non-Catholic ministers concelebrating or distributing communion . . . represent false worship.

The worship is also false when the participants or the choristers chant more about Christ the Man than about Christ the Son of God, more of the Church as a community of people, than as a house of God, more of this life than the next. Worship is surely false when a young man, having rejected Sunday Mass after high school, can write: "I don't see any purpose for having a Church anyway. Since we are all saved anyway, how important could it be?"[7]

Is there a plan to deal uniformly with such false worship? One prominent archbishop suffered over several years with public misuse of the liturgy by Jesuit pastors. He was not the only one. Two theories have made the rounds about episcopal authority, both of which subvert the Catholicity of the Church: (1) the "progressive" theory asserts or suggests that Church authority derives from the Christian community and can be exercised only by the sufferance or consent of that community or of the divines who allegedly speak for the masses; (2) a "traditionalist" theory agrees that it comes from God but is exercised by incompetents who (a) are afraid or unable to exercise their authority as it was conferred by Christ or (b) purposely let their office passively allow a latitudinarian Catholicity to emerge without openly disavowing vital Church documents. Both schools of thought are cynical, one using the battering ram of their ecclesial power to neutralize or debilitate the authority inherent in the episcopal office, the other lowering esteem for bishops by accusing them time and time again in public of malfeasance in office.

Whether one likes it or not radical liturgical innovations or abuses and the willful mistranslation of liturgical texts do undermine the faithful's sense of the sacred and their respect for the truth of what the Church has taught about the eucharist, the heart and soul of its divine worship. A priest who presides at many weddings – and funerals today – notices irreverence and worldliness before the Blessed Sacrament, especially by the young, that was unthinkable a generation ago.

The new *Catechism of the Catholic Church* (No. 1899), reaffirming the ancient teaching of Peter and Paul, makes the correction of such faith-lessness a special work of the hierarchy *in toto et exclusive.* "Let every person be subject to the governing authorities. For there is no authority except from God, and those that exist have been instituted by God. Therefore he who resists the authorities resists what God has appointed, and those who resist will incur judgment." (Rom. 13, 1–2; 1 Pet. 2, 13–17).

There is some truth to the proposition that the pope does not know what is going on in Rome. Considering the vast bureaucracies now in place everywhere, this is hardly surprising. Allegedly, John Paul II was annoyed that a Roman cardinal approved "altar girls" without his express permission. And the complaints of bishops are legion of how Washington bureaucrats publish position papers diocesan leaders never see. How times have changed!

The Bureaucratic Church

When John Cardinal Farley became the archbishop of New York in 1902 his chancery office consisted of one priest (Msgr. Patrick J. Hayes), one diocesan lawyer, and two secretaries. When John Cardinal O'Connor succeeded to that see in 1984 his chancery office was twenty-one stories high. Bureaucracies tend to have a life of their own, regardless of who sits in the presidential or episcopal chair. Harry Truman once jested, during the inauguration of Dwight David Eisenhower: "Wait till he pushes the button in the Oval Office and finds that no one answers!" In 1997 the U.S. bishops acknowledged that the catechesis going on in the Catholic schools across the country was seriously flawed faith-wise, a defect in a major American Catholic bureaucracy which Rome documented as early as 1972.

The modern bishop's early task, therefore, is to supervise, and to reform when necessary, the various diocesan agencies which stand between him and his pastors. It is common knowledge since Vatican II that parish priests have been reprimanded by bishops for bucking the directives of this or that diocesan agency head, even when the pastor wanted Roman norms obeyed, e.g., first confession before first communion for eight-year-olds. Archbishop Thomas Molloy of Brooklyn in olden days was wont to instruct curates who complained about their pastor: "The pastor is always right. You'll be a pastor someday." Whatever the truth of that legend be, the modern situation is radically different. Although a pastor – along with local bishop and pope – has exclusive and ordinary jurisdiction within the Church, he is subject today to more bureaucratic controls than his predecessors ever were. The new power of diocesan and religious agencies in the governance of the Church presents new problems to bishops and to churchgoers, who depend on bishops for the faithful representation of Catholic teaching and discipline.

Every bishop of a diocese, no matter how good a chief executive he may be, suffers at times from the innocent mistakes or the malice of his subordinates. Because of the treachery of his finance officer Christ suffered agony and throughout Church history popes have not always been well served by staff.

In our time John XXIII discovered, too late, that the planning of Vatican II got away from him and went beyond anything he had in mind when he convened it. Given the persuasive mood of the electronic media, disrespect for the papacy within the Church grew to be a major dysfunction. Historically, the word "reform" (the Gregorian Reform, the Tridentine Reform, etc.) meant "change" in accord with the mind of Peter. Popes no longer can count on this. Paul VI had reason to be unhappy with the composition of the Birth Control Commission, which he left to others. And the failure, after more than ten years, to implement authentically sections of the 1983 *Code of Canon Law* (e.g., on religious houses, on marriage tribunals, and on colleges) is attributed to weakness or dissent within the papal and/or national bureaucracies.

Certainly, today's headlines in the secular and religious press feature disrespect for authority down the line of the Church: "Can the Pope Command His Flock,[8] "A Flock at Odds with Its Shepherd.[9] "When Shepherds are Sheep,[10] "Wolves in Shepherds' Clothing." *The Economist,* pointing to the American role in the Roman quandary, opines that the NCCB in Washington, D.C., "will try to ride out the crisis by putting the best face on things and pretending that there are no real problems, only misunderstandings." The internecine debates between Catholic academicians and journalists which foment such editorial barbs, have depleted the devotional life of the faithful. For all the study, communication and political activity at "high" levels, less and less do the laity experience the sign of the cross, genuflection, benediction, the stations of the cross, the rosary, and the blessing of expectant or now mothers.

Bureaucracies seem to go on forever, as everyone knows, whether they are bastions of intransigency or revolution, whether they represent a New Deal for government or a New Freedom from government. Prior to the creation of the NCCB (1966), Church bureaucracies were small. (In the 1960s, it was possible to open a new diocesan agency, e.g., a Family Life Bureau, on an initial budget of $500.) Today, the NCCB's annual budget surpasses $40 million, and its secretariats exercise a hegemony over the doings of diocesan bishops that its predecessor (NCWC) never had. Unsurprisingly, the most powerful Catholic lobbies for special Church interests are found in Washington – the National Catholic Educational Association and various learned, liturgical, and charitable societies, the Jesuit Conference, and a host of others. If the older agencies were less influential on Catholic thinking because of small budgets and powerful controls at the episcopal and papal levels, the newer bureaucracies, with richer endowments and a new spirit have become a "second magisterium."

A more radical explanation for the present Catholic divisions can be found in the paradigmatical shift of priorities within the Church from "saving souls" to "saving the world." Neither Vatican II nor recent popes made this dichotomy a question of "either/or" (that would have made no Christian sense); but certain elites now insist that Catholicity to survive must lower its sights and its norms. Thirty years ago sociologists Rodney Stark and Charles Glock opined that the only Christian Churches to survive will be the ones that sought the good life here. All Churches, they thought, will have to make the "forthright admission that orthodoxy is dead." Philip Gleason summarizes the argument and mind set of the new elite classes as follows:

By the 1850s the Church was sufficiently well-established to assure its survival. This permitted attention to other kinds of problems. At the same time, the older type of controversial apologetics was becoming outmoded, as Protestantism continued on what Catholics regarded as its course of inevitable decline. It was no longer sufficient to defend the authentic rule of faith against misguided fellow Christians. The task of the Catholic apologist in the new era was to justify religious faith itself to unbelievers, to present the Christian message in ways appropriate to changing circumstances, and to suggest ways in which the Church would respond to the needs of the world being reshaped by the forces of modernity.[11]

Since the critical issue for a mature Catholic people, it was said, would no longer be rival Christian creeds but unbelief in general, "saving the world" seemed like the chief apologetic tool for rebuilding faith in Christ. Does the hierarchy really believe this?

This line of apologetic thought originated with mainline Protestant pundits who in the nineteenth century were dissatisfied with the logic of their own faith. "The Social Gospel Movement" became their early twentieth century apostolate. For them Christianity became "the highest democratic morality" and John Dewey emerged as its prophet,[12] and in due course "the movement" divested pews of Sunday worshipers. It is now the popular religion of secularists.

This shift in Christian priorities never received then the sanction of the Catholic community for two reasons: (1) the Church's strong emphasis on Eucharistic worship and the sacramental system continued to make "saving souls" her primary mission; and (2) her clear teaching that the reconstruction of the social order was the apostolate of well-trained and pious Catholic laity. After World War II, however, important Catholic intellectuals, those especially trained in secular universities or those who were in doubt about "the truth" of the Church's doctrinal propositions, raised the socio-political reform of the world's public institutions to a new level in the mission of the Church.[13] Their influence since 1965 over the internal management, and the public posture, of the Catholic Church, became triumphal. Social action came to rival fair in the creeds for prominence in Catholic catechesis. In many respects the bureaucracies overcame Rome's priorities. Sunday worship, the worthy reception of the sacraments, especially the Eucharist, penance as the ordinary instrument of reconciliation, the sacredness of the priesthood; the indissolubility of marriage, marital chastity and other sacred devotional beliefs and practices suffered at the hands of the Church's professional class.

The dilemma of twenty-first century bishops is this: How will they recover their mastery of the Church's priorities? And where will Rome find bishops capable of reinforcing Roman policy? Will bishops find ways to bring their own bureaucrats to the "obedience of faith"? And when is the pope going to return to the "autonomy" of National Episcopal Conferences?

On the right answer to these questions rests the recovery of the Church.

F I V E

The Priest — Shepherd or Hired Hand?

> The Good Shepherd labors zealously for his flock in union with
> the bishop and the pope. The Hired Hand impairs his office and
> his flock by disrespecting the teaching office of the Church, and
> by neglecting his priestly responsibility to form his people in
> "the obedience of faith." (Rom. 1, 5).

A bishop pastor of a large city parish once instructed a new chancery
official, undoubtedly to help the young man keep his Catholic priorities in
order, as follows: "The linchpin of the Catholic Church is the pastor – the
Pope in Rome, the Bishop in his Cathedral, the shepherd of every diocesan
parish. On these three rest the well-being and Catholicity of the Church."

Priests and laity of the World War II generation, as those who had
gone before, accepted this proposition as a Catholic given. Especially
since historians had attributed the strength of the American Church to the
effectiveness of diocesan bishops and parish priests of the late nineteenth,
early twentieth centuries.

Something happened to that concept on the way out of Vatican II,
because two years later the new National Conference of Catholic Bishops
authorized a study, published as *The Catholic Priest in the United States:
Historical Investigations,* whose index of 900 items failed to mention
"parish," "parish priesthood" or "parochial work." Ever since, the phrase
"Catholic pastor" has become an elusive term. The idea, therefore,
deserves another look, not only on behalf of the Church's mission to God's
people but for its Catholicity.

The Bishop's Point

The Catholic pastor – from John Paul II to every would-be imitator of the

Curé of Ars – is the central figure in the existence and conduct of the Catholic Church. Any debasement of his status and dignity, including that by a priest himself, jeopardizes the credibility of the Church.

Pope and bishops may contract with other qualified people to teach under Church   auspices, to succor the needy, and to manage her temporalities, but the pastor – called simply "the parish priest" in many places – is irreplaceable, without peer. Without him the Church cannot function legitimately or properly.

In a community of truly Catholic faith, the phrase "He is a priest" speaks volumes to believers and for the man himself. In a godless society (as the Church understands God), the priest is looked upon as just another citizen with a man-made job. Neither is he "sacred," nor is there a "sacred" for him to represent. At the worst, in the language of a virulent secularist, he is a threat to modern society. John Paul II, in the opening lines of *Pastores Dabo Vobis,* looks at him differently: "Without priests the Church would not be able to live."

The Second Vatican Council also reaffirmed the necessity of pastors in *Lumen Gentium* when the Fathers declared that Christ, the Church's "Eternal Pastor," established Peter at "the head of the apostles and set up in him a lasting and visible source and foundation of the unity both of faith and of communion" (No. 18). Furthermore, bishops are vicars of Christ in their diocese, and "in virtue of this power bishops have the sacred right and duty before the Lord of legislating for and passing judgment on their subjects, as well as regulating everything that concerns the good order of divine worship and of the apostolate" (No. 27). Priests, too, "exercise the function of Christ as Pastor and Head in proportion to their share of authority" (*Presbytorum Ordinis,* No. 6). The Council spoke of service, consultation, participation, collegiality as elements in the proper exercise of his office, but all Church documents are careful to protect the authority of the pastor to act *motu proprio* as necessary in order to teach, to rule, and to sanctify the faithful. The Fathers made clear that a pope is outside – and not a member of – his College of Cardinals,[1] and the local bishop is independent of his board of consultors. Arlington's Bishop John Keating, in urging parish councils in his diocese, also made the following disclaimer for the pastors: "Pastors have certain responsibilities which are theirs alone. They have duties which must be exercised personally in virtue of the mission which they have from Christ in ordination and from the bishop through their appointment as pastor.[2]

The new *Canon Law of the Church* (1983), implementing Vatican II, specifically states that the faithful "are bound by Christian obedience to follow what the sacred pastors, as representatives of Christ, declare as teachers of the faith or determine as leaders of the Church" (Cn. 212). Those pastors alone, pope and bishops especially, have "the supreme responsibility to teach, sanctify, and rule the faithful in Christ's name" (Cn. 376).

The New Questions

Almost every interested Catholic, beginning with John Paul II, is talking today about the shortage of priests and about what their absence will do to the future of the Catholic Church. Are there human causes of this crisis or ways to make the priesthood attractive again to young men, as surely it once was?

The pious look upon the shortage as a cross from God. But how did the American Church fall into this institutional morass?[3] Fewer still are willing to probe further. Why should a manly human being aspire to devote his entire life – celibately – to a Church role which, throughout the recent years of his boyhood, has been denigrated, deflated, and debunked not only by those who reject the very notion of priests but within the Catholic sanctuary itself? Reports of various kinds, including those of ecclesial bodies, attribute this shortfall of priests to the collapse of Catholic discipline before the secular culture or to a moral failures of one kind or another within the Church. There is truth in these assertions. Yet, historically, confusion or doubt about the faith itself – either Christ's teaching or the Church's – is what undermines priestly performance. Many bishops allege today that their serious problems involve priests, not the laity. Furthermore, the believability of the priesthood comes into question whenever questions arise in rectories over what Catholicity – the papacy, or the Eucharist really means. Any overhaul of priestly thinking that excludes Catholic faith and places self-anointed men solely in charge of determining who God is and what he has revealed, or that stresses Christ the man virtually to the exclusion of Christ the Son of God, or that speaks of the Church as people more than as the house of God, or makes the priest more a delegate of the community and less a vicar of Christ, places the Church in trouble with God and his people. Those popularizing such a new gospel would solve the present priest problem by marrying them off, or by ordaining women, or by creating "lay pastors." Would these concessions to secularity motivate a potential Isaac Jogues to leave his homeland and to die, if need be, for Christ?

The Way We Were

No system or organization, even the priesthood, is ever perfect. Still, the American parish may be "the highest achievement of the American priest," as it had been called in 1905.[4]

The special bonus of the American Catholic system, which continued beyond World War II, was the relative freedom of the pastor to run his own parish. It took a little doing to make it so.[5] But by the turn of the twentieth century, the pastor was "a little bishop," whom cardinals treated with respect. For one thing he had stability in office.[6] For another, bishops depended on pastors for support of diocesan causes. Third, the majority of veteran pastors, as "men of authority," also commanded large amounts of local loyalty, and bishops, as a rule, had a healthy regard for the pastor's "ordinary jurisdiction." Pastors were practically "irremovable," except for grave cause. (The obvious dysfunctions of any system – incompetent or lazy pastors – reflected not so much on the system, as on the bishop's failure to use his authority to correct or persuade his errant subordinates.)

In important respects, therefore, the office of pastor was insulated from undue harassment or abuse by curates, by religious, or by laity prone to demand what Church law or a pastor's priorities said they could not have. Brooklyn's Archbishop Thomas Molloy may have overdone it a bit with his advisory to a disgruntled curate: "The pastor is always right. You'll be a pastor someday!" The unhappy curate, principal, corporate executive or political "boss" of that day might complain, or move elsewhere, but a pastor's authority was rarely undermined by his superior.

The underside of this nineteenth-to-twentieth-century parochial success, however, was that mega-parishes sometimes became status symbols and sinecures more than missions. Older priests came to enjoy the benefits of their predecessors' labors, much the way prelates savored benefices in the late Middle Ages. By the 1950s pastors had ceased giving strict orders to their curates. They might propose tasks or at times express annoyance, even bark a bit, but by and large *laissez-faire* became the order of the average pastorate. If the nuns did not wish the priests to teach in the school, that was the end of the matter as far as certain pastors were concerned. A handful of responsibilities were still mandatory and widely respected (e.g., Saturday confessions, rectory duties, parish events), but parish priests were mostly on their own, unless they also had teaching or other assignments. Parishioners came to them (home visitations were a thing of the past), making many rectories busy places. And a function of being a good curate was to protect the pastor from those burdens which transcended administration.

A pastor's priority, which in 1910 was on "the work to be done," shifted to what the priests and others felt about the work in the post-World War II era, especially if it seemed mandatory. The lazy priest was far more noticeable in many rectories than violators of the Ten Commandments. A pastor could still effectively ask for the removal of a curate, but he had little influence over how much work the priest actually did in his house. Nonetheless, so many first-rate parish priests were available everywhere that the "good" parishes remained good. *Laissez-faire* also extended to the bishop's level. If no one disturbed him, then he disturbed no one. Episcopal visitations became perfunctory, more like social meetings than serious supervision of pastoral performance. The superintendent of schools was a more likely overseer of parochial education than the bishop was of the priestly mission. The system continued to work well because tending to the basics remained an ingrained sacred trust for most priests: a decent worship, sound teaching, dutiful sacramental and social life, exemplary behavior.

From the priests' point of view, the most noticeable dysfunction amid such ecclesial prosperity was the length of time required for those in large dioceses to become pastors in their own right. In the nineteenth century, a priest might become the pastor of a small parish in two or three years, and then be transferred to the metropolitan area by the time he was thirty six. By World War I he might still receive a large city parish in his early forties. At World War II time, he would be almost thirty years ordained, or fifty-five years old, when he was called upon to govern a rural parish. The pastoral care of the faithful sometimes suffered when a curate, who had served a single city neighborhood for twenty or more years, was passed over for succession in the pastorate there, in favor of a stranger, because at sixty he was not old enough to merit the assignment. The over-aged curates of the day were, however, too disciplined to be outraged at the prevailing conditions or at a bishop who was not creative enough to find adequate remedies for an obvious evil. Their response, too often, was early retirement from hard work. This situation set the stage, after Vatican II, for a revolution in priestly expectations and behavior.

The Diminishing Status of Pastors

Any octogenarian priest who is still interested will find himself in conversation these days with priests a generation younger who do not wish to be pastors or who already have abandoned the role. If he also moves around the country, he will discover this to be more than a local phenomenon. The United States may be too large for generalizing about the low morale of the clergy, especially when so many young enthusiasts are evident in every diocese. Yet, being "boss" of a parish is not what it used to be, either in its status or in role-playing, a phenomenon new to the twentieth century, during which practically all priests, even the incompetents, yearned for the bishop's call to pastor.

The tendency nowadays to correlate high morale with the ecclesial shift in priestly style and manners, from sacred persons in cassock and Roman collar to "hail-fellows-well-met" in secular clothes, is presumed to enhance self-esteem, allegedly a prized stepping stone to a more fulfilled life of Church service. But how is self-esteem an adequate priestly goal when "emptying oneself" (Phil. 2, 7) is the New Testament model? Freedom, comfort, and shared authority have been offered, too, as bonuses for the "renewed" priest, but for a pastoral role which of its nature demands duty and sacrifice? Has the reinforcement of a new American spirit by new methods of training future priests or updating veterans really worked to the Church's advantage?

Another factor complicating morale has been the rising status of priest-specialists vis-à-vis parish priests out in the field. Once bishops began to feature (and to honor) chancery officials as the important men in their lives, the pastors (certainly the curates) lost diocesan status. Patrick Cardinal Hayes of New York (1918–1938) made bishops only of active pastors, whereas his successor Francis Cardinal Spellman (1939–1967) mostly promoted chancery priests. As the Church's bureaucracies grew, so did the bishop's reliance on what social scientist Charles Murray calls "the cognitive elites." After the New Deal, such elites were not without influence on secular politics, but they were counterbalanced by the grass roots wisdom of "party bosses" and district captains, much as – within the Church – seminary professors and chancellors were offset by large numbers of dominant pastors.

Today, the pastor's likely difficulties (or a priest's) are his diminished Mass attendance, the rising costs of maintaining Church agencies, the increasing taxation or special collections imposed by diocesan headquarters, the absence of well-trained American priests as curates, the plethora of foreign-born externs who do not intend to establish roots or to Americanize, or the dearth of religious, who once were "the heart" of parish life. The Church has recovered from deprivation and poverty before, and so have disciplined priests of faith, but this time it is not going to be easy.

The more pressing problem is that of the pastor or a priest (in communion with his bishop) who is deeply mired in ambiguity about how far his authority extends to decide the meaning of the word "Catholic," or to determine, against recalcitrant opposition, how his parochial community should normally worship, believe, or live, or how much support he will receive from his bishop in doing what the pope says. Challenge to pastoral authority is the order of the present day. The contestation may be expressed in "power-sharing" language, but it really challenges the pastor's fundamental authority. By training, a Catholic pastor realizes the limits of his authority over unbelievers, non-believers, or recalcitrant sinners; now he must face commonplace doubts about his doctrinal and disciplinary authority over a community that is still described as "the faithful.[7]

Post-Vatican II Revolution

The post-Vatican II decline in priestly/pastor status began simply enough with theories, proliferated throughout the Church's infrastructures, that Catholic doctrine had it wrong when it insisted that a priestly hierarchy is the magisterial guarantor of God's Revealed Word, or that Christ appointed bishops as governors of the Church. Catholics were commonly taught during the 1970s, in college or seminary classes, that what the risen Christ likely had in mind as his replacement was a congregation of followers who worshiped God and did good works in his name. Not much more. Certainly not a community with a priestly caste, or a Eucharistic sacrifice, or an *ex opera operato* sacramental system celebrated only by priests, or moral absolutes taught by them. According to Joseph Cardinal Ratzinger this revisionism, viz., that the Catholic Church is largely a human construction, became a dangerous *dubium to* make its rounds at the parish or school street level.[8] A "humanly constructed" Christian community might grow naturally, so the theorizing went, to need supervising "presbyters" (i.e., a Greek word for "old men"), but hardly a divinely sent "holy father" in Rome or anywhere else.[9]

This revolution was justified in the name of Vatican II, which supposedly decreed major accommodations to the demands of secular culture, in the hope of an increased influence for the Church over worldly institutions and the enhancement of the quality of life on earth, particularly that of the poor and the oppressed. Those who feared evil consequences from activating these theories within the Church were called "prophets of doom." Yet, the results have been a diminution of Catholic faith and piety among large numbers of actual and would-be Catholics, a proliferation of dissent against Catholic creeds, and a disobedience of Church laws, to an extent proportionately unknown to America since the early days of its first bishops.

The American bishops sensed this post-Vatican II threat inherent in the theories going around their dioceses as early as 1974. In preparation for the Third Roman Synod, which resulted a year later in Paul VI's deservedly famed *Evangelii Nuntiandi,* the NCCB sent its episcopal delegates to Rome with this advisory: "The emerging question for the Catholic community may well be whether in the future, as in the past, it derives its fundamental beliefs and attitude from the traditional value system of Catholic Christianity or whether its beliefs and attitudes will be drawn more and more from the secularistic, humanistic value system around it.[10]

Wrong Practice Makes Malpractice

The failure to perform the duties assigned to, and expected of, a public office is malpractice. A certain amount of it goes on in families everywhere. Determining the degree to which it must be in evidence before it becomes a menace to society, involves human judgment of a non-infallible nature. Still, like so many social conditions that cannot be defined empirically, people know malpractice when they see it. Certainly, the Church of the United States is worse off than it was in 1962, not because of anything the council fathers said or wrote, but because their words were misinterpreted and misused and because the authority that belongs to pope and bishops was equivalently "hijacked" at lower levels. Worse in the process, the public laws of the Church on worship, doctrine, and discipline were violated with impunity.

As events unfolded, however, the local pastor today can do little about these divisions, which appeared almost everywhere, except to exacerbate them, if he was one of those priests inspired or trained to keep "pluralism" alive among Catholics, after the manner of the Church of England. Although such divisions are often presented as mere differences of opinion between "pluralists" ("the best and the brightest") and "fundamentalists" ("the narrow-minded"), the real issue was, and is, the true meaning of the virtue of faith and its content.[11] If something contrary to faith, or at least indeterminate about faith, is taught or done in violation of Canon Law at a neighboring parish or in the next diocese, it is almost impossible to insist on universal Church norms of belief and practice.

To the charge years ago that the Church was undergoing a "crisis of authority," Jesuit Cardinal Jean Danielou, himself a scholar, responded that the divisions were due rather to the lack of the use of authority by bishops and by Rome. That was his early post-Vatican II judgment. As years went by, the bishops actually allowed their authority to be used to legitimize the status of "pluralists" within the Church. They drew their preferred experts mainly from dissenting professional associations. This not only gave status to dissenters, but it also led to the quarantining of competent "defenders of the faith" and excluded these latter from having any serious influence on the trend of national decisions by hierarchy.

The faithful pastor at the local level suffered from all of this, notably by loss of authority over clergy who were trained in the new order, and over religious who taught in his schools. This did not happen everywhere at first, nor does it happen everywhere now, but significantly so across the country.

The process of debilitating the pastorate (and the parish priest, too) occurred in many places in three stages:

1. By bishops weakening *motu proprio* their own authority, that of Rome, and of every pastor, whose office is only as effective as the bishop's.

2. By secularizing the priestly office.

3. By feminizing the Church.

1. Weakening Pastoral Authority

The year 1967 was a critical turning point. Cardinal John Krol had it right: If bishops, who owned the Catholic University of America, could not terminate the employment of a non-tenured professor of only two years' apprenticeship, what was the use of being its board of trustees? Especially since trustees at Yale or Harvard were free to do precisely that, without having to explain why they did it. In 1967, however, someone persuaded CUA's rector, and others, against their better judgment, that letting Charles Curran's contract expire would somehow be un-American. Subsequently, Curran found the way to bring the bishops to heel by organizing priests and religious, especially in the Washington, D.C., area, to march on picket lines in protest against the very idea of bishops having anything to say about the Catholic qualifications of a professor. The bishops capitulated.

Cardinal Spellman said he was too old to get into another fight. Archbishop John Dearden, newly elected President of the NCCB, was hardly an influence on behalf of Rome, and his fellow Clevelander and friend, Atlanta's Archbishop Paul Hallinan, might even be called the main Curran partisan on CUA's Board. Cardinal Krol himself capitulated to his follow bishops, wrong-headed though he thought them to be. And Boston's Richard Cardinal Cushing roared that he did not know why bishops were involved at all because they knew nothing about running a university (As if this was the principle under attack from the Curran faction). Later, Cardinal Patrick O'Boyle summed up the rout with the pithy line: "We ate crow!"

Within weeks of that debacle the forces of autonomy against episcopal hegemony gathered again. This time it was the Jesuit college presidents, and Notre Dame's President Theodore Hesburgh as their host, at Land o' Lakes, Wisconsin (July 23, 1967), to declare the freedom of Catholic higher education from hierarchy's oversight. On October 14, 1967, the Immaculate Heart of Mary Sisters followed suit celebrating a "Charter Day," whereon they declared that no longer would IHM leadership permit Rome (or the local bishop) to determine "the essentials" of the Church's religious life. This community paved the way for the breakup of convents and parochial schools all across the country. (When the Congregation for Religious directed the IHM's to observe Roman norms, NCCB president Dearden wrote to Paul vi against the letter's sternness.) These autonomies of special Catholic interests from papal and episcopal authority are more firmly in place now than they were thirty years ago.

During the years between 1967 and 1982 American Catholics saw the growing use of contraception among Catholics, the explosion of annulments, the wipeout of the Sacrament of Penance, opposition to the *General Catechetical Directory* (as there later was to the *Universal Catechism),* studies of both religious life and seminary training which managed to paint an optimistic picture little resembling the reality, and a host of disciplinary problems. Tensions developed early between Rome's universal norms and episcopal conferences which regularly sought leeway in their application (e.g., dispensations or reinterpretations of what was about to be promulgated in the new *Code of Canon Law* [1983], or in later Apostolic Constitutions like *Ex Corde Ecclesiae* [1990], even on the English translation [1993] of the new *Catechism).*

By 1982 the bishops in conference were ready to discuss "The Role of the Bishop in the Contemporary Church," which they did behind closed doors in Collegeville. The then-Archbishop James Hickey favored the consultation process inherent in good government, a judgment with which anyone of sense would agree, but he also made clear that certain authoritative aspects of the Church were reserved to bishops alone, such as teaching in Christ's name. He asserted that those who "teach in the Church's name" should be accredited by Church authority, as surely as chemistry teachers were by the state. (These were points Paul VI had made earlier.)

However, the prevailing voice of that meeting was John Cardinal Dearden, the founding father of the American post-Vatican II ecclesiastical machinery. Brought back from retirement to give the keynote, the Detroit archbishop – in contrast to Hickey – stressed almost exclusively the virtues of the "listening" bishop, who shared responsibility and consulted. No reservations were indicated. At one point in the address he jibed at the relationship of Rome with a national body of bishops, by recalling Rome's anxieties about the old NCWC (1919): "We can smile at the reports drawn up during the stormy days when a small delegation was endeavoring to save the NCWC from suppression. One quotation from a report has these sentences: 'They [i.e., the Holy See] are always talking about the autonomy of a single bishop. It's a smoke screen. What they mean is that it is easier to deal with one bishop than with a hierarchy.'"[12]

Indeed, under Dearden's administration of the NCCB (1966–1971), which had an anti-Roman flavor characteristic of him, the episcopal "listening" favored the Church's pluralists, viz., those who held in disfavor many views of Roman authority. Even a bishop-in-the-field could be called "absolutely stupid" by a bishop-bureaucrat if he stood in the way of what became Washington priorities.

To this day official Catholic circles do not correlate the breakup of the Church's doctrinal unity, nor the statistical declines, with policy decisions made between 1966–1971, and reaffirmed thereafter year by year.

The national episcopal machinery was in such a hurry to make changes, some quite dubious from the beginning, and so forcefully, that thirty years later, many individual bishops feel bound to rubber-stamp decisions which make them unhappy. After the November 1966 meeting, for example, Archbishop Elden F. Curtiss of Omaha, discussing liturgical translations, summed up the mood: "We have been fighting about this for several years and arguing and discussing it. We have made our interventions and we tried to get a response. The body of bishops generally wants to finish it and get on with it. So I think this is the reason there has been so little debate.[13] In short, a small committee with "experts" chosen by a few leaders, tends to remain in command despite unrest among bishops in the field.

What has this to do with pastors and parish priests? Such episcopal practice, widely publicized, makes it seem that the local pastor, too, is not the final word in his own jurisdiction, especially if he rejects the recommendation of a parochial committee or council which considers itself independent of the pastor in matters of Church governance. The average pastor today deals with priests, religious, and laity who, by what they notice going on at large, no longer think that a cleric, even it he is a bishop, has any right to require acceptance of what the Church prescribes about first communion, general absolution, or liturgical norms, or teaches about worthy concelebration or communion, marital responsibility, or "the Catholic conscience." If some of those who have enjoyed "consultant" status at the national level, say that bishops no longer control the Church's highways and byways, what makes a parish priest feel important? "Reformers" have come to think that they represent the Holy Spirit refashioning a Church that never should have come to be in the first place.

In some respects, the secular world has succeeded in turning the Church upside down. Ever since the Freudians and Rogerians came to dominate the culture with their stress on the subjective and to make personal feelings the important elements in the determination of truth in the formation of character, or on good citizenship, and ever since hierarchical structures came to be looked upon as instruments of oppression or "guilt machines," the officers of secular society have courted the unhappy and the discontented more than those seeking only to do what is objectively good. In recent years censure has gone out of favor, unless the wrongdoing offends the secular agenda. This ideology has achieved great influence today on the governance of Catholic institutions, where obedience to Church Law is not necessarily a high priority and when the demands of ecclesial authority are deemed to be politically incorrect by secular standards. If many of the best and brightest Americans now eschew vital civic roles because the world in which government officials must function is morally topsy-turvy, it should not be surprising that a pastorate fashioned in the secular mode is not the desirable thing it once was.

2. Secularizing the Priestly Office

"Come Follow Me" was an invitation for the Twelve to undertake Christ's redemptive mission to God's people. Their relationship from the beginning was patriarchal/filial, just about what He meant when He spoke of "my" or of "your" heavenly Father. Many latter-day Christians will have none of this traditional understanding of the priesthood, in part because it suggests dependence on the arbitrary will of someone else or on a lack of self-determination. In their mind it is also opposed to the contemporary plurality of interpretations of God's alleged Word about ministry. Such views are old news to the Church, although rarely expressed in modern times until the post-World War II period.

By then American priests were enjoying more of life's comforts than their lay counterparts, more than their predecessors. Not simply because of their "star status" in every neighborhood, but because of improved rectories and a new freedom of operation. (Priests were, however, no more exempt from the crosses of life than others.) Celibacy in those generations was not the cause of crisis the secular world makes it today. Busy priests had little time, then, to feel sorry for themselves, and knew where to go for help, even to the bishop or the vicar general, who were usually solicitous for every priest's well being.

Almost without careful estimate of what hasty change could do to the status and mission of parish priests, bishops introduced terms of office, personnel boards, multiple discussion groups, preferential options, salary emoluments, leaves of absence, and so forth. These perquisites were presented as real answers to off-expressed personal problems (e.g., over faith and/or being under authority), which all people experience at some time or another under any system. Concessions, however, never seemed to help some priests. Almost immediately, curates became harder to handle once they were made "associates" (no matter the age), no longer .assistants." (In the professional world, an "associate" earns his status over time.) The strange aspect of this "modernization" is that, although these proposals were given by priests' councils as options, bishops often followed them as bounden duty. One archbishop, succeeding to a see where "terms of office" did not exist, refused to introduce them because he looked upon the oversight of all diocesan pastoral needs, and of priests especially, as his personal responsibility. Another bishop told his seventy-five-year-old pastors that he would speak with the pope about compulsory retirement, not adverting to the fact that he, no less than the pope, need not accept a priest's compulsory "letter of resignation." More than a few priests, arriving in the pastor's chair in their fifties, were forced out in their sixties to start all over again in an entirely new place, denied the opportunity to enjoy the harvest they had sown.

If currying favor with the bishop was the earlier way to gain a good assignment or to escape an unpleasant one, the new game involved playing the politics of the personnel board, whose well-intentioned and apostolic-minded members often had their own agendas for the diocese.

While checks and balances between centers of political power, or "divided government," as it is sometimes called, represents enlightened political wisdom, there is no philosophical or ecclesiological principle, let alone empirical evidence, which verifies that a committee system is proper for, or superior to, patriarchy (or matriarchy) in the management of a family, or of Christ's Church. A Church that claims that her hierarchy is of divine institution must be careful about a "committee" tampering with a pastor's office or his staff without his knowledge. A personnel committee which supplies a bishop with information he might not otherwise have is a procedural improvement. A personnel board, which manages the bishop's priest-placement process, stands between a pastor and his bishop (or vicar general), after the manner of a corporate enterprise.

At ordination a priest gives himself in "reverence" and "obedience" into the hands of the bishop alone. To obey a bishop is more in accord with that commitment than to obey a committee or a staff officer who would have a pastor bow to the chancery's prudential judgment on free matters. In former days a chancellor would permit the pastor to decide whether a suicide was entitled to Christian burial. A father-son relationship with a bishop may not make priestly morale in a diocese better, but it does maintain a certain sacredness between the two that cannot be realized through a negotiating committee. Nor do we hear that the present abundance of committees raises priestly morale. The contrary seems to be true. Employment practices borrowed from a modified capitalistic enter-prise, where making or dividing money is the objective, designed to mute class distinctions, or instill a sense of self-fulfillment in subordinates, and improve corporate productivity are not exactly what should define the kinship of a father with his son. These devices by themselves are uncon-nected with "self-sacrifice," "obedience" or priestly "mission." In fact, they more often take away from the priesthood the very qualities required for exercising a – sacred vocation properly and for finding satisfaction with it.

3. The Feminization of the Church

One of the more disparaging statements made about religion, even of Catholicity, is that it is mostly women's work. It is so by the nature of femininity, some would argue. Cursory observations of Catholic life in many countries of Europe lend *prima facie* support to this theory. The fact that such an assertion has never been made convincingly about the Church in the United States is testimony to the well-rounded formation of Catholic character here by American bishops and their priests.

Before God, men are no less bound to His worship than women, nor are they less obligated than women to obey His Laws and those of the Church. Neither in the order of grace nor of nature are men dispensed from fulfilling the different roles that God has ordained for them. God shows no partiality here. Radical feminism, whatever its role in reducing sexuality to sex or in weakening the link between womanliness and marriage, or with motherhood, clearly seeks to unseat men as authority figures. The feminist campaign targets are not just fathers of the household, but priests of the Church as well, especially the Holy Father. God as Father of the human family might even be the ultimate object for a fall.

Men and women are often defined today as male and female, without reference to their fatherhood or motherhood; in radical feminist circles marriage is often mentioned without its natural link to parenthood or even to heterosexuality. Such feminism associates authority with more power, not with God's truth or right. Its partisans seek parity of political power with men, perhaps even more power, although domestic and maternal ties will always place limits on the political entanglements of most women. Their irreplaceable motherly presence in society can never find a fitting substitute in males.

Although extreme sexual formulations can hardly be defended within the Church, feminism nonetheless has impacted negatively on the conduct of pastors, even bishops. By pursuing the ordination of women with social force, in spite of explicit magisterial teaching, its protagonists tend to eviscerate the term "shepherd" of its Christ-like meaning. This destructive privilege was reserved in earlier centuries only to unbelievers, heretics, or schismatics.

Today, pastors tiptoe around the feminist issues (so do official documents), by frequently placing unconditioned emphasis on women's rights without corresponding reference to their Christian duties, and seemingly join the chorus of those who oppose discriminating judgment about sexual roles in the marketplace, in public service, in the worship of God, or even within marriage. Motherhood and fatherhood are rarely discussed in depth. References to the indignities heaped by feminists on manhood or on good men are never heard, while silence over the lack of respect frequently shown to fathers in mother-dominated households merely reinforces the impression that women *per se* are victims and men somewhat unworthy of respect for the role most of them exercise responsibly. A great deal of rhetoric in this vein is sometimes expressed at bishops' meetings. The suggestion occasionally appears that women would be more comfortable with the Church if more of their numbers were diocesan pastors, chancellors, or tribunal judges or if hierarchy only reeducated their priests accordingly or persuaded Rome to overcome its outdated attitudes by conferring priestly jurisdiction on those without holy orders.[14] In Catholic circles discussion of this subject turns at times into a rally for a secular political judgment rather than a search for the correct fulfillment of Christian revelation.

These thorny issues are not going to be resolved by the Church as long as they remain political; nor as long as the only correct answer seems to be to divide the priesthood in Solomonic fashion between so-called chauvinist men and feminist women; nor as long as the absolute demands of God's Word as the Church understands it are not the framework within which sincere believers work out how best to do what God wants them to do. St. Paul, in spite of his dismissal as an authority on matters sexual, speaks more wisely on this subject than his critics. Those who would rewrite Ephesians 5 find it is easy to grant that in modernity, free or not, it is appropriate to remind husbands (as if God is demanding it) to "love your wives" (since men tend to be careless in this regard); but inappropriate to remind wives to "obey" or "be subject" to their husbands in the proper place and time? Good women do this all the time, even as chauvinist 'Enry 'Iggins reminded his Fair Lady of her special tendency to "do precisely what she wants!"

The secular world cannot be held to account for its double standards, or for its hypocrisy, because it no longer believes that words ever mean absolutely what they say (e.g., "until death do us part") or because ambiguity and equivocation are acceptable, if carried on for a politically correct cause. The Church, however, may not permit her sacred institutions – marriage and the priesthood being only two – to appear as man-made constructs rather than as the God-given supernatural realities they are. She does not allow this to happen, at least not among her own, when she is sure of herself. In 1930, for example, Pius XI had no trouble articulating the role of fatherhood: "If the husband is the head of the domestic family, then the wife is the heart, and as the first holds the primacy of authority, so the second can and ought to claim the primacy of love.[15]

Even when new questions arise about the sacraments, Church

teaching remains constant, however the language or arguments are modified. Canon 521 of the new *Code* speaks simply: "To assume the office of pastor one must be in the sacred order of the presbyterate." Canon 517 says such authority can be shared, but if, due to the shortage of priests, "the pastoral care of a parish" is entrusted "to some other person," even a deacon, the bishop is to "appoint a priest endowed with the powers and faculties of a pastor to supervise the pastoral care."

It is this determination of the Church to hold fast to the revealed realities upon which its very nature and the Word of God is based, which "reformers" seek to erode. "Change the Church's practice and the Church's teaching will change" was a principle of revolution enunciated early by the likes of Hans Küng and associates. Under this rubric began simulated concelebration of the Mass with the non-ordained (or non-Catholic ministers), eucharistic reception without absolution from mortal sin, general absolution as licit apart from personal confession of sins, declarations of nullity for valid marriages, ambiguous translations of biblical "hard sayings," secularized religious life, women as administrators of parishes (with a priest as curate), and so forth.

Tearing down the walls around that exclusive "man's world" in the Church and making the definition of priesthood sexually neutral is the latest assault on Catholic doctrine. Already 80 percent of the laity engaged in Church ministry are women, according to one bishop addressing a national meeting of his peers in 1996. How often do churchgoers see a man in the role of their parish's eucharistic minister?

The Catholic Theological Society of America (in a 1996 convention report) deduces that John Paul II's belated approval of altar girls is a theological harbinger of women priests to come. Is it?

The First World has been moving toward unisex for a half century and toward a femininized culture in which women will be honored if they are less than truly feminine or if they limit their motherly role in their daily life. John Paul II warned about the pitfalls of that feminism which encouraged "a renunciation of femininity" or an "imitation of the male role." Such an ideology may please "iron ladies" who seemingly never appear lovable, but it also repudiates the street wisdom that says that working women prefer men bosses. Apart from the homosexual implications of unisex, a "disorder" of nature *ab initio,* "women-power" does not necessarily beget women influence" especially if "iron ladies" are its chief witnesses. The complementary masculine/feminine structures of the Judeo-Christian tradition may have bestowed power on men to wage wars, to levy taxes, and to gain a great deal of attention from history buffs. Still, mothers, the child-bearers, the nurses, the teachers, and the nuns are the ones who mostly ran the world of the streets, where human beings learned how to be human, a lesson many children no longer learn.

In post-World War II Catholic circles, a man, challenged to prove that he was "the head of the house" was commonly caricatured as defending his superiority in this way: "I make all the big decisions, she makes the little ones. She determines where we live, where the kids go to school, and what we eat. I decide whether Russia should be allowed into the United Nations, or whether the A.F.L. should merge with the C.I.O." That crack contained more of the real world than sexists, male or female, would like to admit. The eternal question remains: Does the battle of the sexes really exist? Obviously, from the time of Adam and Eve, with women, usually mothers, winning more often than the radical feminists want youngsters to know. If the children of Catholic immigrants once credited the Church with their social success, chances are that this or that local pastor received honorable mention for the accomplishment. But, more commonly, it was "the nuns" – and mothers in the home – who were the greater influence during husband's and children's formative years, a power of women over people more significant than any man's power over things. (This was so noticeable by 1950 that Philip Wylie made a national reputation decrying the putative ill-effects of "momism.")

The Church cannot control the reigning ideologies of the secular order, but by now she ought to know how to handle her own false prophets. If the purpose of temporizing with those Catholics who have a "conscious bias" against the priesthood (John Paul II's term) is to effectuate their conversion, the effort is failing. New priests are not only fewer, but the morale of the "reformed" clergy has never been lower, if reports of the NCCB (1989) or the National Catholic Educational Association (1990) are correct. Martin Luther denigrated the ruling role of the priest with his line," we are all consecrated priests by baptism," but the modern issue is whether the priest, as "the man of the Eucharist" (John Paul II's term), is Christ's vicar in the apostolate of redemption and salvation. Even the appearance of compromise over the manhood of the priesthood is bound to raise the next questions: Whether the priesthood has direct connection with Christ; whether Christ is really present in the Church or in the Sacrifice of the Mass.

Pastores Dabo Vobis and the Faith Problem

That something should be done about these matters is obvious to John

Paul II who, when he wrote *Pastores Dabo Vobis* in 1992, took note of the depth of the crisis over the priesthood from early Vatican II days and the marked difference in the kind of priests who were appearing on the scene then, as compared to thirty years earlier. Even though his problems are similar to those of his predecessors from earlier centuries, this pope is not expected to do anything impetuous.

During the fourteenth century days of Urban VII (1378–1389), the Church was in decline because ecclesiastics had allowed themselves to be held hostage by underlings or politicians. Princes wanted less Church influence on the conduct of states, French cardinals (and the king) kept the pope in Avignon and out of Rome for seventy years. Freewheeling clerics, then, fixed their eyes more on money than on souls. University personnel (e.g., Paris's John Gerson) argued that Christ's authority was vested in the Church's people, not in the pope, and therefore exercisable without necessary reference to the apostolic patrimony. During this so-called "Avignon Captivity," according to Philip Hughes, hierarchy surrendered their rights and jurisdiction "wholesale," authority which their predecessors valiantly fought to have recognized in the public arena.[16]

History never quite repeats itself, of course. Catholic kings are not around anymore to threaten prelates. Only, the officers of the secular state have a grim, if subtle, way of burying the Church behind her own walls, while they reach over bishops to change the minds of people about religion. The modern state is insidiously antithetical to Catholic piety, a virtue that every pastor must cherish. Its "cognitive elites," including Catholics, are prone nowadays, as they were in the days of imperial Christianity, of conciliarism, of Protestantism, or of Gallicanism, to propose marriage of the Church to the reigning state, a temptation prelates of old found hard to resist. But as one sage reminded them: "If the Church marries herself to any era, she'll soon be a widow." Why? Because she stands outside and above secular culture of any kind, even one of her own making. When certain popes mistakenly thought they should dominate the state because they were vicars of Christ, their successors felt the force of state power seeking to fit the sacred into its secular mold. Whenever the state trivializes capital sins or makes trivial sins capital, the Church has lost.

Masters of secularity think that the idea of sin (an offense against God) is just about as ridiculous as the idea of God becoming man to redeem the world. What has this to do with pastors? If the decline in congregational faith among Protestants is a paradigm, then it was the "treason of clerics" which brought it about, as Anglican priest-theologian

Eric Mascall was wont to say.[17] Mascall saw the process at work among Catholics after Vatican II, in the willingness of "enlightened clerics" to spread a view of Christ as one who is not our God nor our teacher; and to explain Christian events rationalistically, as if the explanations provided by the Apostles, Evangelists, Fathers of the Church, or the magisterium of the apostolic successors were intellectually incompetent. The loss of faith in the real Christ, and in the Church as his real sacramental presence, began in her heartland after the recent Council – within those houses of learning and formation entrusted with the initial and ongoing training of priests and religious. The results of the treason were symbolized almost overnight in little things. Bishops continued to wear cassocks, but many younger priests divested themselves of clerical clothing, almost as rapidly as younger religious women exchanged community garb for secular attire. Then came the priestly downgrading and the belittling of those pious practices which, while not the necessary effects of faith, do reflect the efforts of earlier priests to keep God's presence felt in the lives of their faithful: holy water fonts at the entrance to a Catholic home, bowing the head or signing the cross as one passed a Church, blessing of new mothers and their infants, benediction and adoration of the Blessed Sacrament, devotional novenas to Our Lady and the Saints, scapulars, etc. In due course, as these pious practices fell into disuse, there followed Mass without vestments or creeds, Holy Communion to habitual sinners and non-Catholics, dissoluble marriages, and the end of confessional lines, just about the time that large Catholic families disappeared. When the flight of religious from religion began, colleges, too, founded by a saint or a living martyr from one of America's great communities, muted their Catholic identity or, like the twenty in New York, had themselves declared by the state nondenominational and no longer juridically Catholic. These shortfalls were not sanctioned by Vatican II, yet they were frequently claimed as legitimate fruits of the council, especially the result of the Church's "openness" to the world on rational terms, and to autonomous decision-making below the level of pastors' jurisdiction and, therefore, of no need of pastors. Many years ago an obscure academic, reviewing Karl Rahner's theological superiority over the German bishops, recapped a new elitist view of Catholicity:

> Openness means facing the deep religious problems of contem-
> porary life – acknowledging, for example, that it is not easy to say
> exactly what "God" means today. To say whether the orthodox
> formulas are not mainly empty and to say precisely when love of

neighbor is not sufficient religion. Similarly, we have no adequate ecclesiology for the increasing number who are "selective" in their faith, who cling to some doctrines and reject others. We are already an ecumenical Church, in the sense that we are solidly pluralistic. If we are courageous enough to accept organizational and doctrinal pluralism more forthrightly, letting more ways of following Christ just be and interact, we could really start to think of ourselves as united.[18]

Most Evangelical Protestants would reject this inane logic, which divests the creeds and Church teaching of meaning, and reduces the sacramental system to a series of empty rituals or superstitious acts. For Catholics who think this way, St. Paul's "one Faith, one Lord, one Baptism" (Eph. 4, 5) no longer endures as a rule of faith. The right of the Church to vivify these three aspects of authentic Christianity – unilaterally through pastors – is denied. The faith-problem transcends any failure in the human governance of Christ's Church.

In Summary

The critical questions facing all contemporary Catholic pastors are two:

1. How much of the faith preached by the Vicar of Christ can their parishioners believe, in view of the way bishops or pastors are often contested in their household, or by the quality of parish life they are likely to hand on to their successors, if the present divisions continue;

2. How can that discipleship which characterized the American Church through most of the twentieth century be restored, that which is consistent with mind of Him who told His first followers, "If you live according to my teaching you are truly my disciples" (Jn. 8, 31)?

Doctrinal purity and discipleship go together – injury to one weakens the other – hardly a desirable condition for the Mystical Body of Christ.

Deny it as many may, contradictory pluralism on matters of faith and morals is entrenched in the post-Vatican II Church and a form of heresy. A kind of Peace of Augsburg now rules in the United States, the quality of the Catholicity in a given place depending on who is in charge of the local Catholic community. Europe's political leaders once decided to give civil legitimacy to the religion professed by the local reigning prince or duke. *Cujus regio, ejus religio.* Identify the prince of a place, and the people's religion was officially predetermined. This Solomonic solution was denounced by believing Protestants, while Pope Innocent X (1644–1656) excoriated it as "null, worthless, iniquitous, frivolous and without authority!" Yet Augsburg was nothing more than statutory recognition by politicians of religious pluralism over which popes and bishops no longer had any say. Henceforth, Church membership was to be a private affair, doctrines were of no social significance, and the secular state became, in effect, the arbiter of religion whenever churches were unwise enough to intrude on the public square.

Princes of the realm no longer exist in the West with power to seize monasteries or send a bishop to the tower for head surgery or imprison a pope. The Church's privileged place in secular society was lost at Westphalia, but bishops at least were left free to deal with the Church's own, at least in theory. New "princes" were bound to arise, notably in the academy of Germany for the Protestant Church, but also within Catholicity on the continent. In those years the caretakers of the Church at any given time often lacked the fervor of their Jansenist enemies or the intellectual/polemical skills of a pagan Voltaire or the will-to-win of a politically determined Bismarck.

Something of the kind has been going on in the modern Church. A different kind of Catholicity has unfolded in various segments of the Church, depending on who controls a specific place – a pastor, a prior, a college president, and so forth – with bishops no longer having a firm hold on the consciences of Catholics. This veritable revolution in the United States institutionalizes a nominal Catholicity here for the first time, one that has long been a characteristic of "Catholic" countries in Europe.

A social scientist, asked to comment on the present state of the Church, might express surprise that anyone is upset by this turn of events. Changes in types of government and in ruling classes go on all the time, he would say. Vilfred Pareto dubbed this as the "circulation of elites," a Machiavellian case of "foxes" in a nation's political structure outsmarting the "lions" in power, or of the latter eventually running over the former. In this theory, revolution was likely to appear at critical points of history, when the "ins" miscalculated the popular support enjoyed by the "unfriendly outs." The Pareto analysis claims to explain the dissolution of the Roman Empire, why republics replace monarchies, or how democracies end up totalitarian. It suggests, too, that a fox-like "cleverness" in politics, exercised at the right moment, prevails over the sheer "strength" of officeholders, as symbolized by lions, and has a certain relevancy to secular governance, whose main function is to create or maintain order within a country and to defend people against outside enemies.

The Catholic Church, however, has been created to sustain much more than social peace. She was ordained to instill the Word of God among men and to engender sanctity at least among her own. Granted that, as a human institution, a certain discipline is necessary in order that this be done effectively, but the message matters for the Church, not the social process. And to protect the Gospel and the creed, she may call on the disciplinary customs of an age or draw on the wisdom of her own tradition.

Whether secular society likes it or not, or particular Catholics either, Christ's mission has been entrusted to consecrated priests. John Paul II insists: "Without priests the Church would not be able to live!" In the pursuit of their vocation, therefore, in the Pareto scheme, priests must be both "clever" and "strong." When they are "foxes" to the exclusion of their "lion-like" qualities, "the message" becomes blurred. A "treaty of Westphalia" situation cannot long continue in the United States without the witness of the Catholic Church to Christ's mission becoming irrelevant to the lives of her own people. Nominal Catholicity will replace the deep Catholic piety of those trained in the unified American Church of the earlier twentieth century.

What can Catholics do about this crisis?

Renewing the Pastor's Role

The renewal of priestly status in the Church, the reaffirmation of the parish priest's role and authority, and the reversal of the downward trend in seminary enrollments are top priorities for action by the pope and bishops. Part of the process involves scholarly restatements of the Catholic tradition, going back to apostolic times, and orchestrated recalls also of saintly testimony about priests. But re-enhancement of the office in the lives of priests themselves is also essential. The sacredness of the priestly vocation demands it. If a priest is a vicar of Christ, he must learn to think as such.

To reinforce priests in this endeavor, however, structures must be developed, beginning at the seminary level. It is worth recalling that sound doctrinal and moral formation, episcopal supervision, rectory living, and wearing cassocks or Roman collars, for example, only followed long centuries of poor training and unworthy priests.

As the abuses of the post-Vatican II years mounted, one American cardinal had reason to instruct the Apostolic Delegate: "You clean up the mess in Rome, and I'll clean up my archdiocese!" Reform, whatever its inspiration, is accomplished only through the proper laws with sensible enforcement by a society's highest authorities.

The scandals of recent years are due mainly to the fact that those whom Peter and Paul called evildoers have often been indulged or even rewarded, while the faithful sons and daughters have been ignored or discounted. The disorder, most noticeable of all, has been the fraternal relationship that developed between Church bureaucracies and notorious dissenting bodies within religious and academic communities.

On the other hand, rarely is an apology tendered for the hurt inflicted by a bishop who removed a good pastor after four decades of service for being strict on decorum during worship, on the theologian forced out of his university tenure for criticizing some of his community "leadership" (a post he could retain if he left the order), on the university president forced to retire when dissenters became the dominant force in his congregation, on the priest who never recovered his parish although the Holy See directed the bishop otherwise, on the theologian denied a seminary post because he was considered a papalist, or on a faithful journalist terminated as editor of a diocesan newspaper because a timid bishop caved in to pressure from a handful of priests. These are only a few of the wrongs that have been perpetrated on the Church's faithful by one or another office-holder, with hardly a thought within the community of defending the righteous against the misuse of office by the unrighteous. What was once called "the blackboard jungle syndrome" in major cities came to prevail, once students (some commentators called them hoodlums) took the peaceful management of public education in metropolitan areas away from their teachers and the municipal fathers. The office of pastor suffers similarly whenever Catholic anti-establishment figures ignore the legitimate directives of bishops or refuse to obey, or make threats against his governance, or disdain the office publicly even when he does what Church law requires. Once unchallenged or uncorrected, such misconduct radiates throughout a parish or a diocese.

Reform, according to the authentic norms of Vatican II, begins when all Catholics, including pastors, recognize that the present crisis begins with lack of supernatural faith in the truths of the Church as expressed in her ordinary teaching and ends in disobedience of the pope and the bishops in union with him. Our crisis, therefore, is not one of exhaustion from a frustrating contest between tradition and modernity, liberals and conservatives, Americans and Romans, as it is sometimes made out to be. It results from a lack of virtue within the Catholic community, and perhaps of God's displeasure.

As long as the crisis continues, it is incumbent on those who have full confidence in the "faith of our fathers" to continue witnessing their faith boldly. By so doing they will suffer, as St. Athanasius did in the fourth century at the hands of Arian confreres, as Thomas More and John Fisher did a millennium later under England's headhunting Henry VIII, as the Curé of Ars did in post-French Revolution days when bishops seemed more nationalist than Catholic, and as St. Elizabeth Seton did from the Protestant crusade against her newfound faith. Who else will?

Believing Catholics will reject the pessimism of those who think that the battle for the American Church has been lost, or of those who confront the present controversies more in anger than with hope in God's Providence. The faithful certainly must continue their efforts to regain assent and obedience as attributes of the Church body, until pastors are once more able to teach, rule, and sanctify as Catholic wisdom ordains. Only under those circumstances, and with God's help, will the Church of the United States have once more the quantity and quality of priests the "faith of our fathers" engendered.

Of course, nothing is perfect within the Body of Christ as long as human beings are part of it. But that does not mean that the Church lacks a sacred nature, its priests too, or that seeking perfection in this life is not her *raison d'être*. Henri De Lubac had it right: "The Church which we call our Mother is not some ideal unreal Church but this hierarchical Church itself; not the Church as we might dream her but the Church as she exists in fact, here and now. Thus the obedience which we pledge her in the persons of those who rule cannot be anything but a filial obedience."[19]

These words are meaningless if the contumaciously disobedient or the scandalous sinners, especially consecrated religious persons, dominate Catholic sanctuaries or the designated halls of learning the faith; and if the faithful, including priests, are left to shift for themselves in their quest for holiness and eternal salvation. The gates of hell are prevailing, at least momentarily, when pastors watch the Church overrun by norms and sanctions invented by the secular state to keep God in his heaven and to mute Christ's presence in the public square. Since the princes of academe now take pride in their secularity, as the princes of the realm once did, it is incumbent on the pope with his bishops to restore the priesthood, the pastorate especially, to its full dignity and authority, leaving to practicing Catholics, taught and inspired by such priests, to bear such witness to the faith that the altars and the pulpits of the twenty-first century will be filled to overflowing with worthy Vicars of Christ.

The Bishops and the University[1]

"When bishops, after due consideration, are convinced that the orthodoxy of the people under their care is being endangered, they have the right and duty to intervene."
Delegates of the Catholic Universities of the World,
Rome, November 29, 1972

If the Catholic Church is to have a Second Spring in the United States bishops must accredit colleges as Catholic. Those institutions which refuse such certification should be identified and the Catholic community so notified. The story of the betrayal of Catholicity on the Church's college campuses needs retelling in detail. Dissident theologians would be no threat if they were working in a secular college and religious orders would be held to public account for their stewardship of those institutions which canonically are still theirs.

The nub of the crisis of faith debilitating Catholicity is illustrated first in an interchange between two priests. On June 30, 1998, John Paul II declared that Catholics who deny or doubt articles of divine and Catholic faith, or doctrines taught definitively by the Church's teaching office, are subject to appropriate punishment.

On July 7, 1998, priest Richard McBrien of Notre Dame University told the press that he is not worried: "They'd have World War III on their hands if they suddenly decided to declare war on theologians!" Also, in the various questions that might be raised were these two to meet officially. Who is declaring war on whom? Who is defending the faith? What faith? Is doubting or denying the Church's definitive teaching in a Catholic setting wrong? Why is a theologian who denies or doubts articles of defined faith teaching at a Catholic university? Who hired him? Who will fire him? What is wrong with firing him? Or are the Church's colleges no longer Catholic in practice? Subject to decreditation? *Is the pope irrelevant to its teaching or governance?*

Is Christ also irrelevant, making Fr. McBrien a legitimate alternative to the vicar of Christ?

Did Christ empower theologians to speak for Him, especially if they contest the pope on his definitive teaching?

The Church's Economy – Catholic Higher Education

When a kingdom finds itself at war, defeating the enemy is its highest priority. As the book of Revelation (12, 7) remembers: "War rose in the heaven, Michael and his angels fighting against the dragon; and the dragon and his angels fought, but they were defeated."

The internal enemy of the American Church is her vast system of higher education. The system grew as much from the drive of bishops as from the inspiration of those confessors and martyrs who placed the first shovels in the ground. But today that system fights bishops and pope. The fathers and mothers general of religious communities are sometimes blamed for the secularization of colleges which once boasted about their Catholicity. Perhaps. But the bishops now can return the favor by reclaiming the colleges for the Church's faith and the religious communities to Christ's evangelical counsels.

Why have American bishops, who played a leading role in the establishment of the largest system of Catholic education in the history of Christianity, become peripheral, if not alien, to what goes on within Catholic campuses when their presidents and faculties no longer will guarantee that the teaching they provide is Catholic, as understood by the pope and hierarchies in union with him?

Why do bishops, who originally gave episcopal permission for their creation, now absolve themselves of responsibility for the authenticity of their Catholic witness?

The Catholic college for many years was the center wherein the Church hoped that its future leadership would develop the mind of Christ, as mediated by successors to the Apostles. Its Catholic graduates were expected to leave their campuses as the leaven of Catholicity in a world unfamiliar with Christ, and its non-Catholic student body to acquire respect for the Church. The Catholic college has no other religious reason for existence as Catholic. Given its origins, this college cannot be ideologically neutral to the Church which gave it a name. If the phrase "Catholic University" was an oxymoron to an unbeliever like George Bernard Shaw, "secularized Catholic college" is an oxymoron to any believing vicar of Christ.

The long-range effects of permitting colleges to retain their name but go their own way in opposition to Catholic integrity are three: (1) it undermines episcopal authority, (2) it renders Catholic doctrine ambiguous, (3) it blurs the identity of Catholic institutions everywhere.

A case study in detail of how bishops have dealt with what the present pope calls their "counter-magisterium" may contribute to better decision by magisterium in recapturing the governance of the Church's teaching office. The story is not pleasant.

Undermined episcopal authority. Canonically defined, bishops (1) govern Catholic worship; (2) determine what the message of Christ is; (3) create or approve instruments for its authentic transmission; (4) define the priesthood and religious life, whose personnel serve in schools established to hand on the Catholic faith. Worship and service to God by the Church cannot truly proceed if the hierarchy, in union with the pope, does not have the final word on what it means to be a priest or religious, on the parameters of authentic Catholic theology and on the definition of a Catholic school, whatever else may be its secular function. Without such authority acknowledged, in practice as well as in theory, a Church can hardly be classified as legitimately Catholic.

Since Vatican II, the National Conference of Catholic Bishops has weakened the foundations of ecclesiastical authority – that of the pope in Rome and the local pastor, too – by three incautious decisions, all coalescing strangely in 1967.

First, by deciding that it was un-American to terminate Charles Curran from his teaching post at the Catholic University of America. Nineteen years would pass before Rome declared him unfit to teach Catholic theology and forced his firing. But by 1968 "little Currans" had multiplied all over the Catholic landscape, sometimes as religious superiors, even as columnists in diocesan newspapers. *Humanae Vitae,* the Church's teaching on sexuality and matrimony was a prominent casualty of widespread dissent.

Secondly, in the same year, by virtue of its own authorized studies of the priesthood (all faulty) and for five years thereafter, by intervening in the contest of wills between the Sacred Congregation for Religious over the essentials of religious life, bishops rendered two papal letters defining these essentials dead on arrival – *Ecclesiae Sanctae* (1966) and *Evangelica Testificatio* (1971). As a result, the fertile field of religious vocations suddenly became barren, and the splendid Catholic school system, a century in the making, was depopulated by half. Although many solid voices were raised against these compromises, they were excused by others as the result of uncertainty about the meaning of Vatican II documents.

Thirdly, it is hard to understand, thirty years later, why bishops would permit Catholic colleges to remain unresponsive either to their founders or to the law of the Church – to be autonomous and beyond oversight by her highest authorities. By permitting this to occur, the episcopal conference, fully conscious of the negative consequences, *has weakened support for the special authority of all priests.* An imprimatur of this kind confers legitimacy on a rival teaching office in faith and morals within the Catholic household. If an academic can be independent of his bishop, any Catholic can.

Bishops did not drift into this situation perchance. Leading members of the new NCCB (1966) entered into a peace pact with their Land o' Lakes antagonists right from the beginning. They also obstructed the efforts of two popes to keep Catholic colleges within the fold. They allowed defenders of Catholic identity to shift for themselves, helpless against the punitive power of organized dissenters now in control of colleges. Secular collegiate dogma insists there are no demonstrable religious certainties anywhere, and that no higher education, worthy of the name, claims anymore that there are.[2]

American bishops, who did well against anti-Catholic forces in the nineteenth century, do not do so effectively in the twentieth century with Catholic secularists who seem certain that many teachings of the Church are uncertain.

Ambiguous Identity, Ambiguous Doctrine. A Catholic school which is obscure about its commitment to the teaching authority of the Church is also imprecise about its fidelity to the faith, whose truth is guaranteed, not in an academic seminar, but alone by the witness of bishops in union with the pope. From New Testament times onward, given individuals and communities have picked and chosen elements of Catholicity which gave them comfort, while ignoring what they did not like or found onerous. But Catholic moral persons – colleges – which institutionalize this kind of "cafeteria Catholicism," as it is called, constitute a support system for Catholic deviance at best and agnosticism at its worst. Is this why Christ founded a Church? Or Catholic religious a college? Bishops who, however reluctantly, tolerate the inculcation of contradictory pluralism of belief in schools which identify themselves as privately owned and Catholic, repeat the mistakes of European hierarchies, going back to the time of Arius. Once upon a time, Rome gave up trying to energize the French hierarchy against Jansenism, leaving that body to its own devices, a Church which today has hardly 10 percent of her baptized membership attending Sunday Mass.

The particular danger to the American Church of collegiate ambiguity is that 230 of these structures are scattered over thirty-one states.[3] While this network of Church colleges is the largest in the country, 93 percent of them are small to by American standards, most of them very small.[4] The small colleges educate 75 percent of the total 600,000 Catholic enrollment. If Georgetown, Notre Dame, Fordham, and the other twelve larger schools gave up their Catholic identity – because they do not need bishops anymore to survive economically – the Church's patrimony in higher education would still be salvageable. Most smaller colleges, since they could not really endure as Catholic in the face of episcopal censure, could retain the ability to regroup on behalf of excellence in Catholic witness, as they want to be in teaching and in learning. New Catholic universities, worthy of the Church's learning tradition, might emerge from clarification of what that tradition expects and the Church demands. And they would be as accountable to bishops for their authentic Catholicity as they are to civic bodies for their secular quality, no matter what AAUP or ACLU – both godless agencies – think.

The Slippery Secular Path

As late as 1991 Avery Dulles, S.J., summarized the secularization process in American education in two sentences:

1. As going from "the slippery path that led from denominational to generic Christianity, then to vaguely defined religious values, and finally to total secularization."

2. "Many competent observers are of the opinion that this drift is by now inevitable in practically all Catholic universities.[5]

Protestant universities led the way, according to George Marsden, a student of these matters, who in the same year as Dulles, while at Duke University, asked a comparable question about his own tradition: "Why has Christianity, which played a leading role in Western education until a century ago, now become entirely peripheral in higher education and, in fact, come to be seen as absolutely alien to the educational enterprise?[6]

The first steps down this slippery path were taken by American

Jesuits, as early as 1958, when their college presidents eased their way out from under the jurisdiction of their religious superiors as a prelude to breaking their direct link with hierarchy. The course was later set in concrete for the entire American Church when a mere eight Catholic college presidents (dominantly Jesuits), their religious superiors and/or staff (twenty six in all), decreed at Land o' Lakes, Wisconsin, that Catholic college institutions henceforth were to be independent of episcopal supervision, and of Church law, too. Their action was called a pursuit of excellence, but really it was a quest for secular blessing and secular money. A college or a university is merely the highest level of someone's system of education. There is no intrinsic incompatibility between its academic excellence and fidelity to its founder or sponsor. It is not an independent world of its own. It can be state owned or privately owned, a German, an American, or an English model, operating under a secular or a religious charter. Each system socializes its faculty and student body according to its own philosophy of education; the private system is likely to be more flexible in practice than a state system.

By Vatican II, however, the blessings being proffered to higher education by the federal government, fundations, and the AAUP tempted leading Catholic higher educators to trade their birthright in order to gain those perquisites. Within a very short time Land o' Lakes' partisans developed a new legal argument – never used by Catholics throughout the century before – that once a Catholic college incorporates under civil law, it becomes primarily a public institution serving a civic purpose, requiring the severance of the college's juridical tie with its religious sponsor.[7]

The Roman Response

In hindsight, Church authority lost the war at the very moment of its declaration at Land o' Lakes. At the time bishops could not measure the depth of academic hostility to episcopal oversight. But when they began to negotiate with unequals on the terms of their own surrender, the die was cast.

Beginning in 1968 the Congregation for Catholic Education, headed by Cardinal Gabriel Garrone, began to engage in a battle of words with the Americans. Meetings were held all over the world – Kinshasa, Kyoto, Caracas, finally in Vatican City, where in 1972 an International Congress of Catholic Universities assembled. At this meeting presidents agreed that bishops had the right to intervene privately or publicly, as critics, whenever they were unhappy with what was going on in Catholic colleges.

But by that time, the juridical issue had already been settled, the Americans said: "Autonomy is the issue and it is ours."

Three years earlier (February 15, 1969), in response to Garrone's questionnaire, two opposing university presidents defined the Holy See's new problem.

Georgetown's President Robert Henle, S.J.: "Magisterium is effectively present in the Catholic universities through the conscience of individual Catholics." He further added: "It is very important that the atmosphere on a Catholic campus be ecumenical and open, that it not be burdened with legalisms and juridical limitations."

St. John's University's President Joseph T. Cahill, C.M.: "The magisterium is concretely present in the Catholic universities as the most important guideline in the teaching of Catholic theology and, where the sciences teach, of Catholic philosophy.[8]

Contradictory notions of the Church, to say nothing of Catholic higher education, are evident in these two views: one stressing the individual, his or her subjective views of Church teaching, with no mention even of a correct or rightly formed conscience, nor of binding Catholic truth, nor of responsibility for its faithful transmission; the other tying the university into the Church's Body, to its teaching, and to its lifestyle. Each of these views, once institutionalized, changes the religious practice, not only of its putative young believers but of the Church itself; one socializes the student into a form of "pick and choose" Catholicism; the other, whatever the students' personal choices may eventually become, forms and indoctrinates collegians about Catholic faith and morals, with the same assurance of truth as when it guarantees facts about the solar system. And, since Catholic college graduates are the ones most likely to head up the Church's infrastructures – the parishes, the offices, the seminary faculties, the charitable agencies, etc. – one need speculate little about the kind of future headship each theory of formation will produce.

When leading Land o' Lakes' delegates returned to Washington, D.C., after the 1972 meeting and used a press conference to announce that Vatican officials agreed with the Americans, Garrone was so angered that he sent a letter to all delegates in which he specified the following: Each Catholic college president was (1) to set out in statutes or other documents its Catholic character and commitment "without equivocation"; (2) to create instruments of self-regulation in faith, morals, and discipline; (3) to keep in mind their "relationship with ecclesiastical hierarchy" which must characterize all Catholic institutions. Cardinal Garrone also reminded college presidents that they were not "outside" the reach of Catholic law.

By and large the cardinal was ignored, and the American hierarchy stood mute.

By 1980, work was well under way on the new Code of Canon Law. "The Learned Societies" resisted "the college canons" every inch of the way. When the new code appeared in 1983, and canons 796–821, against their wishes, specified that no school could claim the name Catholic without the consent of competent ecclesiastical authority; that those who teach Catholic theology at the college level, or above, needed a mandate (license) from the same authority; that bishops have the obligation to take care that the principles of Catholic doctrine are faithfully observed in those institutions, these canons – though the Church's universal law – became inoperative in the United States from the beginning. The American bishops remained uninvolved.

Six years later (March 1, 1989) the Holy See, on its own initiative, upped the ante for Catholic college presidents and their faculties by requiring a profession of faith "in any university" for new teachers dealing with faith and morals, and an additional oath of fidelity for anyone assuming an office to be exercised in the name of the Church. The appropriate university personnel were expected to affirm their faith in what the Church teaches as divinely revealed, to accept all that is taught definitively concerning faith and morals, and to adhere to authentic hierarchical teaching, even when it is not proposed definitively. The oath of fidelity, additionally, calls upon certain officials to preserve the deposit of faith and to foster the discipline of the whole Church and Christian obedience to the Church's shepherds. In one place, they are told to shun those who teach contrary to faith. The response of the American Catholic education community – from the important members of the Catholic University faculty to delegates of the Catholic Theological Society of America (CTSA) to university presidents – became one of hostility. Notre Dame University's president simply said No. Msgr. Frederick McManus, CUA canon lawyer, and a leading voice against Roman interventions on many occasions, was even alarmed that pastors might be forced to take these oaths.

At one point, Ralph McInerny, president of the Fellowship of Catholic Scholars, asked a critical question: "Why in the name of God should a Roman Catholic theologian have trouble declaring himself loyal to the Vicar of Christ on earth? He is ashamed to because – here is the tragic truth – to do so would be a lie!" A Dominican theologian pressed the question differently for the members of the CTSA at one of its meetings: "it is inconsistent for theologians to maintain, as a lot of them are doing here, that they participate in the *magisterium,* and yet refuse to take an Oath of Office!"

Ex Corde Ecclesiae

On August 15, 1990, following twenty-two years of discussion by Vatican officials with university personnel, John Paul II issued *Ex Corde Ecclesiae,* an Apostolic Constitution on Catholic Universities, which has the force of law for the Universal Church.

In this document, John Paul speaks of the Catholic university, therefore, as "born from the heart of the Church." His concerns extended beyond research labs and creative scholarship, to youth. The pope expects that these future Church and civic leaders will be introduced for the first time in Catholic colleges to an advanced exposition of Catholic doctrine and to what the pope hopes would be an exemplary model of the Catholic way of life. John Paul II also went beyond expectations to what he demanded of Catholic higher education doctrinally, morally, and worldwide.

General Principles for a Catholic Institution

1. *"Fidelity to the Christian Message as it comes through the Church."* (No. 14).

2. "An institutional commitment," i.e., "an academic institution in which Catholicism is vitally present and operative." (No. 14)

3. "A relationship to the Church that is essential to its *institutional identity* – one consequence (being) *recognition of and adherence to the teaching authority of the Church in matters of faith and morals."* (No. 27).

4. "Bishops should be seen not as external agents but as participants in the life of the Catholic university." (No. 28).

5. By its very nature, each Catholic university makes an important contribution to the Church's work of evangelization – a living institutional witness to Christ and his message." (No. 49).

Article I: Their Nature

1. "Are to be applied concretely at the local and regional levels by the Episcopal Conferences. (No. 2).

2. Catholic universities other than those established by hierarchy "will

make their own general norms and their regional applications, internalizing them into their governing documents." (No. 3).

Article II: Institutional Nature

1. A Catholic university is linked with the Church either by (a) "a formal, constitutive and statutory bond" or (b) "by reason of an institutional commitment made by those responsible for it."

2. Every Catholic university is to make known its Catholic identity either in a mission statement or in some other appropriate document, unless authorized otherwise by competent ecclesiastical authority – to provide means which will guarantee the expression and preservation of this identity.

3. "Any official action or commitment of the university is to be in accord with its Catholic identity."

4. "The rights of the individual and of the community are preserved within the confines of the truth and the common good."

Article III: *Establishing a University*

With the consent or approval of hierarchy of one kind or another.

Article IV: *The University Community*

1. Teachers and administrators must be informed of "their responsibility to promote or, at least, respect that (Catholic) identity."

2. Theologians are to be faithful to the magisterium of the Church.

3. "The number of non-Catholic teachers must not be allowed to constitute a majority within the institution, which is and must remain Catholic."

Article V: Within the Church

1. Each institution is to maintain communion with the Holy See and Diocesan bishops.

2. Each bishop has the right and duty to watch over the preservation and strengthening of the institution's Catholic character.

Ex Corde Ecelesiae took effect on the first day of the academic year 1991, and to this day remains a dead letter of unenforced law.

The Ongoing American Response

The first response by college presidents to the invitations of the Holy See was no; the last response to the requirement that the universal law of the Church be adapted to the local American Church is No. And the NCCB supported the Land o' Lakes college leadership the second time, as it did at first.

In 1995 an NCCB Committee proposed a substitute compliance with "the Law" that (1) a college profess its Catholic identity in a mission statement; (2) that it hire faculty with that mission in mind; (3) that a bishop, if he questions the orthodoxy of a teacher in a theology department, follow the 1989 "Doctrinal Responsibilities" process[9]; (4) that a plan of conscious-raising on social and ecumenical issues be programmed for the institution; (5) that an adequate campus ministry exist; (6) that periodically the college review its congruence with *the ideals* of *Ex Corde Ecclesiae*; (7) that dialogue between presidents and bishops continue in the atmosphere of mutual trust. (There was no mention of a "license" [mandate] for teachers of Catholic theology, as required by Canon 812. This idea was tabled by the Committee "indefinitely.")

The only juridical part of this NCCB memorandum on *Ex Corde Ecclesiae* is the one which binds a local bishop to follow quasi-legal procedures should he choose to challenge a president or member of his faculty for public scandal to the faithful. There are no restrictions on academics. It suggested that works of peace and justice be programmed into the college agenda, but no requirement that the Church's creed, code, and cult also be programmed. The college presidents – in the face of *Ex Corde Ecclesiae* and Canon Law – had demanded *laissez-faire* government from bishops, and "leave-us-alone" government is what they received. The American bishops remained the outsiders.

A year later (1996), the controversy over what right bishops have to determine when a college is Catholic assumed Hegelian proportions:

1. The "Land o' Lakes" thesis is that bishops are outsiders and have nothing to say; the Catholic thesis is that they are insiders, and so have a good deal to say;

2. Ongoing dialogue, based on trust, will bring about good mutual relations and a satisfactory *status quo,* even though it will always fall short of what the pope thinks a Catholic college is;

3. Theoretically, better arguments, not law, will reconcile major differences but, true to the German philosopher's *realpolitik,* the better

arguments are likely to be found on the side of those who have the political strength to frame the question their way, or the power to implement the answer; if, for example, "the thesis" under discussion is "autonomy" or "academic freedom," the party of the second part automatically becomes "the antithesis" and always remains an interloper, seeking to deprive someone of his rightful property or jurisdiction – even if he is a heretic. At the June 1996 bishops' meeting in Portland, Oregon, the "thesis/antithesis" parties assembled to resolve the dilemma. Bishop John Leibrecht, who chaired the NCCB Committee designated to find an answer, justified ongoing dialogue with, and conciliation of, dissenting institutions. He argued: "The bishop's crosier is not meant to be a big stick but the staff of a shepherd," unaware that the staff really was an instrument for keeping the sheep together, without their consent, if need be. Cardinal Adam Maida rose in support of Leibrecht. He thought that dialogue should always lead to compliance, unmindful that compliance is never the object of Hegelian discourse, only more dialogue.

Other bishops, uncomfortable with the "antithesis" role they were playing, reversed the argument. Cardinal Anthony Bevilacqua asked: "We hear about academic freedom, but what about the rights of the faithful? Students at a Catholic college have a right to be taught in accordance with Catholic teaching." Over-reliance on dialogue, he thought, was "evading" their responsibility to enforce the Law of the Church

Bishop Charles Chaput questioned, even more deeply, whether "dialogue" was the correct episcopal response to the dissent that is presently "emphasized or tolerated" on Catholic college campuses. Dialogue only obscures the problem; he said: "It seems to me that we're always giving in as if we're worried about them. They should be worried about us!" The ordinary of Rapid City (now in Denver) is surely right if Christ is both the alpha and omega point of conversation in any Christian dialogue worthy of the name. The authority of bishops to insist on correct doctrinal and moral teaching is the Church's authentic "thesis." If this proposition has a genuine antithesis," it is St. Anselm's "faith seeking understanding" of its mysteries, exploration within the Church, and always under judgment by magisterium. The American antithesis, viz. the claimed right of public dissent within the Church by Catholics, may be acceptable to Hegel but not to a pope.

The difficulty of bishops governing the Church, as bad as it seems when they are not sure themselves how to proceed, was compounded by the tendency of the media to prejudice every case in controversy against authority figures. So it was, at the June 1996 bishops' meeting. Journalist

Gerald M. Costello classified the Maida stress on "dialogue" as a "moderate" position, while Chaput's "law enforcement suggestion" was called "extreme."[10] Labeling of this kind, commonplace in secular politics, is pejorative when issues of Catholic faith and morals are at stake, although it is used widely by in-house dissenters to label John Paul II as an arch-conservative and an extremist besides.

Faulty Dialogue

The mistakes were at least three:

1. *The terms of the dialogue were all wrong.* – The assumption was wrong that every Catholic college – St. Joseph's College in Maine with its 700 students, Allentown College in Pennsylvania with its 1,500 students, St. John's University in New York City with its 19,000 students – is a Rockefeller University, housed in a giant laboratory on a lakeside or riverside, staffed by creative thinkers working abstractly on multi-million dollar technological wonders, seeking the inner secrets of outer space, inner space, or God's psyche. Creative thinkers of such kind would likely receive the blessing of every bishop. Catholic hierarchy has no desire to oversee scientific computer sheets.

The starting point of dialogue in the Catholic case must be the fact that our colleges, all of them, are fundamentally teaching institutions. Forming the minds and characters of eighteen-to-twenty-two-year-olds is their primary business. By definition as Catholic, whatever else they do, colleges are witnesses to, and teachers of, the creed, code, and cult of the Church. And just as the secular aspects of their curriculum and teaching are accredited by outside civic agencies competent to make proper judgments, so are bishops the final judges of whatever is the college's Catholicity, especially if the educators can no longer be trusted. Bishops should be as free as civil servants to propose recommendations or corrections and to see that public regulations and policy are observed. (Furthermore, in a healthy Catholic situation, bishops should not have need to enter a courtroom or a quasi-courtroom to exercise their rights and responsibility.)

In former days things were never perfect in the management of Catholic colleges, neither in their academic performance nor in their religious dimension. During the 1920s, Jesuits complained constantly about both to Fr. Wladimir Ledochowski, their general in Rome. If, at that time, a bishop also experienced distress over one of his colleges, a chat on the phone or at a convocation was usually sufficient to resolve a present or emerging difficulty. This informality became no longer possible once Catholic colleges began to ape the worst features of secular higher education, as the young Robert Hutchins observed they were doing in the 1930s, nor after the American Catholic faculty network grew beyond 16,000 in number. What changed for a certainty were the present adversarial attitude of academics toward hierarchy and the diminished role assigned to bishops today, viz., as facilitators in a process of communication, not as legislators of a Church.

Complexity in any social situation demands system and law, making *laissez-faire* government, at least at a national or continental level, utopian. In the presence of complexity, and as evidence of good Catholic faith, one would think that Catholic academics would act as cooperatively with their religious leaders to an extent no less respectful than the obeisance they tender servants of the civil order. The assumption that they may freely defy the one without penalty but comply to the other with few questions is surely not a fitting end to a Catholic consultation process by believing Catholics.

2. *The process of consultation is all wrong.* Bishops have often been troubled by their national bureaucracy or its leadership. This is not surprising. Every highly endowed officialdom tends to extend and perpetuate its controlling influence over its proprietors. Once bureaucracy feels self-righteous, it sometimes turns against those who pay their salaries, especially if they find congenial allies on the board of trustees. Leaders create bureaucrats, but in time they may, in the Church's case, urge bishops against Rome.

While Vatican II clearly designated bishops as "legislators" for the Church's apostolates *(Lumen Gentium,* No. 27*),* American bishops, in dealing with the college situation, failed to follow normal legislative procedures. Usually, lawmakers, under leadership, if they recognize a *prima facie* social evil, prepare a "bill" to correct whatever harm to society they see pending. Then, in executive session, they hammer out details for a statute and reconcile differences, as best they can. In due course, they hold public hearings: (1) to round out or complete the factual picture; (2) to obtain suggestions for rejecting, modifying or perfecting the proposed law; (3) to provide the public, and those about to be regulated, advance knowledge of what to expect. When debate among legislators comes to an end, a vote is taken, the signature of the governor or president is sought (or denied), and if given, effective implementation begins on a prescribed date. At no time do regulated parties have the right of veto over an enacted law, although the opportunity is not denied them to appeal to a higher authority.

During the quarter century, after the Land o' Lakes declaration of independence – from episcopal oversight, the NCCB never held public hearings or initiated a public debate to find out (1) what was really going on in Catholic colleges so as to suggest new oversight that was never necessary before or (2) to learn how to remedy actual abuses inimical to the faith, moral life, and worshiping habits of the Church. While individual bishops were involved, the basic work of implementing *Ex Corde Ecclesiae* was delegated to an *ad hoc* committee, whose chairman at the time was the superintendent of elementary and secondary schools in St. Louis for almost twenty years. This committee had seven bishop members. One of these (Bishop James Malone), according to his own statement at the 1995 NCCB meeting, sought a dispensation for American colleges from the requirements of the new code (1983). John Paul II turned that request down. Fifteen other members, resource persons, or staff are mostly members of the Land o' Lakes' family, including William Byron, S.J., Edward A. Malloy, C.S.C., J. Donald Monan, S.J., Sr. Alice Gallen, OSV, Msgr. Frederick R. McManus. The chosen project director for the input into the *Ex Corde Ecclesiae* implementation was Fr. Terence Toland, S.J., who sifted the documents and testimony pertinent to the hierarchy's legislative judgment. Prior to his appointment, he was director of a Jesuit retreat house in Maryland.

Not surprisingly, opponents of the Land o' Lakes ideology, although making presentations to individual bishops, abstained from embarrassing themselves by involvement in this preset process. The Fellowship of Catholic Scholars, which was effectually an offshoot of the Roman consultation process, through its president, wrote to solicit a meeting with the NCCB President, and was told to function through "the Learned Societies." Still later, another Fellowship president, realizing that dialogue went on only in one American direction, wrote to Cardinal Pio Laghi, successor to Cardinal Garrone once removed, soliciting dialogue at least at that level. He was referred by Laghi back to the existing episcopal machinery.

During the week of September 25, 1996, six weeks before the bishops' November meeting, Professor Gerard V. Bradley, law professor at the University of Notre Dame, mailed to every bishop the Fellowship of Catholic Scholars' "suggested Ordinances." Based on the text of *Ex Corde Ecclesiae*, they required full adoption of its requirements as a matter of ecclesial policy without setting a fixed timetable for its implementation. The Fellowship proposals differed substantially from those of the Leibrecht Committees insofar as they made juridical demands on Catholic colleges, e.g., that a majority of faculty be Catholic, and recognized not only for being academically "outstanding" but also for their "probity of life."

Approximately ten bishops acknowledged receiving the Fellowship presentation. President Bradley also sent a press release, and his document, to Catholic News Service, the communication arm of the United States Catholic Conference, so that the Catholic reading public might be apprized of the Fellowship perspective. His letter was not acknowledged, nor was he interviewed by CNS.

3. *The unspoken assumptions are all wrong.* Those assumptions, mostly secularist, include the following: (1) that no theology can be truly Catholic anymore; (2) that Vatican II so changed the ground rules for Catholic thinking and behavior that a sectarian approach to modern problems is obsolete; (3) that the only way for the Church to proceed with the Vatican II agenda is with ecumenical and cultural sensitivity.

If the Catholic college remains outside the oversight of bishops, or is dispensed across the board from assent and obedience to Catholic definitions and law, then it is not possible to define anything as Catholic with certainty – neither priesthood, nor marriage, nor episcopacy, nor the Ten Commandments. In Rome, of all places, Jesuit William Byron, former president of the Catholic University of America, stated the new understanding as follows: "The role of the teacher of theology is not to proclaim, but to explain the faith, hoping for a response not of faith, but of understanding.[11]

If there is no Catholic theology – which once was looked upon as "the soul" of the institution bearing the name – then it is not possible to expect other faculty mer or administrators to care about Catholicity one way or another. Therefore, the daily prayer of the Church instructing bishops (Feast of St. Ambrose) to "refute falsehood, correct error, and call to obedience" is an unanswerable request. In such a case, their witness to the Catholic belief system and to the holiness of their people demanded by *Lumen Gentium* (Nos. 39–42), will assure their successors of masses of secularized and/or nominal Catholics.

Fr. Bryan Hehir, who has exercised extraordinary influence in the councils of American bishops, said not long ago: "Vatican II recast the very ideas of the Church, and the context of lay-religious relationships, so that the terms of discussion in the 1940s and 1950s were not those of the post-conciliar period.[12]

This statement is false, if *Ex Corde Ecclesiae, The Catechism of the Catholic Church,* and such papal documents as *Veritatis Splendor* or *Evangelium Vitae,* mean what they say. More than twenty years ago, Cardinal Ratzinger placed his finger on the modern problem: "I wonder at the adroitness of theologians who manage to represent the exact opposite of what is written in clear documents of magisterium, in order afterward to set forth this inversion with skilled dialectical devices as the true meaning of the documents in question.[13]

Currying favor with the media masters of secular America is an equally dubious ploy. At this critical hour of American Catholic history, the words of Christ suggest a more appropriate strategy: "If your right hand causes you to sin cut it off and throw it away. It is better for you to lose one of your members than to have your whole body go into Gehenna." (Mt. 5:31).

Argument or Illusion?

Within eight months of the promulgation of *Ex Corde Ecclesiae,* Joseph Cardinal Bernardin appeared at the same Fordham University Conference, in which Avery Dulles adverted to the creeping secularization of Catholic campuses.[14] There the former NCCB president announced that there was no turning back from a mixed sectarian/secular identity model for Catholic higher education, i.e., toward the old Church model. In his view the sectarian model, such as institutionalized by evangelicals and fundamentalists, is unsuitable for Catholics because it tends to be too defensive – Catholic colleges were never fundamentalist – and by that fact alone lacks credibility in the present-day public forum. Bernardin placed his confidence in good public relations between bishops and educational leaders, symbolized by his own annual luncheon with local college presidents. These events, he averred, facilitated quiet solutions to thorny problems, helping to resolve them before conflict situations (with their tensions) arose and before open disagreements eroded public confidence in the Church. His regard for the Land o' Lakes's redefinition of Catholic higher education is positive, expressing the opinion that the policy of bishops in France and Great Britain seems sound, since it leaves concrete application of Catholic principles to those engaged in the day-to-day operation of these institutions. (Neither country has the large American system.)

With canon law for Catholic colleges already on the books[15] and an *Apostolic Constitution* recently promulgated, the Bernardin presentation was remarkable for his confidence in "going ahead," and in the ability of good "public relations" as a solution of the Catholic dilemma in a Land o' Lakes choice. It is not as if the cardinal did not know the issues. As far back as 1976, one Catholic university president, at the suggestion of Rome, brought to his personal attention Paul VI's anxieties about the Church's substantial difficulties with post-Vatican II Catholic higher education, expressed first to Jesuit Rectors:

> Some Catholic universities in recent years have thought that they can respond to the questions of man and the world by weakening their Catholic character. And the consequences? They have helped in the weakening of Christian values by putting in their place a humanism that transforms itself into a true and real secularization. They have helped in the lowering of standards of behavior in the sphere of the university campus by letting the fascination of many virtues drop out of the students' sight.[16]

The pope of Vatican II continued, touching the heart of this matter for these seventy Jesuit college presidents throughout the world (by and large Americans), and addressing the core of the papal problem with their performance:

> Likewise, in teaching, in publications, in all forms of academic life, provision must be made for complete orthodoxy of teaching, for obedience to the magisterium of the Church, for fidelity to the hierarchy and the Holy See. Nor should there be any license for doctrinal "relativism" or moral permissiveness, incompatible with the character of a university that wants to be called "Catholic." Blind imitation of others, in doctrine or in morals is far from the spirit of the gospel which wishes us to be "salt of the earth," under pain of being cast out and trodden underfoot should we ever forget it (cf. Matt. 5, 13).
>
> Furthermore, those who do not share with us the stance of the Church demand of us extreme clarity in expressing our viewpoint so as to be able to establish constructive and trustworthy dialogue. Cultural pluralism and the respect due to each individual among the brethren should never make a Christian lose sight of his obligation to serve the truth in charity (cf. Eph. 4, 15) to follow that truth of Christ which alone gives us true freedom." (cf. John 8, 32; Gal. 4, 32; 2 Cor. 3, 17).

By that year, however, with NCCB help, the American die was cast in favor of the Land o' Lakes's philosophy. Cardinal Bernardin *did* express the concern of bishops about the long-range negative impact on the Church of defective theological training given to Catholic graduates by non-Catholic divinity schools. He confessed that today's Catholic college presidents share with bishops his concern about this turn of events. Yet, by the time he was speaking, the defective doctrinal formation of graduates of Catholic colleges was the more serious pastoral concern. The hierarchical magisterium looked less than "vigorous" by making no move to prevent the results which Richard John Neuhaus predicted were the inevitable result of the Land o' Lakes formula.[17] Most of the "lunches" between college presidents and bishops since 1970 have been friendly interpersonal exchanges of hopes and wishes rather than a submission of minds and wills to the norms and laws of the Church. The fact that classroom champions of a "new order" usually indoctrinate students to think as they did, to believe in "scientific" religion, not the content of Catholicity, was never discussed. By 1991 the diplomatic relations between bishops and academics had devolved into trading of words or the signing of letters, while the realities of a given situation remained precisely where they were.

Cardinal Bernardin's fear of "the fundamentalist trap" was also a strange one, in view of his strong feelings about the necessity of the Vatican II Church being a vital force in shaping the country's secular policies. Whether prelates today like it or not, Catholic political influence has never been at a lower ebb, and the most respected religious power block in the nation is the Christian Coalition, dominantly Evangelical Protestant in its constituency. It is somewhat peculiar that Catholic elites do not have public concern about the "secular humanist trap" which, after the 1960s, became a far more dangerous temptation for Catholics than eighteenth-century Protestantism because it allowed Romans to keep their nomenclature, as long as what they did advanced the secularist agenda.[18]

The Free Choice of the Bishops

College presidents have made "free choice," secularly defined, their operative concept in this power struggle with the magisterium. Two popes and many cardinals have tried persuasion to return American Catholic colleges to the household of the faith, but the relevant presidents have rebuffed them repeatedly. Since bishops are dealing with a general strike against the Church, some bishops wish to exercise their own "free choice" under Catholic law, viz., to decide how their parents and diocesan high school graduates can find a truly Catholic college.

Five steps are available to these bishops:

1. *Oneness with the pope.* As difficult as it may be to obtain unity among 300 bishops, or oneness with the pope in such a large episcopal body, the future of the American Church at the parish level, and of their own apostolic priesthood, depends on the right decisions made by such a unified hierarchy. The time is ripe for great bishops to arise. The Holy See, knowing the mistakes of Church history better than anyone, realizes that a significant moment is here and that the norms of *Ex Corde Ecclesiae* must prevail over the secularist standards of the National Education Association, and of the American Association of University Professors, which are nothing more than secular faculty unions. If "doctors" of the Church fiddle with more placebos, the Church's sickness will not be cured, and the twenty-first century will witness far more serious obstacles to the catechesis of Catholics. The academics of our day are content with episcopal placebos, but they claim no responsibility for the salvation of souls. That by itself is a sinful state of mind.

2. *Denationalize the problem.* Strictly speaking, the Catholicity of a college lies within the pastoral jurisdiction of a diocesan bishop. The faithful have a vested interest in knowing what he, above anyone else, is doing to protect their baptismal right to have their children formed in authentic Catholic faith and worship. A national body of bishops can no more guarantee the Catholicity of Walsh College in Youngstown, Ohio, with its 1,600 students, than the FBI can guarantee the safety of the residents of New York's South Bronx. The American Church does not have a central government, and, even if it did, it could not protect the Catholicity of Walsh College. Rome can only look to the local bishop to do that – if he can. The Land o' Lakes group seized the initiative from Rome and the local bishop, when they found bishops willing to deal with their unilateral demands only through the National Catholic Educational Association first, and later through its birth child, the Association of Catholic Colleges and Universities. During this process, several hundred little colleges were swallowed up in a runaway eddy created by a handful of large colleges. The present confrontation magnified is the result.

Diocesan bishops may not care to assume such a responsibility at this late date, especially those who are inexperienced with the task. But the authenticity of the Church is best tested in the local diocese, not in the offices of the United States Catholic Conference.

3. *Enforce Canon Law.* The NCCB should require that the *Code of Canon Law* and *Ex Corde Ecclesiae* are in force, as of a given date, for all colleges which wish official recognition as Catholic. Institutional commitment to the teaching authority of the Church, declared publicly in a mission statement of some kind, the requirement that teachers of theology are to be faithful to the magisterium, and need a license from competent ecclesial authority to teach theology, and that believing Catholic teachers of probity must form a majority of the faculty are the essential elements of the understanding.

4. *Effective administration.* College presidents should undertake an internal review of the composition of the board, faculty contracts, hiring and termination procedures, promotions, faculty and student associations, and numerous other housekeeping details, which reflect or detract from the Catholic commitment. Yeshiva University, Howard University, Evangelical, Harvard, Yale, and Princeton possess infrastructures which protect their ethnic, racial, religious, or secular identity. This necessarily may be an enormous burden on presidents of the larger schools, and certainly on anyone whose institution has become more secular than Catholic. Some presidents may opt out of the Catholic system over these complexities. This is a small price to pay in a Church that is unambiguous about its purpose and nature, no matter how much religious clarity is resented in a secularized world and no matter how ambiguous Catholics individually are in their personal lives.

5. *A Vicar for Education.* Such a person would be to a bishop what a commissioner of education is to the governor of a state. He oversees the application of public law to the institutions covered by appropriate statutes. Relations with college presidents are professional, standard operational procedures are taken for granted, and mutual interests are served. In the Church situation, the concept of a Vicar formalizes what once was carried on by a bishop informally; a recognition, too, that in recent years Church authorities have neglected to oversee the ecclesial stake in Catholic higher education at the very moment it became necessary. During the post-Vatican II period bishops often were forced to take an active interest in the day-to-day problems of their diocesan educational system, rarely reflecting that their difficulties at that level originated on a college campus somewhere, if not in a local religious house.

With errant and erroneous teaching on Catholic colleges in mind, Paul

VI instructed Apostolic Delegate Jean Jadot in 1975 to advise American bishops to appoint a vicar for doctrine, if they could not deal with this important matter personally. No bishop in attendance paid attention to the request. Nonetheless, that ignored recommendation has relevancy to any effort to restore full Catholicity to the Church's college system. College presidents, out of habit, will object to such vigilance, especially those whose faculties are in the forefront of movements to pressure secular governments to correct social evils of one kind or another. A good president, in the face of a factual report which raises questions about the Catholicity of his college, should be as distressed as the bishop and to no less degree than after a state commissioner told him the college library was inferior. A president who is hostile to the very idea of such oversight from the bishop's office demonstrates, better than a report, that restoration of an authentic sensus fidei on every accredited Catholic campus is a necessity not just a desideratum.

In the United States two words have been out of fashion in episcopal circles since 1919 at least – *laissez faire* and "gradualism" – the first, because it justified entrepreneurs doing whatever they wanted to do with their property, public be damned; the other because it was a hypocritical device used by capitalists, labor barons, and racists to assure government overseers that, on their own and eventually, they would undo the evils they perpetrated against their fellow citizens and their country. Pius XI buried both evasions of responsibility in *Quadragesimo Anno* (1931), and every NCCB pastoral since 1966 has called for action by secular government to right civil and social wrongs traceable to society's evil structures. Every contemporary recovery program rejects "Let me do what I want" and "Let me recover in stages" as a first or last step in dealing effectively with anti-social behavior. Yet this is what Jesuit and other college presidents expect Rome and national hierarchies to allow.

If Church authority needs convincing beyond this that college presidents have seized the higher ground above bishops in determining what is acceptably Catholic, to the deconstruction of the Church's nature, the following anecdote may help it face the present *status quo* realistically: A chief officer at a major Catholic university in the Midwest, alarmed at the possibility of episcopal intervention in the internal affairs of his institution, vented his fears to the president, who happened to be a major Land o' Lakes zealot. The executive later reported to others publicly the comforting words of the President: "What is the worst that can happen? The pope will tell the world we are not a Catholic University. No one will believe him!"

The Bypass of *Ex Corde Ecclesiae*

On November 13, 1996, after six years of study, the American bishops by a vote of 224-6 decided not to implement the universal law of the Church concerning Catholic higher education. Rather than enact ordinances to authenticate the Catholicity of campuses which bear the Church's name, they agreed to continue the informal relationships they had developed since 1967, in the hope that college presidents would do better in the future to witness their Catholic commitment. At no time did the bishops seriously or in depth discuss the doctrinal, moral, or liturgical shortcomings of the remarkable system that had been bequeathed to them by their predecessors. At that meeting episcopal spokesmen expressed gratification that the climate of "revolt" and "suspicion" in the college ranks had lately become one of "mutual trust and cooperation." One cardinal said, "This was the best document we could possibly produce at this time'; another thought a victory of sorts had been achieved by getting into the text a footnote which promised to study at a future date the requirement of Canon Law that campus theologians have approval from "competent ecclesiastical authority." Although six years of study had gone by, more than six bishops over the years had at one time or another expressed unhappiness with temporizing further with the college establishment. Still, very few Catholics will know who finally voted for what because NCCB procedures, unlike those of modern legislative bodies, do not allow for the publication of the voting lists whenever legislation on issues critical to the Church's well-being is enacted or tabled.

In summary, the governing structures of *Ex Corde Ecclesiae* are not implemented for the United States. One prelate was reminded of the way the English hierarchy (up to 1535) satisfied the lusts of Henry VIII for power over the Church in the hope of keeping him within the fold. A canon lawyer, asking how a national hierarchy could dispense itself from the Church's universal law, responded that an unenforced law gives a new twist to the real mind of the Supreme Legislator. That reasoning suggests a duplicity – perhaps a certain pharasaism – in Church headquarters.

An additional puzzlement, beyond the failure to investigate what really goes on throughout the nation in Catholic college classes or on campuses, is the reluctance of bishops to face up to the judgment of highly placed academics that hierarchy is incompetent personally (for the most part), or by office, to make decisions about scientific theology or about permissible Catholic lifestyles. These elites have no intention of ever taking direction again from bishops about what a Catholic college should look like, or what its content should be.

The bishops' meeting had hardly ended when the *Chronicle of Higher Education* published (November 22, 1996) the reaction of several well-known Catholic university figures to what had gone on in Washington the week before. Richard McBrien termed any oversight by bishops of what goes on at Notre Dame, or anywhere else, to be "odious." He added: "Bishops should be welcome on a Catholic university campus. Give them tickets to ball games. Let them say Mass. Bring them to graduation. Let them sit on the stage. But there should be nothing beyond that. They should have nothing to say about the internal academic affairs of the university or any faculty members thereof."

Former priest Daniel C. Maguire, presently teaching moral theology at Marquette, saw value in Catholic universities because they "take religion seriously." Still, in his view, these are American universities, and "the Catholic element is adjectival and secondary." He added: "it is not on that basis we got millions of dollars for student aid and research." Maguire's final word: "I am a pro-choice theologian. The university has lived with that for 25 years. I defended mercy death before I had tenure, and I got tenure."

Joseph A. O'Hare, president of Fordham, which by law in the state of New York is "non-denominational," not Catholic, thinks consistency in Catholic teaching will come about on campuses from good relations with bishops, not from a legalistic approach toward college administration. He does not mention, however, that Fordham is riddled with dissent. And O'Hare himself is long convicted by his own words as a defender of "selective obedience" by post-Vatican II Catholics in the face of Church authority.

Defenders of the *status quo* post-Vatican II may insist that McBrien, Maguire, and O'Hare are extreme voices of discontent. Yet anyone who has been exposed to a Catholic university campus for any length of time knows how widely situated and virulent is the anti-hierarchy animus in Catholic college faculties. The hostility to serious episcopal oversight is well-developed there. Faculty members or institutes or even colleges, known to prize Catholic orthodoxy in the teaching/learning situation, even when their public posture is non-argumentative, are considered having a narrow scope and alien to the American learning mainstream. The reality, which bishops do not wish to face, is that the secular collegiate model, with its agnosticism toward revealed religion, is presently normative for campuses which owe their existence to Founders who deemed the secular model inadequate for fully rounded Catholic in principle to be hostile to Christianity.

Rome Rejects 1997 U.S. Proposal

In May 1997 the Holy See sent back to the U.S. bishops the agreement they had made with American Catholic college educators on the implementation of *Canon Law* (1983) and *Ex Corde Ecclesiae* (1990). This pact, approved by the NCCB at their November 1996 meeting, evaded the demands that Rome enunciated first during the pontificate of Paul VI and which John Paul II imposed canonically on all such institutes by 1990. While Cardinal Pio Laghi's letter of rejection was not admitted to be such, and while the American response from the NCCB to the congregation was irenic in tone, the latest Roman intervention indicates that the pope is not about to free the 234 American Catholic colleges, all but a dozen of which are comparatively small, of their Church obligations, so long as they keep calling themselves Catholic. The American counterproposal of 1996 had stressed the voluntary relationship of Catholic college presidents to the Church; the Roman rejoinder in 1997 insists upon the juridical nature of this relationship, and that college statements of "ideals and principles" are not sufficient to describe their ties to the Church's hierarchy. The Catholic juridical order requires the acknowledgment by such colleges that Church norms bind their presidents, boards of trustees, and faculties.

Laghi's letter restated the Roman position: (1) that the connection of a college with the Church must always be juridically affirmed, i.e., there must be a legal acknowledgment by the college that it is as readily bound by *Canon Law* as it is by civil statutes; (2) that the "essential elements" of this juridical relationship must be spelled out in a written mission statement; (3) that those who teach any of the theological disciplines must receive a license from "competent ecclesiastical authority"; (4) most significantly, that the U.S. bishops reexamine their 1989 arbitration machinery ("doctrinal responsibility") for resolving episcopal disputes which favored mis-teachers of Catholic theology. This arbitration procedure adopted then by the national body interfered with the right and responsibility of a diocesan ordinary to deal with local theological problems as they arose within his personal jurisdiction. Rome was now asking the U.S. hierarchy to review its 1989 policy.

The first practical result of this Roman action was the immediate creation of a subcommittee of four bishops, all with doctorates in Canon Law, headed by Philadelphia's Anthony Cardinal Bevilacqua, to develop "the Ordinances," the likes of which Catholic college presidents have been rejecting for thirty years. Well-documented doctrinal, liturgical, and disciplinary abuses on Catholic college campuses since 1962 make clear that, in Rome's view, the long-range reform of Catholic higher education in the

Catholic mode is not possible without the force of Church law. And without such proper reform, Catholic higher education no more serves Catholic purposes than a first-rate Catholic ministry on the secular campus, and is significantly worse whenever Catholic professors teach in opposition to the Church. In specific situations, the resources of the Catholic community could be used to better advantage. The potential misuse of episcopal authority in a given moment or case no more justifies *laissez-faire* government in ecclesial matters than governmental malfeasance does in the civil order. Indeed, compared to the outrageous behavior of "cognitive elites" against three popes, the American hierarchy has been a model of restraint and decorum, especially in the face of contumacious defamation, even betrayal, of the Church's teaching office.

Given the extant record of widespread doctrinal dissent, Rome is insisting that any college claiming the name Catholic must at least have a school or department of authentic Catholic theology, staffed by a faculty licensed by competent Church authority to teach ecclesiastical subjects, and that liturgical and other laws dealing with worship and established Church teaching be enforced on Catholic-college campuses. Whether those same college presidents will submit themselves to episcopal oversight, as promptly as they do to correction by the state and other chartered agencies, remains to be seen. Educational malpractice and "quackery" are closely scrutinized in the one world; why not distorted Catholicity in the other? In civil matters college administrators have no choice but to conform to public law or suffer stiff penalties; in the present ecclesial atmosphere, the Holy See has simply requested that American bishops ask college presidents once more to comply with Church law.

Now that Rome has spoken again, Jesuits and other religious communities, still the leading voices in most Catholic-college affairs, are forced, if they care, to examine the reasons why they freely chose to administer their once-religious foundations by secularist norms. By so doing they forfeit their freedom to be truly Catholic and deny to the country the plurality of educational models, of which our political leaders, and their predecessors, once boasted.[19]

How strange that the sages of Land o' Lakes are at peace with federal/state commissioners of education and their professional aides de camp, who tell Catholic educators what they may or may not do in matters that touch upon civil mores, but are at odds with bishops who would define for them what is and what is not truly Catholic? Why are these commissioners and allied professionals of the state interior to the workaday world of Catholic education, while bishops of the Church are held to be outsiders? The wrong answers here imply more than an embrace of a new political order. The nature of the Catholic faith, and their obligation to it, eventually become the issue.

By tacitly concurring over many years in the Land o' Lakes' choices made by religious superiors/presidents, the bishops have compromised their own role as legislators for the Church and as guardians of the faith. In some respects they have mimicked the worst features of secular governance, whose officials frequently negotiate downward the meaning of necessary public law in order to satisfy the wants and pleasures of "veto groups" that wish to be a law unto themselves. Given the present climate, therefore, it will be as difficult for bishops to enforce Church law on college presidents, as it is for Catholic academics to comply with it. Grave inconvenience does not, however, justify indigenous lawlessness in any society.

Even the recent demand of Rome that bishops return to the bargaining table implies that an equality of Church roles already exists, hardly what the title "hierarchy" really means in the Catholic tradition or what Christ intended for the Apostles or their successors. Media may see the argument to be about a methodology of governance, but it really involves decisions concerning the content of God's revealed Word, or whether there is such a Word at all. Bishops can be good debaters and facilitators, but primarily they are decisive teachers and decision-making legislators for the whole Church.

Obviously Rome is seeking compliance with Church law, not negotiating downward toward a diluted form of Catholicity. To some the ongoing contest appears to be simply a test of wills over the power to rule; but it is also a test for both bishops and presidents about their Catholic faith.

What is Catholic faith? Who defines it? And who is dispensed from its binding authority? The easy answer for Catholic nominalists is to produce a document containing sophisticated Catholic words which will comfort nervous Roman ears but still leave college presidents and faculties free to choose their own contradictory interpretation. It is hard to believe that John Paul II will permit such pharisaism to prevail.[20]

A profound moment of truth, therefore, has arrived for American bishops and for college presidents. Either the Catholic college, a creation of the Church community, is an American institution energized by the norms of Catholic faith, or it is not. Either the bishops under the pope are the final judges of what is Catholic about one of the Church's major teaching bodies, or they are not. Either college presidents and boards of trustees accept "the obedience of faith" inherent in their public commitment to Catholicity, or they do not. Either maintaining a cross on a campus committed to secularism is hypocrisy, or it is not. Either pretending that Catholic norms govern college life, when they do not, is the Catholic community's hypocrisy, or it is not. Can Catholic educators take the patrimony of the Church's earlier generations, generated out of their poverty and piety, and squander it to achieve state-like, not Catholic, objectives? in the last analysis, pope and bishops govern the Church and its subsidiary agencies, or they do not.

Let us understand why the Church stands at a dangerous crossroads in this quarrel of college presidents with Rome about the extent of episcopal jurisdiction over the Catholicity of their institutions. The presidents operate out of the post-Christian world view that colleges belong to secular society and, as public institutions, they must conduct themselves according to rules of the civic order without reference to their Catholic obligations. Like individual citizens, Catholic colleges are free, of course, to be as religious as they choose but only privately, and within the limits set by secular mores, not by their Catholic faith. In the worldly scenario, Church authorities are pressed to close their eyes to what professors teach about worship and doctrine, in spite of the fact that these credal forms have a precise and objective content as geography.

Let us understand, further, that the forces of counter-magisterium will not make concessions to hierarchy of their own free will. Cardinal Bevilacqua's new Ordinances of 1998 were hardly in bishops' hands, certainly unread by many, when a major Jesuit rejection was already made in print. *America* magazine called those proposed norms "unworkable" and "dangerous" (November 14, 1998). Why unworkable? Because they would require Catholic theologians to obtain a license from their bishop to teach the Catholic faith, would have a college president make a profession of faith, and insist that a majority of faculty and Trustees be "faithful Catholics." In the mind of Jesuit America, Rome's and Bevilacqua's terms ar simply unthinkable in a culture which finds no verifiable truth in religious propositions. Why dangerous? Because Cardinal Bevilacqua, like John Paul II, is forcing Catholic colleges to choose authentic Catholicity in faith and practice at the price of sacrificing some of the world's benefits of not being really Catholic: (1) money from corporations, foundations, and governments which they would not receive it they were authentically Catholic; (2) a pluralistic image, not unlike that of *Princeton or* Yale, which are committed institutionally only to the religious of secularity, a temptation attractive to some Christians from the time of Judas; (3) losing the approval of the secular establishment in general.

Thomas Reese, S.J., *America's* new editor, hopes that wisdom will return in time to both pope and hierarchy because – as he told an another audience the same month – saluting the pope when he speaks is no longer a workable response by Jesuits or Catholics, unproductive when he brings up subjects like women's priestly ordination, and dangerous to the future of the Church.

Present-day elite Jesuit opinion is contrary to what America Press said in 1960, when Jesuit George Bull was called upon to answer a question in pamphlet form: "Why A Catholic College?" This Fordham professor took credit then (in the Church's name) for moving young Catholics rather successfully into the mainstream of American socioeconomic life, but recorded pride also in placing them on the upward mobility track as fully believing and practicing Catholics. The George Bulls of that day agreed with the Psalmist (127, 1): "Unless the Lord builds the house, those who build it labor in vain."

Obviously, a secularist ideology is unacceptable to Rome. Not only because it impedes the right of the Church to be Catholic, but mainly because it denies that anything the Church says about the divine or the human is true, until a group of professors says it is true. Such an approach makes Christ irrelevant to his revelation: "I am the way, the truth, and the life. No one comes to the Father except through me." (Jn. 14, 6). It also divests of meaning any Catholic institution established specifically to further Christ's mission. As a consequence, a secularized Catholic college becomes an *Adversary* to the creed, code, and cult of the Church which gave it birth and name – a veritable Satan (the biblical word for "adversary") to Christ himself: "Every kingdom divided against itself will be laid waste, and no town or house divided against itself will stand." (Mt. 12, 26). Secularist forces outside the Church surely debilitate the influence of revealed religion in the country as a whole, but empirical evidence also indicates that autonomous Catholic institutions play a devilish role in the same process, not merely by leading young Catholics into a way of life declared immoral by the Church, but by muting or disputing the truth of the Church's creeds in the classrooms. Individual professors do this, of course, but so do institutions which sanction the teaching of disbelief.

Beyond formal teaching, sarcastic and cynical lectures under Catholic auspices, which make fun of or belittle the Church and her conservative bishops, also do a great deal of damage to the religious psyche of would-be Catholics. "Conservative" Catholics are not the Church's problem, even when they criticize the present shortcomings in the management of ecclesial bureaucracies. The real threat to the Church arises from that

Catholic quarter which accepts privatization of revealed religion as America's First Commandment. Those who call themselves "liberals" are the ones who diminish the authority of bishops to make seriously binding moral demands on the baptized.

Catholics who manage Catholic colleges and universities are major offenders, too, and their influence on the Americanization of the Church has had lamentable results for the faithful. Sins against faith and morals on today's Catholic college campuses are common enough to appall any conscientious bishop. Yet so long as rebellion rules those campuses, so long as the NCCB inhibits the individual bishop's authority over the teaching in his own diocese, so long will the young suffer the diminution of their faith, perhaps irreparably, and their parents as well, perhaps to the point of embitterment or alienation. The unity, the holiness, the Catholicity of the Church are tarnished, and her apostolicity can be called into question. The faithful deserve better than that.

There is no way out of the present divisions between Rome and the American Catholic collegiate enterprise except for all parties to suffer the pain of doing what is right, when so many who have the choice and the power want to do wrong. The Word of God must prevail, even if some refuse to hear it and elect to walk away; and the preachers of that Word must carry the cross of office and endure that pain. (Mt. 6, 31).

On November 17, 1999, the American hierarchy by a majority vote of 223 to 31 approved the application of *Ex Corde Ecclesiae* to Catholic higher education in the United States. Among other things, the following requirements now apply: Catholic college presidents should be Catholic and take the oath of fidelity to the Church; the majority of the college board should be Catholics committed in the Church; the major of the faulty should be committed Catholics; theological faculty members should have a *mandatum* from competent ecclesiastical authority; Catholic students have the right to instruction in Catholic doctrine and practice. On May 3, 2000, the Vatical Congregation for Bishops approved the American application, and authorized the publication of these norms for Catholic higher education in the United States.

What Is the Right Thing?

That to maintain their own identity, Catholic colleges acknowledge their juridical relationship with the Church, and with the successors of the Apostles to whom she was entrusted.

This involves them in a type of internal organization which fifty years ago would have been considered normal. Then, the relationships between college presidents and bishops were *canonical and informal.* The presidents of that day gave high priority to their corporate witness to the faith; and the bishops had no desire (as today they do not) to be part of college management, whether the college be one owned by the diocese, or be one of which the bishop is a trustee. The bishops expected the presidents to watch over its Catholicity.

After Vatican II, however, *in order to establish greater secular credibility, the* presidents made a fetish of their civic legality, and looked upon their canonical status as a demon. They began the process of secularization by reincorporating their colleges with a "lay" Board of Trustees as owners, civilly independent of the Church, even though the Jesuit presidents, together with the Fr. Theodore Hesburghs and their like, continued to dominate the direction of their respective colleges and universities. Later, they used other legalisms, viz,, those contained in contracts with federal and state governments, to keep bishops further at bay from campus doings, even on matters pertaining to Catholicity. And, as if to compound their pretensions after 1967, Land o' Lakes academics slandered bishops with public tales of alleged authoritarian excesses by their predecessors against putatively faultless professors; or they accused Rome of having a legalistic approach to religion whenever it appeared that Church authority was ready to proceed against factual or potential anti-Catholic behavior on a Catholic campus.

An end to the legalistic jousting with "cognitive elites" is the order of the day. The fact that promulgated Catholic law remains unenforced for more than a decade is a scandal. Although the International Federation of Catholic Universities agreed in 1972 that every bishop had a right to make public judgments about heterodoxy on a Catholic campus, no bishop has dared to make them. The process of legalistic circumvention and evasion of Church regulations and law continues to this day. Cardinal Laghi's 1997 demands were hardly public when, as if Cardinal Bevilacqua's appointment had not occurred, leading members of the *NCCBs Ex Corde Ecclesiae* Committee appeared in Rome to enquire what Laghi's rejection of U.S. college arrangements really meant. The impression left behind was that any attempt by Rome to resurrect its 30 year old norms would lead to a revolution in American college quarters. (As if the *coup d'Église* of 1967 had not already occurred and its leaders seriously in command of a great deal of grassroots Catholic thinking by 1972).

If the truth is appreciated, the future relationships of colleges and bishops, whatever else they can be, *must be canonical and formal,* The transition from *laissez faire* for college administrators to episcopal oversight of authentic Catholicity on campus will not be easy, nor will it be effectuated overnight. But the formalities of implementation – as would happen in secular circles in the presence of any new law – must be set in place. The situation calls for machinery of compliance with the demands of the new legislation, not further evisceration of the Holy See's intent that that Catholic colleges must be truly, not nominally, Catholic.

In other words, Catholic colleges, which were always subject to *Canon Law,* must formally adopt procedures to guarantee their Catholicity or forfeit their right to call themselves Catholic. Bishops, who have a right canonically to determine when an institution is Catholic, must undertake this responsibility more systematically. State governments do this all the time whenever corporate bodies wish to engage in "public business" whether it be building a bridge or a bomb, running a hospital or a *drug* company, establishing a military academy or a college. Under Catholic law bishops have the authority to expect authentic worship and doctrinal teaching on a Catholic campus. They do not interfere with the institution's secularity, or its freedom, any more than the state does with religion, when either sets juridical terms for the performance of a public or ecclesial function. Licensing a theologian is no more sinister than licensing a doctor, a lawyer, or an engineer. The difference is that this is a new experience for bishops, and they will have to learn what comes naturally to a president or a governor.

No one on either side of the controversy – no one who is truly Catholic – wishes to see this stalemate continue to the harm of the faith of Catholics or to the country's deprivation of a unique form of higher education. Rome's demands are reasonable, even if collegiate officials and faculties have functioned in violation of Catholic norms for more than a generation. Fidelity to the faith and to Catholic law may cause both sides to lose something of value, bishops some of their once-prized colleges, colleges some of the professional and governmental favors they gained from hiding the light of the Catholic faith under secular trappings. College presidents serve two masters, and they are free to choose to serve one to the exclusion of the other; bishops have only one Master, and have been amply instructed by Christ in Matthew 6, 24, and 18, 9, how to serve him in difficult situations.

S E V E N

The Catholic Bishops at War

"The authority of the Church is the authority of God, who
delegated it to Christ, and Christ in turn to his Apostles, and the
Apostles to the bishops and deacons."
St. Ignatius of Antioch, circa 107 AD

"What is it, Lord?" (Acts 10, 4)

The title of this chapter will surely offend those, including some bishops,
who are content with the Church the way it is, or who do not want a fuss
made over things as they are, because, for various reasons, good and bad,
they are comfortable with detente, or as long as the war remains a
stalemate. But how else can one honestly describe the conditions under
which bishops live except as a state of siege?

Germain Grisez, a profound and pious theologian, summarizes the
present state of Catholic affairs: "Conditions in Catholicism worldwide
are very bad, with a kind of artificial unity masking confusion and dissent
not only on moral questions but on fundamental dogmas like Jesus' bodily
resurrection and the Real Presence of Christ in the Eucharist. The problem
extends not just to the simple faithful and theologians but to people in
authority.[1]

If this be the case, an explanation is needed. Bishops did not start this
war. Loss of faith of this magnitude did not occur spontaneously. Who is
responsible for the decline? And what are bishops doing about it?

For different reasons, inattentive Church-watchers and provocative
agents for a new Church, may look with equanimity upon events of the
past thirty years or maintain that American Catholicity is still better than
elsewhere. But facts do not lie. Grisez is right. The former *Georgetown*

professor is too much of a gentleman to say so curtly, but clearly he thinks that bishops are part of their own problem. John Paul II thinks so, too, and has from the moment of his election told many hierarchies so. Indeed, on his first day in office (October 17, 1978) he warned the cardinals who chose him that the Church did not need "wavering obedience to the magisterium of Peter, especially in what pertains to doctrine.[2] Still, this is exactly what he inherited.

It surely makes no difference what Catholic tradition or what "the good book" says about the Church's teaching office, or about modern bishops' responsibility to the faith, or about their fidelity to those faithful who accepted as true what bishops of old taught them, if the present members of the hierarchy, however inadvertently, are contributors to the "wavering of obedience" deplored by the new pope. Only John Paul II has moved over the years to quarantine the watered-down Catholicity, if not the heresy, that he found in books with an imprimatur, or among teaching theologians, or in the activity of politicized priests. He gained no popularity by enforcing Catholic demands from far away, but, it should be asked, why should any pope's intervention be necessary from far away?

James Hitchcock, a devout historian, has the American Church right. On the basis of recent performance, local bishops, whether "conservative" or "liberal," are not likely alone to set aright the disorder they inherit, no matter how much the pope indicates that reform is necessary,[3] An incoming bishop may face an obstreperous priests' council, or a bad Catholic college, or simply the silly practice of priests not distributing Communion at Mass "because it interferes with the lay role." When has it last been known in priestly circles that a bishop read "the riot act" to an offender? To Mother Angelica most likely, not to Richard McBrien or Richard McCormick.

What seems to have been forgotten in the game-playing since Vatican II is that the pope or the bishop is the Church's "decider" for Christ. Not His "juggler" of special interests or of hostile forces. Bishops are duty-bound to deal effectively with the Church's "black sheep."

When the trouble began in 1966, a certain wait-and-see attitude made sense. Bishops needed time to assess the intentions and plans of those who proposed themselves as champions of "renewal." Somehow, however, alarms should have gone off in many episcopal residences, when their "excellencies" heard *ad nauseam* how Vatican II redefined the hierarchy to be "learners," "listeners," "consensus builders," as if they never consulted anyone up to that time. They could not be sure then that they were being programmed to be non-triumphal figureheads, who never do anything important without gaining the consent of those who live under their guidance or rule. The wide-awake bishop might have realized, in short order, that he was being conditioned to be more a "dialogist" than a decider. He might have got the message once he found out what the NCCB's leading lights were saying *in camera* with theologians as they forged ecclesial strategies for the Church's future.[4] The "successor of the Apostles" could learn, by 1980 at least, that he ought not offer judgmental answers to serious Church situations, unless in "consensus" with theologians; that professors were free to teach as they chose, with views different from those of their bishops, as long as what they taught was not presented as official; and that, while bishops were still free to criticize theologians, but these latter were not to be penalized for their private opinions. Without a by-your-leave to the heritage of Cardinal Gibbons and the Third Council of Baltimore, which created the sturdy American Church, the "renewed" shepherds, at least their leaders, were being counseled by their own experts to debate with their flock before they decided anything for the flock's benefit – even about faith and morals.

This new rhetoric did not cause the war that ensued, but it surely prepared the way. It became an instrument used by the Church's dissenting power-bloc to intimidate Catholic apologists, and by some bishops to gain power over other bishops, and for the NCCB leadership to forestall Rome's interference in American affairs.

It Is War

It is bad enough not to see war coming; it is far worse not to know that an enemy is already inside the gates.

Peter Kreeft has a brilliant six-line thumb-sketch about war. To win it, you must know that (1) you are at war, (2) who your enemy is, and (3) what weapons or strategies will likely defeat him. To lose it (1) you simply sew peace banners on the battlefield, (2) fight civil wars against your allies, and (3) use the wrong weapons.[5] This pious philosopher was speaking, when he said this of the Church's culture war with secular society and its anti-Catholicity. But his comments also apply to the present struggles going on within the Church between the pope and national hierarchies, within various national Churches, even at certain diocesan and parochial levels.

Simple-Simon politicians know that any war is at least half-won if you keep the opposition asleep or discredit it or hoodwink it. In our time, all three things have happened to bishops, as "the Learneds" insisted: "We are the true sons of Vatican II, we are the professional theologians, we will make Vatican II work."

When the "renewal" of the Tridentine Church began in 1965, the hierarchy's casual acceptance of the "reformist" rhetoric neutralized its sacred authority over the Church. The giants of the American Church like Cardinals James Gibbons and Francis Spellman had legions of advisers who enjoyed the bishop's common faith. Both these prelates also had a unique ability to delegate authority to coworkers within their jurisdiction, even as they rendered reverence and obedience to the pope. They "listened" and they "shared responsibility," words which after 1965 took on a different meaning. Overnight, these catchwords were reinterpreted to circumscribe the authority of anyone – parents or presidents included – who under God were personally responsible for the well-being of other people. Change-makers, intent on redefining the Church's way of thinking and of Catholic life, flocked together around bishops, chanting "Listen," "Share Your Authority," "Gain Consensus First." One might have thought that Catholic bishops were holding political jobs in Tammany Hall.

How this "reformed" managerial design worked out in practice is a different story, once the "democratic types" gained power within religious communities, in Church institutions, and inside the episcopal bureaucracies. Sixteen years after he was elected president of the NCCB (1982), Cardinal John Dearden, invited to tell a national assembly of his peers how to be a bishop in alleged Vatican II terms, was still advising: "Listen." However, neither he nor his successors really listened to anyone outside their self-selected bureaucracies and advisors. The NCCB/USCC staff and consultants were largely drawn from elite critics of the Holy See and among established members of "the knowledge class," many of whom had doubts about the historicity of both episcopal claims and/or of apostolic succession.

The Dearden-fashioned NCCB found trouble with Rome almost from the day the Detroit Ordinary was elected to be the American hierarchy's chief spokesman (1966). Rome was not going to make any judgments for the American Church without his intervention or acquiescence. This was exactly what the homegrown dissidents wanted. In 1967, for example, he intervened personally with Paul VI on behalf of LA's IHM nuns, then in the process of rebelling against Roman norms on religious life.

Again, in 1968 a resolution of the NCCB's Administrative Committee, intended for Paul VI, and supporting Cardinal Patrick O'Boyle's handling of fifty-two Washington, D.C., priests who publicly dissented against *Humanae Vitae,* never reached the pope. Dearden, exercising presidential privilege, shelved the proposal "for parliamentary reasons," as he told an angry Cardinal Francis McIntyre. (Dearden, a member of the Papal Birth Control Commission, had voted to change Catholic doctrine on contraception.) No one today mentions his 1976 Call to Action meeting in Detroit. Organized by Church bureaucrats as a showcase of a people's church a-borning, the meeting turned out to be a raucous forum for changing Catholic consciences on morality, especially on sexuality. Even Dearden was embarrassed. But the climate of ecclesial war by then was in place – the beginning of a breakdown in Catholic discipline – bishop against bishop, bishop against Rome, laity against bishops.

Jesuit Thomas Reese portrays a positive picture of what the organized hierarchy has accomplished within thirty years in two books called *Archbishop* (1990) and A *Flock of Shepherds* (1992). These reports confirm the sense of many insiders and outsiders that episcopal leadership had a specific vision of Vatican II and a consistent methodology to implement its priorities. Reese gives due notice, however, of Roman unhappiness with the NCCB's handling of annulments, liturgy, and the American bishops' governance of theologians and religious educators.

In 1994 the NCCB's Doctrinal Committee was commissioned to raise study questions about the Catholic authenticity of certain translations. Three of the member bishops, who asked a lot of Roman questions, found themselves off the committee, replaced by three others disposed to inclusive language. Reese explains that what is sought in the modern episcopacy is "the team player," viz. the man who fits into "the episcopal club." But great bishops fit no such Procrustean bed.

The theological study of the priesthood, launched by Dearden under the tutelage of two Jesuits (who abandoned the Society and the priesthood), turned out to be a disaster, if only because it concluded that Holy Orders was not so holy after all – certainly not instituted by Christ.

The following are a few of the national hierarchy's favorite experts in those early days: one-time Maryknoller Eugene Kennedy, who blamed the malformation of pre-Vatican II Catholics on "people's acceptance of the Church's moral authority on the way they should live their lives"[6]; Jesuit Francis J. Buckley, an oft-quoted questioner of magisterium, who attributed (1972) the Church's contemporary difficulties to .moral conformism and uncritical acceptance of authority[7]; Sr. Maria Augusta Neal, who helped revolutionize mother houses and diocesan catechetical centers almost simultaneously, opined that the task of religious leaders (1969) no longer "is to impose doctrine or values or commitments.[8]

Brother Gabriel Moran, a catechetical expert for many diocesan offices of education, wrote a book in 1971 named *Design for Religion,* which argued (p. 149) that "the supposition that the bishop is the teacher of the diocese and that religion teachers in the schools are an extension of the bishop is a fallacy that must be put to rest." Former Jesuit Bernard Cooke questioned (in 1972) whether there was a definitive biblical basis for the episcopal office itself.[9] David O'Brien, who helped write the history of the American priesthood for the NCCB (1971), told the National Federation of Priests' Councils later that Catholics needed "to find liberation from the heavy-handed ecclesial bureaucracy, the cultural sterility and moral hypocrisy which seemed to us the dominant elements of our Catholic heritage.[10] Much published material, no less anti-establishment, permeated the Catholic lifeline with *imprimaturs* or diocesan protection. The St. Anthony Messenger Press of Cincinnati, for example, in its family magazine called *Catholic Update,* published a major article on birth control (October 1986) by Kenneth R. Overbrook, S.J. He considered Paul VI's *Humanae Vitae* to be the pope's personal theological opinion. The faithful were free to follow another opinion if, after a sincere effort, they failed to follow the papal lead.

Other wrong signals given by NCCB officials in those years were diocesan "listening sessions," like the six held in Milwaukee (1990), where a bishop sat empathizing with Catholics who wanted to be pro-choice on abortion without feeling guilty about it, or at least be pro-choice before they conceived.

Five years later, a group of bishops, of whom Archbishop Rembert Weakland would be the most prominent, met privately over a substantial period of time, raising questions with each other about Rome's policy judgments concerning faith, morals, and liturgy. The content became public at the NCCB's 1990 meeting and, among other things, expressed pique against cardinals and bishops running around their own conference to deal with Rome. The Catholic News Service published the report, an exercise that indicated the unhappiness of some bishops with John Paul II's idea of orthodoxy, while bolstering the lessons that dissenting theologians taught twenty-five years earlier.[11]

The case has been made many times that Rome's oversight of episcopal conferences and bishops' supervision of the American Church left something to be desired. Catholic discipline, the bulwark of practicing faith, suffered everywhere.

Vatican II did legitimize episcopal conferences in *Christus Dominus* (No. 38), but they came into being without guidelines or direction from

Rome. This was an unfortunate misstep, in view of the harm done to the universal community of Catholicity throughout history by national Churches, as early as the fifth century. For one thing, the NCCB assumed several roles and functions that properly belonged to diocesan bishops. A bureaucracy in Washington, D.C., with an annual budget of $40 million, surrounded by the major offices of groups like the Jesuit Conference, Catholic Charities, and the CTSA, turning out position papers bishops-in-the-field hardly had time to read, did little to enhance the central importance of the diocesan bishop in the Church. Many bishops felt they were called together simply to rubber-stamp staff decisions. And on more than one occasion, documents that were rejected by voting bishops entered the Catholic lifelines anyway, via the USCC Committee system. For another, a highly structured conference created an aura, in which an individual bishop, to be in good standing with "headquarters," was expected to be a "team player," i.e., to act jointly with his Washington-based leadership. That is a normal expectancy of all bureaucrats, even back in NCWC days, when one cardinal joked that he paid his diocesan dues to NCWC so that he could ignore its demands. Another archbishop, young enough to be around in those days and also to help establish the NCCB, whose meetings he still attends, made this comment: "There was more freedom when Spellman and Stritch ran things, than there is today!" In 1996, for example, when the NCCB criticized Notre Dame's Richard McBrien's book *Catholicism,* Bishop John M. D'Arcy, the local ordinary at South Bend, disavowed any "input either into the substance or process of the review," although later informed of its progress.[12]

When in 1988, after two decades of tension between Rome and some of its Conferences (even Asian bishops talk autonomy now), the Congregation for Bishops, with the approval of John Paul II, drafted a proposal which reemphasized the rights of a diocesan bishop against his conference and denied that the conference had a "teaching office" in the universal Church. The U.S. bishops reacted strongly. At their November meeting they rejected Rome's proffer by a 206-69 vote, but agreed to study the issue. When the President announced his choices for a study committee on the subject – chaired by him and consisting of his six predecessors in office – Bishop Austin Vaughan rose to suggest that additional members be added because the prelates mentioned were "neither distinguished ecclesiologists" nor "distinguished by their practice in collegiality."

It is an open secret and well documented, even by those in favor of disagreement, that leading members of the conference have been at odds with Rome, and fellow bishops, almost from the beginning – over matters such as the *General Catechetical Directory* (1971), first confession for eight year olds (1976), general absolution (1978), the peace pastoral (1983), the women's pastoral and "doctrinal responsibilities" (1988), over annulments regularly, and now over mistranslations of liturgical texts. The reversal by Rome of its ban on altar girls at the behest of several prelates came as a shock to bishops who, despite social pressures, successfully upheld the Holy See's longtime insistence on altar boys. They were particularly chagrined at the alleged news that the pope did not approve the change personally. Bishops have left national meetings fuming: "It's a disgrace" or "We got the run-around!" Even cardinals have been outmaneuvered by the NCCB staff. Bishop Vaughan once accused his leadership of keeping Roman documents from bishops in the field.

Probably the most egregious act of encouragement to dissent by the NCCB was the passage in 1989 of "doctrinal responsibilities." While felicitously entitled "Bishops and Theologians: Promoting Cooperation, Resolving Misunderstanding," academics are free under its procedures to explain to a bishop the rights of a professor, while instructing him not to do or say anything that might be used against him, or to suggest that he get a lawyer. It had the air of a Catholic *Miranda* formula and could just as easily have been called "An Enforceable Code of Righteous Episcopal Conduct toward Errant Theologians." Rome had three fundamental objections to the document: (1) it placed bishops and theologians on an equal footing as teaching authorities; (2) it gave larger emphasis to a teacher's subjective claims than to the objective content of Church teaching; (3) it created unnecessary legalistic entanglements in the way of a bishop, who has the unique and ultimate responsibility to make his own judgment in doctrinal matters.

Unquestionably, "doctrinal responsibilities" limits the freedom of a given bishop to sanction a teacher engaged in scandalous teaching of the young. It inhibits the bishop from asking the right questions when confronted with well-founded bad teaching. In practice, the proposal contradicts its own credal and canonical system. After certain verbal accommodations, Rome stepped aside and permitted the NCCB to do what it wanted in 1989, but in 1997 asked the Americans to reexamine this document. There is no record of this document ever being used, or of any errant theologian being corrected either, evidence enough that, in this war over faith and morals, bishops are hardly gaining ground. The continued standoff also explains why a large share of complaints go to Rome, a tactic the late Cardinal Bernardin found objectionable and offensive.

Who's Winning the War?

Peter Kreeft had it right: You do not win a war it you close your eyes to it, or make a friend of your enemies, or force your real friends to live under enemy occupation of their homeland. The Church's Washington bureaucracies and their satellites in Catholic universities/colleges/social ministries have been doing this for thirty years. And leading bishops have allowed their exotic belief system and moral code to prevail within the Church.

This is a painful statement to make because it means a family fight is taking place, and electing to fight a brother or sister in a once-loving household is heart-breaking, especially if the parent ultimately will have to choose sides. Church membership can be half saint/half sinner, half obedient/disobedient, half believers/unbelievers, an acknowledgment that people fall short of the Church's demands. But the Church Body itself has only One Lord, One Faith, One Vicar of Christ. It is against these three components of authentic Christianity that dissenters have declared war.

If the reader cannot chose between John Paul II and Cardinal John Dearden, then permit him to choose between Avery Dulles, S.J., and Richard McCormick, S.J. Within a month of each other in 1998, these two Jesuits defined the war.[13] Speaking about the 1997 convention of the Catholic Theological Society of America, whose president he had been in 1976, Fr. Dulles said the following: "The convention speakers mounted a series of attacks on Catholic doctrine more radical, it would seem, than the challenges issued by Luther and Calvin. . . . They rejected fundamental articles of Catholic belief regarding priesthood and Eucharist as expressed by the Council of Trent, the Second Vatican Council, the Synod of Bishops, Paul VI, John Paul II, and the Congregation for the Doctrine of the Faith." If this "attack" does not define a war in being, what other act of Church defiance could it be?

At the other end of the doctrinal spectrum, stood Fr. McCormick, who defended the right of Catholics to dissent from Catholic teaching. Why? Because Vatican II in *Gaudium et Spes* (No. 62) ushered in "a new way of thinking," he says, when the council endorsed the study of "new questions which influence life and demand now theological investigation."

McCormick never specifies what dissent he is talking about? The pope's animadversions on the mass production of nuclear weapons? Or on profit sharing? or on National Episcopal Conferences? or dissent against absolute moral norms? or on contraception? or against the teaching on the manliness of the priesthood? In his generic way, the Jesuit's overall thesis is a declaration of war, even against Christ's right to bind the human conscience without the conscience's permission. McCormick, conveniently, fails to mention that *Gaudium et Spes,* in the very next sentence to the one he uses, specifically distinguishes study of new questions from "communicating doctrine," from "deposit of faith," and from "revealed truth." McCormick knows, too, that the same Council, in *Lumen Gentium* (No. 25), requires "religious assent of the soul" to the Church's ordinary magisterium, a virtue which the new *Catechism* calls "an extension of faith." Here is the exact reason why years ago McCormick's friend and mentor, Joseph Fuchs, S.J., taught that the sin of contraception was not only an immoral act, but also "a sin against the faith." Today, however, the contumacious dissenter would change the Church, instead of interpreting it properly, using, in the words of the Psalmist (55, 22), "speech as soft as butter, but war is in his heart."

Fr. McCormick's provocative dissent in *Commonweal* is a good example of Kreeft's "law of winning or losing a war" at work. He, the president of CTSA in 1970, was driven to his exaggerated counterclaim, he says, by James Hitchcock, once president (1979) and continuing stalwart of the Fellowship of Catholic Scholars, who pointed out that doctrinal dissent violates both the spirit and letter of Vatican II.

The focus thus shifts from two scholars in debate *mano a mano,* to two academic groups and their different relationships with the body of bishops. CTSA has been the lineal son of the NCCB, even though it has been anti-magisterium since 1969; FCS, born at the request of a Roman cardinal that a pro-magisterial voice of Catholic academia be heard in the U.S., has been from the beginning looked upon by NCCB leadership as a prodigal son, if not illegitimate. Not every word from the *Fellowship* is a pearl of Catholic wisdom, but Hitchcock, Germain Grisez, William Smith, Francis Canavan, S.J., John Ford, S.J., James Schall, S.J., Ronald Lawler, O.F.M. Cap., Ralph McInerny, Jordan Aumann, O.P., William Bentley Ball, Jude Dougherty, Thomas Dubay, S.M., Robert Farich, S.J., John Finnis, Joseph Fessio, S.J., John Haas, John Hardon, S.J., John Harvey, O.S.F.S., Peter Kreeft, Henry Sattler, C.SS.R., Paul Vitz, Kenneth Whitehead, and Michael Wrenn, all from the early days, plus 900 more, are hardly intellectual striplings.

Yet, when the first FCS president paid a courtesy call on NCCB's executive secretary in 1977, the official in question demonstrated noninterest in a new group committed to the Church's teaching office. In 1979, the second FCS president met restrained hostility from the then-reigning NCCB president. As the years passed. yet another FCS president, writing to NCCB's headquarters with a recommendation, was told to take the matter up with the learned societies. An archbishop, finding that his nominee to a USCC Committee was not appointed, asked why not? He was told that the theologian had turned the offer down. That was a lie. Later, at a national meeting, one bishop asked another: "Was the Fellowship consulted?" He was told: "They did not wish to participate." That, too, was a lie.

Snippets of history, like selected statistics, or citations of personal experiences, do not tell the whole story about the competence of the Fellowship of Catholic Scholars vis-à-vis CTSA, or the mindset of an episcopal college with three hundred members. In spite of the alienation of vital Catholic institutions from the oversight of the Church's only government, and of 20 million Catholics missing from Sunday Mass, and of nonexistent confession lines, and of empty rectories and convents, and of the loss of political influence in American life, and of euphemisms like dissent (i.e., disagreement) used commonly to legitimize serious doubts and denials of the Catholic faith, self-defense mechanisms for Catholicity are still not at home within the Church's Beltway.

Bishop-watcher Thomas Reese, S.J.,[14] is conscious of Rome's unhappiness with NCCB's handling of critical Catholic issues, but muses, nonetheless, that most American bishops are comfortable with the Church's direction since 1966, and with their National Conference, if their votes in session year by year are the evidence. Reese's judgment is that American episcopal leadership from the start had a specific vision of Vatican II and a consistent program to implement their chosen priorities. *America*'s new editor writes favorably of Cardinal John Dearden's success in guiding the American bishops in the role they play in the American Church, and in his ability to gain consensus with bishops-in-the-field about where the Church is going. Reese estimates this forward movement was made possible by bishops who were "team players," not authoritarians, i.e., autocrats.

Is Reese's judgment correct? Only if groups like the CTSA, whose leading members have dominated Church agencies since 1966, are right, and Rome is wrong.

The contemporary schism within the Church is deeper than that reflected in the debates among different theological theorists or combative "learned societies." Pope John Paul II has remarked on this problem many times, and only recently (January 29, 1997), the Congregation for the Doctrine of the Faith pointed to its fundamental cause: "The true, deep root of dissent is the crisis of faith." Few Church leaders wish to confront this most serious threat to Catholic Christianity in modern times or to admit the role of their bureaucracies in breaking the ties that bind baptized Catholics to their bishops. Churchgoers, however, are well aware that a marriage in which one party is notoriously unfaithful means a disturbed household and estranged family relations.

By 1997, Archbishop Oscar Lipscomb of Mobile, and NCCB's doctrinal chairman, recognizing a problem, traveled to Minneapolis to see what he could do to restore unity to the Church. His audience was a June 6th meeting of the Catholic Theological Society of America, and his hope was that he could develop there "common ground" between bishops and theologians in pursuit of the vital cause of unity. Traditionally that "common ground," at least in the United States, has been understood as comprising the Catholic faith as described by bishops united with the pope. Indeed immediately before the opening of Vatican II, in 1962, the reigning president of CTSA made it clear to a similar convention that the role of the theologian in the economy of the teaching Church was "auxiliary" and "subsidiary" to bishops. This understanding of CTSA's founders in 1946 was canceled in 1968. By 1997, however, Archbishop Lipscomb – sensing a radically different mood in his audience – approached his subject, as he himself confessed, with some "trepidation." He wanted CTSA to face up to the acrimonious polarization that has been occurring within the Church community over such "Word of God" questions as the nature of Christ and of the Church. The source of our present ecclesial difficulties, he told the theologians, was the modern tendency to attach "an aura of infallibility to all magisterial statements, or demanding intransigent allegiance to theological opinions of famous theologians," after the manner of the Dominican/Jesuit fights in the post-Tridentine era over the relation of God's grace to man's eternal salvation.

Although Rome would likely disagree with this judgment, the archbishop of Mobile also asserted that the present Catholic divisions are not due to religious orders, as they once were, but rather to rival professional organizations within the Church. And as if to epitomize the type of opposing forces that are causing the present Catholic difficulties, he cited "the heretics" of the CTSA vis-à-vis the ultra-montanist Fellowship of Catholic Scholars." At that point Archbishop Lipscomb, who had inherited the late Cardinal Joseph Bernardin's mantle as the leader of the Common Ground Initiative, paused and extended a hand of friendship to CTSA, praising the organization's members for their help in combating "the religious illiteracy that is prominent in our midst and at times nurtures misunderstanding and division."

Setting aside the question of whether the present divisions are due to "religious illiteracy" and "misunderstanding," or whether the battles between putative CTSA "heretics" and "ultra-montanist" Fellowship members are to blame for the present divisions, Archbishop Lipscomb's statement inspires other questions to which answers are long overdue for anyone who cares about the Church. Who began the fight against Catholic teaching and discipline? What have been the roles of the pope and the bishops in this development? What will be the final resolution? And what is CTSA capable of doing to heal that breach, given the current orientation of its leadership?

Archbishop Lipscomb's 1997 presentation was not the first time an important U.S. prelate, looking to assign blame for "the Catholic mess," had pointed in the wrong direction. Lipscomb's personal unhappiness with the Fellowship of Catholic Scholars is on the written record. But before him archbishop John May, at a 1989 CTSA convention, also exculpated the CTSA membership of any responsibility. This late NCCB president assured his St. Louis audience that "you have the strong and grateful support of your bishops." Then, lashing out at critics of modern scholars as quasi-McCarthyites, who make sweeping and generalized accusations against theologians without appropriate evidence, May opines: "Very bluntly, I think the Church in the United States suffers from too many anxious warning voices that would divide bishops from theologians." In his original manuscript distributed at the CTSA meeting, the St. Louis archbishop named three scholars whom he considered irresponsible for creating "a cloud of fear that would poison the air in which we do our work." These were the philosopher Ralph McInerny of Notre Dame, the political scientist Father James Schall, S.J., of Georgetown, and the historian James Hitchcock of St. Louis University – all prominent members of the Fellowship of Catholic Scholars. Under legal pressure, the archbishop wrote a letter of retraction to those whom he had, perhaps ventriloqually, vilified.

The issue today, therefore, is not whether the NCCB likes the CTSA better than the Fellowship of Catholic Scholars, nor even whether criticism of NCCB's prudential judgments is an offense on the same plane as challenging the truth of Rome's declarations of faith. But what teaching and what policies are bishops reinforcing when they claim affinity with CTSA (and CLS or ACCU) rather than with the Fellowship and other associated groups like the Society of Catholic Scientists, or the American Public Philosophical Initiative, or the Cardinal Newman Society? Or does marriage to one preclude liaisons with the others? The CTSA has for two decades been agitating within the Church for the ordination of women. Its first favorable report on the subject appeared in 1978. Here is what one Jesuit theologian at Creighton University (Father John Sheets, later auxiliary bishop of Fort Wayne, Indiana) said then about that original study:

> How does the CTSA expect professional respect when it loads a task force with people who have the same views on the subject; and who call in consultants who share these opinions? Much the same thing happened in the study on human sexuality. Has the CTSA ceased to be a body of professional scholars interested in a serious investigation of the truth, or has it become a politicized advocacy group? Every serious body of scholars realizes that truth is not served simply by turning up the volume, hoping to drown out other points of view. Again, has what is supposed to be a body of theologians begun to assume a more direct and extensive role not only in competition with the bishops but sometimes in contradiction of them? These are serious questions.

Archbishop Lipscomb surely was not unaware of this problem as he spoke to the conference of American theologians. Nor is it likely that he was unaware of what Archbishop May had said to CTSA in 1989 – since he had been a priest in Mobile and succeeded May as bishop there when the latter went to St. Louis in 1980. At the very convention at which May played the role of episcopal protector, the CTSA adopted three proposals: (1) it overwhelmingly supported Charles Curran in his contest with U.S. bishops; (2) it called upon the board to address the issues raised against the magisterium by Bernard Haering and 162 other German-speaking dissenters; and (3) its sitting president publicly expressed CTSA's anxiety over Rome's "profession of faith" for theologians.

By 1989 CTSA had compiled a consistent track record of opposition to the pope and the bishops in union with him. In 1974 the CTSA president declared that the institutional Church was "out of phase with the demands of the times," adding later (in 1976) that Vatican II implicitly taught the legitimacy of dissent. CTSA published the book *Human Sexuality,* which was censured by the Holy See and U.S. bishops. Its leading members have predictably opposed Rome's disciplining of dissenting theologians (even in the case of Hans Küng), and criticized an ecclesiastical superior for firing a dissident nun from a major seminary. They have contributed many lectures, articles, books, and reviews to general audiences in support of dissent, and CTSA itself has conferred its highest annual award on a variety of virulent critics of Church teaching and of the magisterium, such as Bernard Cooke, Gregory Baum, and David Tracy.

One of the least remembered offenses by CTSA was its 1990 broadside against John Paul II's administration of the Church, a 4,400 word criticism of his policies. The declaration faulted the Holy See for not paying more attention to the will of episcopal conferences, for not recognizing the autonomous rights of theologians, and for narrow views on feminism and ecumenism. What distressed the CTSA was that the pope was acting as a primate, not as the head of one church within a "communion of churches." By then CTSA was pressing the U.S. hierarchy to go beyond Roman norms and to move toward the limits of a "learning Church" agenda.

If that 1990 salvo against Rome evoked no serious rejoinder from the NCCB, CTSA's 1997 drumbeat for women priests did. In 1990 Lipscomb issued "unofficial" words of regret that episcopal decisions could not always follow CTSA's "abstract theological ideal" (if that is what it really was). But after John Paul II upped the ante on women priests, several bishops came out swinging against CTSA's 1997 barrage on the subject. Cardinal Bernard Law of Boston called the CTSA "an association of advocacy for theological dissent." He lashed out: "How pitiable it is to see the rich Catholic theological tradition put under the bushel-basket of politically correct bromides. What a wasteland is the professional Catholic theological community as represented by CTSA." The mild-mannered new archbishop of Denver, Charles Chaput, even wondered aloud whether or not CTSA's latest dissent "raises questions about the CTSA's continuing usefulness for the life of the Church."

Why did it take so long for the episcopal leadership to recognize the dangers to the Church of an extended misalliance between their conference and the leadership of the CTSA? The leadership of the Canon Law Society and the Association of Catholic Colleges and Universities, whose influence on bishops-in-conference has been equally pernicious, are also overdue for comparable reevaluation.

Long before the Fellowship of Catholic Scholars appeared on the scene in 1977, the American hierarchy had ample warnings from Roman cardinals about misinterpretations and miscalculations by the Washington bureaucracies. The mistake of the Fellowship founders was their presumption that the Washington agencies were interested in such notices. Roman cardinals like Francis Seper, John Wright, Augustine Mayer, Jerome Hamer, Gabriel Garrone, and others rang alarms, but no one in the national Church headquarters of the U.S. paid any heed. It was not Cardinal Joseph Ratzinger, the present head of the Congregation for the Doctrine of the Faith, but his predecessor in office, Cardinal Francis Seper, who made this terrifying observation about bishops as early as 1972: "The bishops, who obtained many powers for themselves at the Council, are often to blame because in this crisis they are not exercising their powers as they should. Rome is too far away to cope with every scandal, and Rome is not well obeyed. If all the bishops would deal decisively with these aberrations, the situation would be different. It is very difficult for us in Rome, if we get no cooperation from bishops."

By the time Seper was uttering these words, the American hierarchy was providing anti-Roman groups like the CTSA, CLS, and ACCU with favored standing within the Church. Their one-sided input and their often "abstract theological perspective" were already significant enough so that they should have alerted the bishops who govern the Church. Much more serious, however, was the unfolding tendency of NCCB leaders to negotiate with "experts" from these groups over Roman definitions and the reach of Catholic law. One prominent cardinal who sought to uphold traditional teaching reported that he was out-voted 4-1 in a committee meeting with his peers, but the vote became 9-1 when staff experts were in the room.

By the late 1960s, negotiating downward was an art form in secular society. Once the Protestant ethic began to show wear and tear, the architects of a new order – savants after the style of John Dewey – convinced opinion leaders that terms such as "the law of the land," "the force of the law," and even "the law of logic" were relative terms, subject to constant reinterpretation. Visionaries and prophets once were wont to call would-be followers to a higher life, realizing that their demands would not appeal to everyone. Populists, on the other hand, looked to ease life's burdens on most people, or keep the peace by mollifying the potentially unruly; they called for more flexibility in governance and a deeper understanding of the people's pleasures and pains. The *descent* from Mount Sinai and the Mount of Olives was a *sine qua non* for these emerging populists, who thought little of the New Testament axiom "wide is the gate and broad is the road that leads to destruction" (Mt. 7, 13), and were totally oblivious to the fact that civility in society requires moral virtue in the citizenry. Today, few will argue that the trend of Western civilization by the late 1960s was downward toward the vulgar, the licentious, and the violent.

The Second Vatican Council never intended for the Church to follow this low road. But many Catholics have done so. A movement developed quickly in learned Catholic circles, a movement which sought to translate the principle of collegiality between pope and the bishops in governing the ancient Church into a principle of fraternity between bishops and academics in governing the post-Conciliar Church. According to this understanding, it was inevitable that episcopal thinking about Catholicity would eventually converge with academic thinking. Is it not strange that Pope Pius X condemned this very idea ninety years ago? In an amazing catalogue of the un-Catholic ideas called *Lamentabile Sane Exitu* (July 30, 1907), the last canonized pope found the following proposition repulsive: "The 'Church learning' and the 'Church teaching' collaborate in such a way that it only remains for the 'Church teaching' to sanction the opinions of the 'Church learning.'"

Unmindful of this warning, the chief organizers of the American episcopal conference turned to their established "learned societies" in 1966 for scholarly input to their post-conciliar decision-making process, and ended up following their lead. Once that first critical decision had been made, a middle-management bureaucracy grew up overnight, under the supervision of only a handful of bishops, gaining monopoly control of "Vatican II renewal." Bishops in the field often complained that they were excluded from having a significant impact at the beginning of decisions in process. (Similar complaints were also made by disenfranchised bishops in other countries.)

Also pushed to the fringes of the Church were those intellectuals, academics, and informed laymen who were never allowed to become Washington insiders, even if they coveted the role. Should the outsiders appeal to the NCCB president, they would be told to go through the learned societies, which by the late 1960s were rarely tuned in to Rome's wave length. When occasionally they appealed to Rome in a formal way, they were informed that the NCCB was the proper conduit for their concerns.

The "closed shop" atmosphere which thus arose was only one aspect of a new Church problem. As soon as the learned elites discovered that consultation could easily be turned into negotiation, they insisted on tradeoffs. When Church leaders showed any openness to discuss the terms under which restive groups would live cooperatively in the Catholic body, they thereby transferred significant power over Catholic life to special interests – especially to those whose asocial or antisocial tendencies make them a law unto themselves.

Juridically, negotiation in any enterprise occurs between equal partners – usually over income distribution, respective areas of jurisdiction, or for the resolution of conflicts. Sovereign states negotiate with each other, or sometimes with criminals they have convicted, in order to obtain specific social benefits. On the other hand, legislators of a given community – in the face of a social difficulty or crisis, and in order to secure community peace – conduct hearings with interested parties to discover facts about wrongdoing and to solicit remedies. But once a viable statute is proposed, legislators debate only with each other about the wisdom of the impending law. Unless they have been corrupted by special interests, they no longer negotiate with those who are about to be regulated.

Yet this is precisely what has happened since the American hierarchy was nationalized, and individual ordinaries became inhibited by their Washington leadership. Evasions of law became widespread, experiments (which were not really experiments) proliferated throughout the Church, American norms replaced Roman norms. When Rome objected to American practices, the NCCB – at the behest of one learned society or another – usually sought dispensations from Rome's higher standards for worship and sacramental life, for the priesthood and marriage, for morals and discipline. These concessions always favored freedom over obedience. (We now concede the full benefit of funeral rites to those whom their neighbors know had no faith or, in fact, had despised the Church.)

The results have been lamentable. In 1960, with a 40 million Catholic population, about 28 million Catholics attended Sunday Mass regularly; by 2000, with 60 million counted as baptized Catholics, pastors will be fortunate to have 15 million regular Sunday worshipers.

Will high Church standards be continually negotiated downward? In May 1997, when Rome told the NCCB president to bring American standards for Catholic colleges up to the norms of canon law and of John Paul II's *Ex Corde Ecclesiae,* Bishop Anthony Pilla announced that he would renew dialogue with ACCU, even though dissent runs rampant on Catholic college and university campuses. And as if to reaffirm the established American approach to Roman restrictions, the new chairman of the USCC's Department of Education solicited forthwith "valued advice, support, and participation in local dialogues" from "CTSA, CTS [Catholic Theological Society], CLSA [Canon Law Society of America], the Men's and Women's Conferences of Religious" about *Ex Corde Ecclesiae.* No other groups were invited to present their views.

We are dealing here with an old story of Church history. In the sixth century, when Arian bishops were fighting Catholic bishops over Christ's divine Sonship, a pattern of response developed which has been repeated in many places over the centuries. Historian Philip Hughes recaps the Arian difficulty as follows: "They [the condemned Arians] would continue to maintain their places, and their offices, in the Church. They would even, for a moment, hold almost all the key positions, and a day would come of which St. Jerome could say: 'The whole world groaned to find itself Arian.'" Fifteen hundred years later, it is John Paul II who groans about dissenting Catholic elites and bishops who give them succor.

Not many months ago, the Jesuit Fathers Thomas J. Reese and Richard A. McCormick announced that their favored changes, *even in* doctrine, will never be ratified by John Paul II (whom they consider reactionary) nor by his successor (who might make the present pontiff look like a "liberal"). Yet collegiality, they believe, is the mitigating influence of episcopal conferences on the Vatican (and Jesuit influence on local bishops) – will in the long run institutionalize their idea of Vatican II renewal.

"Ultra-montanist" may no longer be the term of opprobrium that it was in the late nineteenth century, when loyalty to the pope might have simply meant an oath of allegiance to the Papal States, not a conviction that the pope's teaching of Christ's Resurrection was true. Today, when John Paul II is accused by leaders of the "learned societies" of undoing Vatican II or chastised for publishing a serenely orthodox *Catechism of the Catholic Church* or of expecting those engaged in the ecclesiastical disciplines to profess the Catholic faith, standing with him at the foot of his cross may well be the proper exercise of "the obedience of faith" (Rom. 1, 5) normally expected of all believing Catholics. If a living martyrdom is the price of being Catholic, then so be it.

If a second spring of a pious and vigorous Church American-style is the order of the day – and more importantly a demand of the faith itself – bishops must win this war they have been losing for thirty years. They must have a battle plan and bishop generals who are good at conquering hostile forces. They must be prepared for losses among those who want a deformed Catholicity. They must restore unity with the pope and their authority over the Church. And this means freeing themselves of captivity by their arrogant elites. They must be afraid of nothing, not even the godless media. They need not acknowledge the errors of their predecessors as long as they change their course Romeward. Of old Dennis Cardinal Dougherty ("the grizzly bear"), William Cardinal O'Connell ("one of a kind"), Francis Cardinal Spellman ("the little man with a ten-foot-tall shadow") were great because they left behind remarkably

Churchgoing dioceses. Great men, as Archbishop John Ireland once said, walk in single file, cowards in crowds. It is the pope's responsibility to see that the great bishops rise to take charge of this war.

EIGHT

John Paul II and Diocesan Bishops

*The bishops, who obtained many powers for themselves at the
Council, are often to blame because in this crisis they are not
exercising their powers as they should, Rome is too far away to
cope with every scandal – and Rome is not well obeyed. If all the
bishops would deal decisively with these aberrations as they
occur, the situation would be different. It is very difficult for us in
Rome if we get no cooperation from the bishops.*
Francis Cardinal Seper, Prefect, Congregation for
the Doctrine of the Faith (*Origins*, May 4, 1972)

After years of teaching to the hard of hearing, John Paul II's patience has
finally come to an end. Within three days in May 1998 he dropped a papal
shoe on errant theologians, promising appropriate punishment of those
who obstinately reject a Catholic doctrine that is definitively taught by the
Church as true; and a second shoe on national hierarchies, forbidding them
to attempt binding doctrinal statements without relative unanimity within
their body and then only in union with the Holy See.

This effort to restore teaching and hierarchical unity brought to mind
Christ's final prayer over the Twelve in the Upper Room the night before
he died: "That they may all be one, as you, Father, are in me and I in you,
that they may be one in us, that the world may believe that you sent me
(Jn. 17, 21).

The agents of the counter-magisterium were not appreciative of these
belated efforts to protect the Church at large. They might be willing to
grant extraordinary restraining power to the state during internal strife, but
not to the Church overrun by disbelievers in the classroom or by hirelings
in the pastorate. They reacted as if Christ was content with an unruly
Church, He who once called Peter a devil: "Got thee behind me, Satan.
You are an obstacle to me. You are thinking not as God does but as human

beings do" (Mt. 16, 23). As if abusers of Church office or station are beyond the reach of the Church's law.

John Paul II has now moved to restore order to his Church, where discipleship is mainly measured by the obedience of faith: "If you continue in my word, you are my disciples" (Jn. 8, 31). He tries this in a culture where people are conditioned to think that they are a law unto themselves. Can John Paul II succeed, now that his national hierarchies have failed at the task? Catholic pundits are betting that he cannot because autonomy, even among bishops, is now the rule of modern life, especially in America.

As the Church watches the march of the once Christian West toward universal belief in an old god called Humanity, she is in for the fight of her life. This is no contest over Christ's personality, Mary's virginity, or the pope's infallibility. The very notion of "Our Father Who art in heaven" is the question. In *Gaudium et Spes,* Vatican II called "systematic atheism" the major problem of the Church's present day, i.e., mankind's rush to autonomy from the very notion of God.

If atheism, therefore, is democratic society's threat to all that Christ personified throughout twenty centuries, then it falls chiefly to the Catholic Church to bear the onus of the world's reconversion. She succeeded at her beginning against the virulent paganism of Rome. But if she is to prevail a second time, the Church will need bishops who have the charism and discipline of the apostles under Peter. They will also need the power of God.

Does John Paul II know how to marshal his bishops for this testing? Can he recall them to collegial unity – together with its head, the Roman Pontiff, and never without this head" *(Lumen Gentium)* – in view of the divisions that appeared early during the council between John XXIII and "the Belgian Bloc" of continental bishops and widened during Paul VI's *Humanae Vitae* controversy?

John Paul II faces a faith crisis, to be sure, but he knows that it began with a breakdown in discipline. During his first day on American shores (October 6, 1979), he sized up the new papal challenge: "Our leadership will be effective only to the extent that our own *discipline* is genuine," He used the word, knowing that in ninety days he would be confronting disobedient Dutch bishops, whose bad example eventually infected the conduct of episcopal conferences everywhere

By the 1990s several million central European Catholics had already taken part in a plebiscite against important Church doctrines; an American bishop thought such a referendum might also be good for the United

States. Ninety-year-old Cardinal Franz Koenig of Vienna publicly challenged the pope over his "infallible" ban on women priests; three leading German bishops, who had proposed seriously that divorced but invalidly remarried Catholics are eligible to receive the Eucharist, reasserted their positions, even after verbal censure by the Congregation for the Doctrine of the Faith, "for leading Catholics into sin.[1] French bishops gave qualified approval to the use of contraceptives by AIDS patients, a Spanish bishop, quoted on the same subject, said that "prevention is a prophylactic, not a moral issue," while an English bishop decided that, in those circumstances, the use of a condom "seems to be common sense.[2] Another bishop was removed for pederasty, a U.S. bishops' report provided parents with unsatisfactory advice about the care of homosexual children and, while the Asian bishops have a harmless desire for more autonomy from Rome, the South African bishops issued fuzzy guidelines on the Eucharist that allowed Baptist President Clinton to feel free to receive communion in a Catholic Church.

Taken together, this catena of opinions and events, some of which have doctrinal import, prompted the *National Catholic Reporter* to editorialize (August 25, 1995) that John Paul II is no longer a pivotal Church force, receiving, as he has, episcopal rebukes "almost weekly."

In a Nutshell

John Paul II is now struggling to restore those "plausibility structures" which make the Catholic creed and moral norms credible to her own. Catholic life is not lived by the grace of God alone, nor because one is born Irish, Italian, or Polish. Piety may originate in different places, but it endures to a last anointing only because it is nurtured as true in Catholic homes, in Catholic classrooms, in Catholic parishes by priests, nuns, and bishops who themselves teach and live fully faithful to Christ's Word, as this has been handed to posterity by the teaching office of the Church. Those "plausibility structures" are now in shambles at a time when they are more necessary to faith than ever. A culture which denies the credibility of Christ and penalizes its intrusion into the public life of the nation is hard on Catholics. If they must shift for themselves, unsure anymore about what is true about their faith, they are badly served. It makes no difference what the pope wants or says, if their pastor or teacher at the local level thinks the pope is wrong.

The secular world says it can no longer exist half-slave/half-free. Can the Church exist half-believing/half-unbelieving? Or with anti-popes?

Only within "plausibility structures" – family, parish, diocese – do the preachments of the Church fill lives with meaning, elevate their aspirations for a better life, and ease life's burdens.

John Paul II's work is cut out for him, but his task is not impossible. The only two canonized saints to sit in Peter's chair in the past 500 years were popes who brought the Church out of serious trouble with her own:

> St. Pius V (d. 1572), during his six-year pontificate, enforced the decrees of the Council of Trent against those, including bishops, who thought the content of the Catholic faith was a matter of personal opinion.

> St. Pius X (d. 1914), in his eleven-year reign, created structures, including the first universal *Code of Canon Law,* that helped vitiate the influence of Modernists on Catholic life, particularly their view that much of what Christianity has taught as coming from Christ is untrue.

Both popes placed high value on "the obedience of faith," made good use of religious orders, were judicious in their selection of bishops, and received important help from available Catholic apologists.

Teacher Si, Ruler No?

In recent years, even John Paul II's greatest admirers have been wondering whether the Polish pope was not better at teaching than at governing. Earlier, folklore from Crakow reported that Karol Wojtyla was good at laying hands on people, but not so well on the diocesan machinery. Vaticanologists, in their turn, attributed his administrative shortcomings in Rome to his nationality. "Only Italians know how to run the Church" was their line, forgetting that the disintegration of Catholicity began under two Italian popes (1968–1978). Once in office, however, the Polish Pontiff quickly dispatched Hans Küng as a Catholic theologian (later Charles Curran too), but without influencing the conduct of national hierarchies toward errant theologians. He also withdrew *imprimaturs* but without inspiring bishops to supervise better the Catholic publishers within their dioceses.

In spite of these gestures at governing it was clear from the beginning, however, that John Paul II's priority was preaching. His "traveling ministry" became the hallmark of his pontificate. And although he was good at the spoken word and impressive as a charismatic presence, his critics had a point: no pope can run a universal Church while regularly on the road. Certainly few popes down the centuries ever will have the personal impact on local Catholic communities on five continents that he had. Wojtyla surely had an old pastor's sense that to be a good shepherd he of necessity must visit his people.

Still, the main function of the head of any society is to see that good is done for his people, and evil avoided in that society. At various times he is teacher, legislator, doctor, fireman, cop and warden – and he need be comfortable in all roles. Good governing always involves firm decision-making, often about bad situations. Trouble spots preoccupy the leader's attention, and test, better than anything else, his ability to make his reforms bind on those who work under him, those who in turn are expected to change the misbehavior that created a mess in the first place. John Paul II's problem in 1978 was the cultural approval showered on those who defy authority and the canonization of rebels with or without causes. The inability of society's subordinate office holders to cope with mythologized anti-heroes only compounded the ruling difficulties of presidents and popes. Consider the academic reaction to John Paul II's early censure of theologians Küng and Curran. The entire theological establishments of Germany and the United States rose up in defense of both, while the local hierarchies stood on the sidelines mute. The common assumptions of secular society prevailed: Only peers have the right to judge peers; prophets who speak for God, and bishops, have no standing as judges of ideas.

In these circumstances what does a hierarchical Church do? or a Vicar of Christ? What makes one think that Christ is relevant to egalitarians?

A mere dozen years after the council, the Church's professional "equalizers," who operate on the principle that "the world of the Church should be flat," had already muddied the reason for the very existence of the Catholic Church, and popularized the view that much of what she teaches is unreliable or only the opinion of a pope. So, in the twenty-first century, hierarchical decrees will be mere invitations to study a question until the second magisterium agrees with the first.

What was John Paul II prepared to do under those circumstances? A society with an ambiguous constitution cannot be governed. It is bad enough that Church authority figures everywhere in the West had collapsed before one forceful mini-mob or another, especially on catechetical and liturgical fronts. After a while even bishops began to argue among themselves about what their role was and whether anything any of them had to say was better or more enforceable than what any other bishop had to say. In the process the Church became a playground for the discontented, a debating society for the disbelievers, and the open Catholic mind closed only on comfortable doctrines of personal choice.

While John Paul II can be faulted for hesitancy in some areas of governance, he did become master of one of its facets, viz. the definition of the Church, of her message and her mission in modern language and in Vatican II terms. His teaching is precise, explicit and fully Catholic – about Christ, scripture, the papal office, the Eucharist, matrimony, the priesthood, contraception, indissolubility, ecumenism as well as about penance and the worthy reception of Holy Communion. When he published the *Catechism of the Catholic Church* in 1994, some theological divines were unhappy because "it could have been written before Vatican II." The criticism itself demonstrates how these men misread John XXIII's intent and the Council's documents – and why the Church is in crisis today. Catholic unity – the keystone of "making disciples of all nations" – is possible only through the authentic and definitive teaching of John Paul II.

The chief papal oversight, if that is what it may be called, was the failure to deal with the make-up of the episcopacy. In any area of social life, institutional leaders are only as good as their ability to manage the *de facto* situation they face effectively. Good money makers are often poor money managers. The peacemaker Neville Chamberlain was no match for the warlike Adolph Hitler. "Safe" bishops chosen for safe times are usually failures during battles over faith and morals. Prior to Vatican II, practically all American bishops were ultramontanes. After observing the conduct of European cardinals toward John XXIII and Paul VI in council, some of them came home anti-Roman and in search of their own autonomy from the Vatican Curia. By Paul VI's death many new bishops had been badly trained as seminarians, even in Rome, and comfortable with dissenting theologians like Bernard Haering, C.SS.R., and Joseph Fuchs, S.J. Business as usual remained the rule in the appointment of bishops: Bishops named bishops. There is nothing wrong in principle with such a nomination process, since bishops should know about what makes a good bishop.

The major defect of the process, of course, is the tendency of every executive to choose an "assistant" or "a son," either of whom may be valuable in a subordinate role, without being competent to be a No. 1 anywhere. Even in the peaceful years, when the Church was running smoothly, this kind of promotion system was hardly inspirational. One might think that by 1978 Rome would have developed a new plan for selecting the precise bishops needed to handle war. They did it before.

Granted the fallibility of foresight and the fickleness of luck, the American Church a-building was fortunate when O'Connell appeared in Boston, Dougherty in Philadelphia, Mitty in San Francisco, Rummel to New Orleans, Spellman to New York – all choice appointments if the Catholic patrimony they left behind is the judge. Recently, John Paul II has been accused of "stacking" the American hierarchy with conservatives and, in truth, a renewed effort to choose "orthodox" candidates is noticeable. But "orthodoxy" by itself does not guarantee ability to establish episcopal authority where Church law demands it be exercised. Bishops lost authority to those who out-argued them in public and were more competent in defiance of the law than bishops were at its enforcement. Bishops of the twenty-first century, therefore, beyond their proven theological and rhetorical competence, must have the character to use counter-force, as necessary, against the force of counter-magisterium. Without such bishops, the Church's lawbreakers will dominate Catholic structures at the expense of the faithful's piety.

If John Paul II's sensitivity to bishops and their national conference restrained him from dealing firmly with their vagaries, it remains a mystery why he permitted the Society of Jesus to escape papal control.

Whereas the Jesuits of Trent days were the major allies of the Catholic hierarchy in recovering from the onslaught on the faith of Martin Luther and his princes, the Jesuit body of the Vatican II period is unquestionably the single most powerful anti-papal force in the Church today, as much the source of doctrinal division and impiety within the Church as any other single movement. The legitimacy of contraception, abortion, and sodomy as morally acceptable Catholic options, the collapse of theology as Catholic, the rise of lopsided liberation theology with its anti-hierarchical thrust, the revolt of religious orders (and of women who taught in parish schools), the breakaway of Catholic colleges from the oversight of Church authority with all that this implies, the regular "soft" reinterpretation of papal documents against the obvious meaning of their words, and the isolation or punishment of papal loyalists in their ranks – activities that have drained the Church of its authenticity – all owe their origins or maintenance in significant ways to Jesuits. The latest sortie against Papal authority – a flat contradiction of the Holy See's irreformable teaching on the ordination of women – was led by two Jesuits.[3] Through this entire stream of dissent and disobedience over thirty years, the Jesuits regularly proclaimed their "genuine respect and affection for the pastors of the Church." But, their 1995 General Congregation in Rome made it abundantly clear that, however others define "obedience," Jesuits ("with prayerful discernment") demand freedom to differ with "our religious and Church superiors.[4] They obviously have a limited view of the pope's right to censure wrongdoing.

A year later, Vaticanologist Thomas Reese, S.J., for example, confessed his doubts about the value even of Church penalties because this, in his view, "is burning the bridges of dialogue." Jesuits have been saying this for years. Karol Wojtyla was still a young pope when one of the NCCB's favorite Jesuits, Michael Buckley, insisted that his community was not rebelling against the pope, merely "counter-pointing" him. In the Buckley view, the Jesuit vow of obedience was not of loyalty to him, but of being available for duty whenever he sent them on a mission. The casuistry would have fascinated Ignatius Loyola.[5]

The strange thing about this evolving estrangement of the Jesuits from their pontiff is that Pius XII, a quarter century earlier, severely criticized them at their thirtieth Congregation (1957) for "heterodox mentality" in their midst, which in due course, said the pope, produces "unworthy and unfaithful sons of your Father Ignatius whom it would be necessary to cut off as soon as possible from the Society." After this put-down, dissenting Jesuits went into hiding and remained underground until Vatican II. During the pontificate of Paul VI, however, American Jesuits especially assumed an influential role in the decision-making of their Roman generalate on the side of relativism and autonomy. Two weeks before he died, Jesuit John Courtney Murray, who in 1941 told New York clerics that Jesuits were a model of fidelity to the Church's pastors, acknowledged in 1967 that he could no longer make that claim. In 1968 they moved their distinguished Woodstock Seminary from Maryland to New York, where it became a scandal, closing abruptly after two Jesuit officials with national reputations left the priesthood.

By 1982 John Paul II placed the Society of Jesus into receivership. He sidelined Pedro Arrupe as Father General, appointed two Jesuits of his choosing as temporary administrators, and demanded they introduce reforms consistent with "the exact interpretation of the recent Council," with the requirement, too, that they restore "thinking with the Church" and "fidelity to the *magisterium* and the pope," that they intensify the Society's interior life and that they resist the tendency "to secularize priest's work by reducing it to a purely philanthropic function." The pope could hardly have been more forthright about the misdirection of the Church's most powerful religious order whose educational network throughout the world was second to none – but was by then directed against the Church's definitive teaching and policies.

The papal receivership failed to accomplish its objective. By 1983 John Paul II permitted the thirty-third General Congregation to convene for the election of a new Father General, who would direct the Society on a course different from that of Fr. Arrupe. The assembly met, and only then was it clear that the Jesuit establishment had outmaneuvered the pope. These "insiders" uncovered and elected an obscure Dutchman named Peter Hans Kolvenback "with veritable unanimity," a neutral figure whose priesthood was exercised mostly in India and the Near East, and a tyro in the game of post-Vatican II ecclesial politics. Most outsiders took little notice of the four assistant generals also elected, men who knew their way around the Roman byways. Later, one of these Assistants would remind the General that a 1965 change in the Jesuit bylaws made it possible for him to be impeached by his four aides. Later still, another Assistant General mused in a public interview that the College of Cardinals might well have similar authority to impeach a pope. The Jesuit relationship with the pope had been reestablished, as "dialogic" in nature, not one of obedience.

Why John Paul II permitted the Society to escape his discipline is unclear, especially since Jesuits were capable of doing greater harm to Catholicity than diocesan priests like Khng or Curran. Their network – colleges, journals like *America* and *Theological Studies,* parishes, the Jesuit Conference, have kept a drumbeat going for *avant-garde* causes, unacceptable to Rome, any one of which a diocesan bishop would dare frustrate at great peril, to his reputation. Their command centers have withheld final vows, fired tenured professors, removed from Jesuit houses as "divisive," denied preferential options, transfers, or promotions to fellow Jesuits who were open defenders of papal policies and/or candid critics of their office holders and anti-Roman ideology. Other men religious report similar dissent within their own congregations, but confess that restoration of Catholic order is not possible as long as the pope permits Jesuits to remain disobedient. Considering the importance of religious communities to the front lines of the Church's evangelization mechanisms, such autonomy from papal discipline reflects badly on the governance of the Church.

Appeasement or Cover-up?

Probably the worst thing Christ said about wrong-headed religionists in his company was that they were "hypocrites" (Mt. 23, 27) – "whitened sepulchers full of dead men's bones." These pretenders made religious claims and performed sacred rituals, but believed in neither or, while seeming to be saints in public, they were really private devils. Hypocrites are usually cynics at heart, whose only god is their own self-interest. Nominal Catholicity belongs to the same family, a precious name but one with little meaning any more for its practitioners.

John Paul II's worst enemies would never call him a "hypocrite." What annoys them most is that he believes what he preaches. Even when he utters what, in their eyes, are outrageous dicta, such as his claim that the Church's doctrine on contraception "belongs not only to the natural law but also to the moral order revealed by God.[6] The present pope surely believes what the new *Catechism* says (No. 552) of his guardianship of the universal Church: "His mission will be to keep the faith from every lapse and to strengthen his brothers in it." The pope obviously believes all that he teaches.

But is the Vatican apparatus equally trustworthy? The Council was hardly over when Hans Küng was advising Catholic revolutionists: Pay no heed to what Rome says; watch instead what she does. His point suggested that Rome keeps using her old words, even as she allows their meaning to die. And those who would want more formality in deception, might want to fall back on John XXIII's apocryphal say-so: "What a pope can do, a pope can undo."

The history of the Church, of course, is filled with enough contradictions that a plausible case can surely be made for institutional hypocrisy in high places. Practice does not necessarily follow principle in all cases, as everyone knows. But the conviction that truth or right are of little account to a Catholic is heresy.

Controversies over appeasement and/or hypocrisy in the Church have been bitter since Vatican II. Probably the early wipe out of the Latin liturgy, in spite of the Council ("the Latin language is to be preserved in Latin rites"), was at the start the most heated of all; but arguments soon developed over mistranslations of biblical and liturgical texts, over the virtual elimination of the sacrament of penance during the debates over first confession and general absolution, over Paul VI's failure to give Cardinal O'Boyle full support in his disciplining of priest enemies of *Humanae Vitae,* over Rome's failure to secure the Catholicity of Catholic colleges or a profession of faith from Catholic college professors. One or the other of these fights has been cited as an example of weak Roman governance or the result of the hidden agenda at work of a Roman curialist somewhere.

But when all these controversies are resolved, it is still true that the alleged incidents of maladministration, previously mentioned, mostly concern ecclesiastical law – which is eminently changeable, regardless of whether the effects on the Church are good or bad. But what about divine law? Would ambiguity in papal teaching or performance vis-à-vis the clear law of God be serious misconduct in office?

As an example of that question, consider the manner in which the Church deals currently with the indissolubility of matrimony, which is coming more and more under intense fire. Clearly, marital indissolubility is God's law (Mt. 19, 3–10). Christ criticized Moses for granting divorces simply because the people wanted them. Was Paul VI another Moses, since the rush to annulment began under his watch? Charles Morris's *American Catholic* (1997) made much of "the contrast between rigid Church teachings on divorce and the enthusiasm with which many dioceses hand out annulments." A year later, Notre Dame's Robert Vasoli, in a carefully written volume *What God Has Joined Together: The Annulment Crisis in American Catholicism,* contended that the Church's canonical system, at least in the United States, is directed toward legitimizing divorce and remarriage for Catholics.

Years before Vatican II, selected scholars took stabs at tearing asunder the literal meaning of "let no man put asunder," without having any effect on the indissolubility of Catholic marriage or on the Church's Canon Law. As late as 1968, only 400 formal annulments were granted to Catholics. Today, 40,000 such formal declarations per year are standard practice in the United States, mostly on psychological grounds. Rome has always resisted the trend officially, but when episcopal conferences became involved, it made procedural concessions (later tightened) which facilitated the multiplication of annulments. Since statistics were unavailable in those days, the loosening of the Catholic marriage bond at local levels was not publicly measurable at first. Charles Morris suggests that what went on was hardly honest: "Rather than acknowledge divorce, the Church accedes to the pretense that long-standing marriages, celebrated in Church, ones that produced children, *never happened.*"

But Rome did know what was going on locally. Within six years of the Council (December 30, 1971), the Holy See reprimanded the bishops of Holland for allowing views to develop within their jurisdiction which made indissoluble marriage appear to be an ideal, not a norm, marital consent to seem as something not given at time of marriage, but a contract which evolved over time. In the process, Rome said, Church annulments are treated as it one party or another "can establish by their own [*sic*] judgment if the marriage was valid because it was happy or else null and dissolved because it ended in failure" – as if psychology determines incapacity for interpersonal relationships, as if pastoral concern is an "aid to a human situation without at the same time conserving the revealed faith.[7]

The Apostolic Signatura, the Church's highest court, in its closing remarks, condemned in no uncertain terms a major offense by a national hierarchy within six years of the Council (December 30, 1971):

> It is clear that a particular or local church cannot act in a manner contrary to the procedure and doctrine of the universal Church, taking account only of the particular Church. The only holy Catholic and apostolic Church is made present in the life and activity of all particular churches. Even where a certain pluralism is admitted, there remain essential points in which it is not permitted for any particular church to separate itself from the universal Church and from the other particular churches.
>
> . . . the [Dutch tribunal] judges themselves recognize that their judgments are accepted with difficulty in other regions. In their own country, they are challenged by certain of the faithful who are scandalized to that audacity even fundamental rights are wronged.
>
> . . . . where a judge should refuse to conform, he ought to be dismissed from his charge by a competent authority and the task of administering justice should be given without delay to a more proven man.[8]

In the following twenty years, operating on the same faulty theological principles, American tribunals were blanketing parish Churches with annulments, without effective correction by Rome.

The statistics alone (for the period 1984–1993) are alarming:

Annulment Typ.[9]	U. S. A.	Rest of World
Documentary	182,941 (87%)	26,345
Ordinary	401,306 (74%)	131,741

In other words, American Catholics, which comprise 6 percent of the Church's 1 billion adherents worldwide, receive over 70 percent of the ordinary annulments, justified by the very reasons of defective consent that the Holy See found objectionable in the Holland situation.

As year followed year, the American bishops continued to ask Rome to leave their marriage tribunals alone, sometimes in *ad limina* visits, sometimes during negotiations of the NCCB with the Holy See. And in spite of obvious abuses, their own canonical establishment, as far back as 1980, assured them that "tribunals in the United States are applying the *magisterium*'s own teaching on marriage as expressed by recent popes and the Second Vatican Council."[10]

John Paul II would not likely agree – if all his papal exhortations and lectures since 1980 to canonists, to bishops, and to judges of the rota, critical of easy annulments, are taken into account. Furthermore, the fact that of the 50,000+ annulments worldwide, the Roman Rota annually hears less than 200 on appeal, is an indication of how inadequate the Church's judicial system is to deal with the American annulment explosion. (Out of 40,000 favorable American judgments favoring nullity only 20 come from the United States in a given year, 90 percent of which the Rota overturns!)

Robert Vasoli maintains that the American canonists' argument, viz. that their loose annulment policy is an effort to protect indissolubility, reminds him of the abortionists who claim that they do what they do merely to save the unborn child from coming into a world of pain and poverty.

While the annulment crisis may be the most scandalous example of seeming papal paralysis over God's law in the face of dissident forces, many other items of divine and Catholic faith, certainly of definitive teaching, are victims of stonewalling by religious orders, Catholic colleges, Catholic professors, and some bishops. Laminating dissent and disobedience over Catholic substance with euphemisms like "constructive dialogue" and "common ground," where they compromise articles of faith about the priesthood, religious life, the Eucharist, etc., only tends to tarnish the otherwise brilliant pontificate of the Church's first Polish pope.

The Pope: Supervisor of Bishops

Some years ago a cardinal prefect in the curia told his secretary: "The pope doesn't have to fire those four bishops. All he need do is fire one of them and tell the world why he was fired!" The secretary, having examined complaints against four American ordinaries, made the original across-the-board proposal.

This recommendation was not as crude as it sounds in the telling. The cardinal was old enough to know how Pius XI and Pius XII handled devious bishops and there was no reason why John Paul II could not do in like manner – firmly but with class. And if anyone can handle the modern media, he can. When Bishop Jacques Gaillot, for example, was ousted as bishop of the French Diocese of Evreux, the pope reproached him personally without anger, but let him be chewed out by Cardinal Bernard Gantin, head of the Congregation for Bishops.[11] That is one way.

In most episcopal circles today punishing a wrongdoer, especially one who is likely to fight back and survive, has become almost unthinkable. Which is why "Go to hell!" has become an unbelievable threat and is rarely stressed anymore in catechesis, no matter what Christ said.

"Correction" – "to set things right" – though considered in some circles as a psychological "no-no" – is both natural to humankind and a biblical demand. Correction presumes that there is a right to be done, an evil to be avoided, and that someone is responsible for both. People who recognize their unfortunate tendency to do evil appreciate the value of righting wrong. In a Christian community, especially, where assent to the Church's teaching and obedience to the Commandments are considered acts of virtue, and their denials labeled vice, correction is the responsibility for parents, presidents, and pastors – and for the pope confronting wayward bishops.

What is John Paul II to do in the face of disrespect for his authority by bishops? Nothing, if the issues are picayune or peripheral to Catholicity. Something, if the Catholic faith or the serious discipline of the Church is involved. The integrity of his own pontificate is at stake.

John Paul II has already instructed the Congregation for the Doctrine of the Faith (November 24, 1995) on the urgency of the Catholic Church to recover her authority based on faith, in part because the "dialogic Church authority" practiced since 1965 has undermined episcopal authority and Christ's. In reality, however, authority is never given: It is enacted or earned. So it is surprising in recent disputes how little attention has been paid to the manner in which the Apostolic Church responded to unfriendly challenges to its teaching and piety. The first century had reached its twilight when St. John the Evangelist and his disciples made the following point in the Second Epistle bearing that name: "Anyone who is so 'progressive' that he does not remain rooted in the teaching of Christ, does not possess God, while anyone who remains rooted in the teaching possesses both the Father and the Son. If anyone comes to you who does not bring this teaching, do not receive him into your house, do not even greet him, for whoever greets him shares in the evil he does."

The Church is not a godless state. Keeping God's law is what the Church is about. And the pope is charged to see good done, and evil avoided, by strengthening bishops' will to join him in doing both. Will he succeed?

NINE

The Second Spring

No doubt that the other Apostles were all that Peter was,
endowed with equal dignity and power, but the start comes from
him alone, in order to show that the Church of Christ is unique. .
. . If a man does not hold fast to this oneness of the Church, does
he imagine that he still holds the faith?
St. Cyprian, bishop of Carthage, 251 AD

The Catholic Church rarely remains dead long, although its second Pentecost may not shine as brightly as the first. The rise, fall, then rise again cycle is not entirely in a pope's hands. The American Church is going to find that out. Though far from dead, she has been seriously wounded. Her internal enemies continue to brag that they control her lifelines and her most persuasive voice, that they dominate the thinking of her liturgists, her religious educators and her theologians[1]; that, as Americans, they will not bow to papal disciplinary measures. They make these claims, not as idle boasts of ivory-tower iconoclasts, but with the banzai cries of victors over hierarchy.

It is a shame that someone at the First Synod of Bishops did not think of Pearl Harbor, when they met that week in 1967 to assess the damage already inflicted by the theological bombs dropped on Cathedrals by the Küng/Curran forces. But instead of immediate defense and counter-offense, the prelates waited, and, in short order, religious houses, colleges, and seminaries came under attack from the Richard McBrien/Rosemary Ruether-types who staked out occupation claims over the thinking and behavior of Catholics within those hallowed walls.

The forces of the counter-magisterium were by then developing strategies/tactics in various places that would forestall, if not paralyze, Church authority from imposing its definitions or its governing decisions on priests or laity who questioned the legitimacy or the validity of either. A Catholic association appears here, a theologian there, an academic society now, a prominent pastor then, an article, a book, a published lecture yesterday, today, and a guarantee of more tomorrow – all objecting to the Church's view, on sin and "divine" revelation, "carrying a cross," the liturgy, vows and obedience, chastity, indissolubility, priestly celibacy, the primacy of Peter, *et alia*. Bishops begin to look like rangers at a forest fire – hardly knowing where to begin. Forgetful, too, that by permitting venial sins against the Church to go unattended, they were preparing the way for mortal sins which would be committed brazenly – in no need of confession, absolution, or penance. As a result of terrorist tactics, it has come to pass that *Ex Corde Ecclesiae*, the new Church law defining what a Catholic college is, will not eaily be implemented by the American bishops because an organized collegiate body, called the Association of Catholic Colleges and Universities, will not obey its stipulations!

In 1998 John Paul II took the counter-offensive on the Church's terms. For him this is nothing short of reconstructing the City of God. Some of his structures must be sold, given away or razed. Some need rebuilding. Staff needs reshuffling, too – some retired, some fired. His first project may be the most difficult of all, viz. the re-deployment of unfriendly occupation troops acting as trustees for an alien Church in the making.

John Paul II will also need a "Wojtyla Recovery Plan," one already sketched in the *Catechism of the Catholic Church*. The Church's definitive teaching must bind everyone who aspires to remain in Church employ. Prophets of doom say on record that the Pope's kind of Catholicity has no appeal to moderns. It is too otherworldly and it is too demanding. They are quite aware, of course, that their own "catholicons," a Greek word for "cure-alls," while slaking certain modern thirsts and lusts, also empty churches on Sunday, and divest Catholic rituals of their sacred meaning. The pope, however, is convinced that in the long run the goddess Humanity is not viable for his contemporaries when "Our Father Who art in Heaven" is fairly and fully presented in the one voice of Christ. From the Church's pulpits, classrooms, religious houses, and from her editorial rooms. A good place to start this recovery is in the Mother Houses of the religious orders around St. Peter's Square.

The Authority Hassle

John Paul II will reconstruct very little in Catholicity, however, unless he and his bishops together first reestablish their credibility as the voice of

Christ with their right to "bind and loose" the consciences of Catholics – especially those who are in error or in bad faith. The Christian conscience of the West, for all practical purposes, is dead. Were David around, he might lament: "Rise up, Lord, defend your cause." Or as in the Psalms (74): "Your foes have made uproar in your house of prayer."

The pope has on his hands a public relations problem of the first magnitude. The secularists do not mind his "silly" musings on Mary's virginity or the Sacred Host, if these fables amuse him. But they have roundly defeated him, they think, on condoms, sexual choices, war, the death penalty, capitalism, and women priests. They recognize him as a soldier of Christ, but where are those legionnaires that used to worry heads of state (except Stalin)? Where are his Henry Edward Mannings and his John Henry Newmans or even his John Hugheses? In a real sense he faces war on two oceans – the credibility of his authority inside the Church and its utility to secular society on the outside. To make a dent in the public media he needs more than his own debating voice. First, he must reduce his internal dissenters to manageable size, as Christ once silenced the Doubting Thomases. In today's milieu, the medium – not the pulpit or the rostrum – is the pervasive message, and the medium knows neither God nor Christ. Up to now, the Church has played a minor counter-cultural role there, in part because media-masters play the pope off against his dissenters in a way they would never do to their own cultural icons. Further, the Church lets them get away with these put-downs, as they would not have done earlier in this century. As a result, Catholic bishops spend more time avoiding a bad headline – than they do getting their message across.

The pope and the bishops must reestablish the plausibility of their authority, and do it on the world's center stage. They must declare and defend their rights, as Christ did, and as necessary; they must diminish the ability of homegrown revilers to damage their office and their teaching. In the popular mind, certainly that of elites, any social arrangement based on hierarchy is *per se* undemocratic, turning the self-will of special interests against authority figures into a populist virtue. This is an old French Revolutionary/Marxist notion, of course, and explains much of the hostility toward John Paul II. Its practitioners might still excuse Christ for driving money-changers from the temple because he lived in a primitive era; but expelling Charles Curran from the Catholic University of America was outrageous.

Officers of magisterium must almost go back to Apologetics I because the Christian perspective is different when the world is truly Catholic.

Here, the pope is a servant of God, as are all pastors and parents. He and they are deputed to see to it that, in their community at least, common good is done and common evil avoided. Caring for others makes them, technically, superior to others, but it is the caring, when done well, and the patent suffering that goes with the minding, which brings them reverence. Not their mastery. It is the legitimacy of their authority to make decisions binding others that is denied widely. Today, Christ would do no better than John Paul II.

We hear a lot these days about autonomy in the Church. *De facto*, no one is autonomous of someone's authority. And no one interferes with other people's autonomy more that autonomists.[2] In Catholic circles, some elites exalt movements "from below" against popes, except when popular opinion agrees with the pope. Others stand embarrassed about revelation "from on high," even if it comes from Christ. Suavity of manner is a valued social grace for prelates, but when they use phrases like "I implore," "I encourage," "I recommend" when speaking authoritatively, in the presence of those who pay them no heed (the root words of "obedience") or before those who carry on vendettas against them, they hardly enhance respect for their authority. John Paul II presumes that Church officials are "fraternal and spiritual," but he also warns that "the final words belong to authority, and consequently that authority has the right to see that decisions taken are respected.[3] Do they do this?

The force of law, as an instrument of recovery, cannot be neglected by hierarchy, and hierarchy must defend and justify its proper use at the very time they exercise it. Good teaching, good example, better training, charitable advice, patience, forceful correction, visible support for the righteous, have a salvific effect on three-quarters or more of Catholics who are disgruntled for one reason or another. But virulent anti-Church activists, usually a small numerical cadre, disdain sweet talk and count on total *noblesse oblige* from Church authority while they continue their *coup d'église*. Today's prelates are, by choice, out of practice at correcting those who make their life difficult. Still, defenders of Catholicity, like defenders of honor or self-preservation, must strike the right blow in favor of the faith. And faith in the pope, and in the bishops united with him, is an essential element in Catholicity. Suspension of recalcitrant clergy, interdiction and/or excommunication of *agents provocateurs*, are covered by sections of present Church law that have a New Testament base. Religious wrongdoing cannot be allowed indefinitely to infest the body of the faithful. If even quiet schism becomes an institutionalized status quo, someone has forgotten the words of Christ, "Begone!" "Shake the dust..,"

"Depart ye cursed," etc. The Lord was hardly a tenderhearted moralizer when the well-being of his "little ones" was at stake. Allowing sheep to fall into the hands of wolves, or of untrustworthy hirelings, is a scandal. The only ones capable of quarantining wickedness within the Church, as civil authorities might do with an epidemic, is the Catholic hierarchy led by the pope. And they must take their case to the public and suffer their opposition, if need be, a word must be said here about punishment. The English word derives from the Latin word "poena" – translated as "pain," penalty, or even payback. The price of drunkenness is the hangover, payback time for a crook is restitution, and the penalty for committing a felony is jail. "Do penance" and "let him be an anathema" are the Church's ways, going back to New Testament times, of expressing strong disapproval of ecclesial trouble-making. Sentimentalists dislike the punishment of criminals, even of using strong words against them, though their indulgence of wrongdoing makes life painful for the majority who must endure it.

The new *Catechism of the Catholic Church* recognizes the value and necessity of punishment, administered reasonably by proper authority to malefactors (Nos. 2266–2267), for their own good, and for that of society. Something is radically wrong, of course, with the moral character of Catholics if the Church *regularly* needs external sanctions to keep the peace. Mother Church realizes better than most that Catholics live in a state of only "partial internalization," and need watching. "Lead us not into temptation" is not an idle prayer. Nor was it intended that the House of God look like the house of mammon. Why does the Church decry modern society's destructive individualism, subjectivism, and relativism, yet validate both within her own household? Why do bishops favor so many social controls of political evils, and shy away from controlling evildoers within their family?

Take the case of Lincoln, Nebraska's Bishop Fabian Bruskewitz, who in May 1996 threatened to excommunicate any Catholic[4] in his diocese who played leading roles in various intrinsically evil anti-life movements sponsored there by Planned Parenthood. He received a large amount of private and personal support, but a Religious News Service survey of fellow bishops found that most of his peers, those willing to be quoted, were rather unfriendly to the very idea and considered his action an embarrassment to them. Would his critics be outraged had he pointed the same penalties at racists or anti-Semites? Bishops have changed. Forty years ago, New Orleans archbishop Joseph Rummel excommunicated three diocesan laymen for interfering with his desegregation of the Catholic schools. No other bishop at that time interfered with his judgment, and the secular world only praised his courage.

Rome and bishops will never win the authority hassle by aping the worst features of secular society, i.e., by allowing its own laws or Christ's commands to remain empty words.

A Defense of Authority

There is no Catholicity without the authority of Christ, and of the Episcopacy bonded to Peter's successor. This claim may make the Church appear more confident in her faith than in human experience, more paternal in government than consensual. So be it. The authoritative witness by hierarchy to Christ and Catholic faith takes precedence over speculation used to explain its meaning and over how people react to its creed, code, or cult. The world's smartest men and women make acts of faith in her all the time. St. Augustine had this in mind when he said (*De Moribus Ecclesiae Catholicae*): "There is no sounder principle in the Catholic Church than that authority should precede reason." John Paul II once observed that the trend of revisionists to equate the Church's faith with what people would like it to be, especially when their views are offered in opposition to the magisterium, "is equivalent to denying the Catholic concept of revelation.5

Popes, bishops, or pastors, therefore, cannot afford to leave their authority outside the door when they enter a room to hear what people have to say about the Church, or when they represent what the Church has to say to people. Throughout the centuries prelates have often been discomforted by the way people talked about them, even to their face. James Gordon Bennett used to say of John Hughes: "He is more of a demagogue than a Christian!" Yet, even Bennett appreciated the dignity of the archbishop, and Hughes knew what respect his office demanded when dealing with Bennett.

The line between what a bishop defines as a truth of faith and his prudential judgments about how to protect the Church's political decisions is wide, and disputants on either side can go too far in the wrong direction. St. Augustine, in saying: "Heed your bishop, that God may hear you, too," had in mind episcopal demands of faith. Still, priests, especially the obstinate ones who, facing opposition from a bishop to their practical judgment, lacking the civility to come back another day, must submit to their bishop's decision, if it falls within his competence, not theirs. Christ expected no less of the Apostles.

John Paul II might well become the author of an *Encyclopedia of Catholic Faith and Worship*, if someone assembles his personal papers. Such a compilation could well become the source book par excellence for the twenty-first century, and beyond, of authentic Catholic Christianity. It would be a yardstick by which to judge Vatican II and the Catholicity of all future theological/canonical writing, and prompt historians down the line to designate him as "the Great." Perhaps someone will adapt what was once said of St. Leo the Great (440–461): "[I]t is Peter who is speaking through the voice of John Paul II." But not before he succeeds in having bishops and theologians listen to him. (Lk. 9, 35). Pope John Paul II's vision of Catholicity cannot remain, within the Church at least, just one man's opinion, not the voice of Christ's Vicar.

How is John Paul II going to turn around the present disobedience in faith?

The Preliminaries of Recovery

"Have this mind among yourselves which is in Christ Jesus." (Phil. 2, 6). There cannot be any recovery if Christians do not think like Christians, and walk in the Church as disciples. The key concept, therefore, in any process of construction or deconstruction is discipline. Without discipleship there is no personal achievement – or peace in the Church. The reason the American Church is in trouble today is that forces of disunity – religious superiors, college presidents, and professional academics – have held fast in their "no" to hierarchy, while the bishops and Rome in response have been at odds with each other, one side belatedly prepared to pay some price of defiance, the other still fearful of the consequences of law enforcement. The impression is sometimes left by this or that academic – if, for example, he fights the indissolubility of Catholic marriage with the pope – that he is an equal, free to dispute the pontiff, or as if this were simply an argument over Latin in the Mass.

Disciples are learners. They owe whatever they are to their teachers. If they are apt learners, they follow the rules of their craft, whether it be science, art, politics, or breaking the four-minute mile. In spite of a modern myth that great men or women are rule-breakers, the truth is that, although people sometimes achieve stardom by luck, most "greats" are masters of their calling. (And they acknowledge their debt to those who taught them.) The greatest Catholics are the Church's saints. The greatest

Catholic theologian, Thomas Aquinas, on his deathbed after receiving Viaticum, confessed that all he wrote about the Eucharist was subject to judgment by the Church's teaching office.

The "scientific" method for determining Catholic anything includes a judgment by the Church's magisterium. In all matters that pertain to Catholicity, final decisions about what is true and authentic, inauthentic or counterfeit about a religious order, a college, or an ecclesiastical study is the responsibility of Catholic bishops, and ultimately of the pope.

The American Church has faced crisis before. In its early years (1829) bishops suffered through widespread priestly disobedience and a laity more American than piously Catholic. The first thing the hierarchy did then was to instill responsibility in pastors and teachers. Few Catholics were ever excommunicated, interdicted, or suspended from ecclesial office, but everyone learned the difference between episcopal pleasure and displeasure, and eventually the faithful reaped the benefits that accompanied practicing Catholicity. Bishops were not always liked, but by and large, being hard to bully, they earned the respect of their community – even from those who ineffectively challenged their authority or teaching.

In more recent times, the National Conference of Catholic Bishops has faced far more serious and organized challenges to their governance of that Church, which now claims 60 million adherents. In 1982 they faced up to malefactors in their ranks, at least in theory, when they summarized Catholic teaching on the episcopal role in the salvation process. At their annual meeting that year in Collegeville, they recapitulated not only their episcopal obligations, but bishops' rights: (1) to foster and safeguard the unity of faith; (2) to uphold the special discipline of the Church; (3) to educate the faithful, especially the poor; and (4) to promote the Church's apostolic activity. In an explanatory note, taken from the Second Synod of Bishops (1969), they stressed two points: (1) "the faithful are bound to accept the teaching which the bishop proclaims in the name of Christ on matters of faith and morals"; (2) "the task of giving authentic interpretation of the Word of God, whether it is in written form or in the form of tradition, has been entrusted to the living teaching office of the Church alone." Rejection of these principles by dissenters and lack of correction by bishops are what has weakened the faith of Catholics at this time.

To avoid confrontation with bishops, non-conformists do not always reject Catholic teachings out of hand. But the self-righteous among them do re-label magisterial proclamations as ideals or suggestions, not as matters of obligation; or nuance their obvious meaning away from orthodoxy, especially if these doctrines be applied to Catholic institutions.

One readily comes across today statements like the following: "Fordham is not a place to indoctrinate, proselytize, or impose religious tests on faculty or students." Or, we hear how Catholic hospitals are free to sterilize those who have serious reasons to request the procedure. Archbishop John Quinn, from a Jesuit base in England, criticized the pope's curia and called for wide-open debate on women's ordination and birth control. Andrew Greeley once opined that selective Catholics have as much a handle on God as the magisterium. Such voices must not be allowed to go uncriticized by Churchmen.

Discipline will never cure the incorrigibles, but they surely can be marginalized. Neither Hans Küng nor Charles Curran have the same influence on Catholic circles as they did before the pope "fired" them. Before any "Wojtyla Recovery Plan" is undertaken, certain assumptions must be taken for granted by those responsible for its implementation:

1. Bishops, collectively and personally, must be one with the Holy See in recognizing the deformation that stares them in the face. If the situation is otherwise, the inevitable result for generations to come will be the nominal practice of the faith by fewer Catholics, as in continental Europe;

2. Agreement together that the core issues dividing Catholics involve the content of the faith itself and the authority of the hierarchy to define that faith, not simply a "renewal" of style;

3. Determination at the papal and episcopal levels that organized dissenting activists, who claim squatters' rights over Catholic institutions, be treated as antagonists;

4. Notice to all and sundry that the promotion of contradictory pluralism within the Church over and against definitive Church teaching is intolerable and subject to public correction;

5. The acknowledgment before all, with conviction, that the cure of Catholic malaise is primarily the responsibility of all pastors, notably diocesan bishops through appropriate teaching, reconciliation, and disciplinary procedures.

Not by good will alone does a father raise a family effectively or a teacher educate his class or a general win a war or a shepherd lead his flock to the fold. The ruler must rule, and if he faces disorder, he must be competent to find his way through the chaos successfully. No one in authority takes pleasure in conflict, or lives comfortably with those who hold him in contempt. Sinful creatures do fight, do dissent, do mistake their own way for the Church's way. Bishops must deal with God's undisciplined children who are more than ecclesial gadflies. However good they may be in conversation or in preaching, bishops will be judged for the Catholic quality of their pastorate. Indulgence toward institutional unbelief or evil has little support from the Church leaders of New Testament days. Christ himself had his unpopular moments, and for similar reasons.

The following scandals must not be repeated: Jesuit Robert Drinan held political office in Congress for ten years (1971–1981) against the direct order of his Father General in Rome, and against the Canon Law of the Church which forbids clerics to hold political office. The alienation of Catholic colleges from the Church by the obstinate refusal of their presidents to subscribe to the requirements of *Ex Corde Ecclesiae* or canon law must be terminated. Simple words of exhortation are no longer sufficient to ameliorate the effects of imbedded scandal. Teaching is easy, but "teaching them to observe" tests the character of the episcopacy. Bishops must no longer act as if their antagonists are their co-equals, or that radically irreconcilable doctrinal positions can be syncretized simply by conversation that does not and in the obedience of faith" (where is the open quote mark?) (Rom. 1, 6).

The Seven Keys of the Kingdom

The Keys of the Kingdom – the authority to bind and loose – were given to the pope and the bishops in union with him. To no one else. They must be properly used, of course, but someone else's idea of the appropriate should not interfere with their effective use, especially when the integrity or survival of Christ's Church is at stake.

The second spring of a revitalized American Church calls for bishops or pope opening doors that have been closed to them by those under their jurisdiction who reject their teaching or defy their law.

> *1. The Holy See must insist, once universal policy or law is established, that every National Conference of Catholic Bisbops, as well as each diocesan bishop, apply the policy or law without equivocation, ambiguity, or "benign neglect" of enforcement.*

The Holy See must also oversee Roman institutions of learning and seminary training so that they become models for bishops and major seminaries everywhere of how the Church's universal norms are implemented and how Catholic institutions should be managed. The source of many Roman problems is Rome itself. Religious orders in particular, especially those with pontifical accreditation, must become exemplars of Church holiness and obedience and administer the institutions in their care according to Church law. The Society of Jesus, which brought the Church through Tridentine reforms, must be returned to obedience.

2. Bishops once again ought to instruct the faithful personally about the meaning of the articles of the Creed and the relationship of doctrine to the Catholic way of life.

St. Alphonsus Liguori thought that the ability to teach and preach well was essential to an effective episcopacy. As early as the 1840s, New York's Bishop John Hughes was preaching in public halls about Christ's divinity, Mary's virginity, the Eucharist, and papal infallibility. A generation later, Bishop James Gibbons, while still in Richmond (1876), published The *Faith of Our Fathers*, which by the time of his death in 1921 had gone through 110 editions. Catholics today have only the vaguest idea of Catholic doctrine. It is not surprising, therefore, that they seek legitimacy from bishops to have a second spouse, an abortion, or to keep intact their hatreds of different classes and races. St. Paul and St. Augustine appeared in Church history at the right time.

3. In the present trying circumstances, bishops are more likely to initiate recovery by the proper and judicious use of their legislative judicial. and executive authority. Lumen Gentium *(No. 27) reaffirmed these episcopal rights and responsibilities. An important element of this authority is the clarification of disputed issues without undue delay, lest dissenting opinions over time gain wider acceptance than they already have.*

The number of countries that were once Catholic but now lost to the Church by timid or incompetent governance is not small. Today's bishops must be prepared to dispute and refute, publicly as necessary, those who lead the faithful astray on matters of doctrine or threaten the Church's well-being by their disobedience. Doubts about or denials of the Church's definitive teaching are widely disseminated by Catholic publishing houses. Texts used in Catholic classrooms for religious and theological studies should have explicit and carefully given approval. Catholic publishers of such books should be wisely monitored. Report of scandalous behavior should be dealt with in timely fashion, according to law, and appropriately in manly fashion, making sure that the reputations of the priestly and religious bodies as such are vigorously respected.

Directives from the Holy See should be vigorously enforced. And the superiors of religious congregations should be closely supervised in the interest of uniform implementation of universal law. The day that religious congregations function somewhat outside the general law should be at an end.

>   *4. Bishops should reward the Church's Catholic apologists with recognition and approval and withhold both from dissenters, at least.*

The body of academics most neglected by bishops since Vatican II are those scholars, writers, and journalists who have been in the forefront of defending the faith and John Paul II. This neglect has not gone unnoticed. The July 8, 1974,issue of *Time* magazine cited Bishop James Rausch, Bernardin's successor as general secretary of the NCCB, as having explained how the American bishops had begun to wield hierarchical clout against "the right" (usually those pro-Roman on doctrinal issues) which their predecessors in pre-Vatican II days used against "the left" (usually those pro-Roman on social issues). The 1970s were the very years when American norms on annulments, women's rights, and experimental catechetics, were high on the Church's Washington agenda.

Appointments of dissenters as advisors to bishops, or as lecturers in episcopal assemblies, workshops, clergy conferences, seminaries, or as drafters of Church documents, with *Origins* giving more than ample dissemination to their views, have created the impression that a counter-magisterium (John Paul II's term) has achieved a certain legitimacy. The basic principle of the natural law is "Do good and avoid evil." In Christian language this axiom may be rephrased to say "Reward the good, punish the evil." The Roman Missal celebrates 200 saints on the altars of the Western Church, most of whom were confessors or just holy people, a third of them shedding their blood for the faith. It is difficult to reconcile a great deal of what goes on within many Catholic institutions or in chancery offices with the daily prayer of the Church.

>   *5. Bishops ought to provide well-advertised support for Catholic colleges and universities that have kept their Catholic identity in the fullest sense, and exhort and assist all others to preserve, enhance or recover their commitment to the Catholic Church and her faith. Institutions that have abandoned their Catholic commitment should be identified.*

Moreover, the Catholic University of America must be a paradigm for truly Catholic higher education. This it has not been since 1965. Bishops should restore confidence in its faculties of Catholic theology, philosophy, and canon law, which have been pontifically certified. They should not permit the work of such faculties to be offset by other schools, particularly of religious studies, where dissent often reigns. Teaching in all seminaries should be conducted in full accordance with Church doctrines and norms. No theories should be presented for possible acceptance at Catholic colleges and universities that are manifestly in conflict with binding Church doctrines and norms. Bishops cannot supervise unless they know what is going on in Catholic colleges, and often they do not want to know. Their most dangerous antagonists may be those of whom Christ spoke sarcastically: "This people honors me with their lips, but their hearts are far from me. In vain do they worship me, teaching as doctrines human precepts." (Mt. 15, 8–9).

> *6. Only those persons who have a significant public record of active fidelity to the Church's teaching office should be appointed to Church positions, especially at the episcopal level. All practices that tend to demean or weaken Church authority should be reviewed and revised as necessary. The requirements of religious garb for priests and religious when "on duty" would be a fitting beginning of reform.*

> *7. Since the state of the Church is no better than the state of her parishes, diocesan ordinaries must review all policies and practices already in place to ensure that these enhance the sacred status of pastors in particular, and of parish priests in general. Any custom that secularizes a priest's divinely conferred status and role should be reversed.*

Pastors must be held to account for their stewardship in a consistent manner. As a general rule, however, their word, supported by the bishop, should bind curates and those religious who serve under them. Priests must be assigned to pastors already trained to live an exemplary life and to serve them in obedience. Bishops should be friendly with all their priests, but with their pastors especially, those who have ordinary, not delegated, jurisdiction in their respective territory.

A man or woman of authority may technically be a superior, but he or she is also a person of presence. Great leaders exude presence. No one takes them for granted or underestimates who they are. Those to the office born share one notable characteristic of Jesus. They act like men of authority.

Men of authority, when they are good at what they are supposed to do, bear with equanimity the suffering that goes with their office. These men are often held in awe, even by those who do not like them. When Cardinal Manning spoke, the British prime minister listened. When Cardinal Hayes blessed churchgoers, they automatically fell to their knees. When Cardinal Dougherty told his flock what he thought of the *Philadelphia Enquirer*'s publisher, the man took a vacation. During the exercise of their episcopal office, provincials and college presidents bowed in their direction, not the other way around.

To Recapitulate

It is a sin to trivialize the revolution going on within the Catholic Church by calling it a tug of war between those who have institutional authority and those who claim charismatic power over its destiny. or as between higher clergy and lower clergy. or as a variation in the clericalism/laicism battles which plagued Europe a century before Martin Luther. If any of these were the case, the only question would be: Who runs the Church? And the modern answer might be equally simple – a priest democrat or his equivalent, certainly not a priest monarch. Recently, the *Boston College Magazine* posed the dilemma this way: "Pluralist Democracy the Greatest Challenge to Catholicism – America is the Test Case." In that journalistic circle, the contrast was two neighboring pastorates: one clearly governed and dominated by a priest-pastor, the other chaired by a nun "pastoral/administrator" (with a circuit-riding priest on part-time duty for sacramental purposes) who shared the management of the Catholic community with representatives of the people.

The stereotyping is inexact, of course, false in many cases. But is "management style" the source of the Church's depression? Or would lay trustees be its salvation?

The present Catholic war is not driven by the old clericalism v. laicism dichotomy. These were derogatory terms invented to indict clerics who invaded the laity's worldly turf, or laity who took possession of the sanctuary. The most zealous laicists were often priests and popes who cheerfully sacrificed Christ for the favors of secular princes. Unadulterated laicists really did not become "trustees" of the Catholic Church until the French Revolution, when Humanity became god, and the secular state appeared as its church. Sociology became the queen of the sciences, and reading people's minds – or that of the likes of Jean Jacques Rousseau – developed into the new revelation. At various times lay trustees ran major segments of the Church – with the encouragement and consent of the clergy – to the detriment of pious Catholicity.

Whenever the City of Man or any of its proxies stands over the City of God, the state sets the norms for the Church's acceptable behavior. Sins against humanity, politically understood, take precedence over sins against God, the bible disappears from classrooms, counseling rooms replace the confessional box, and less and less do priests wear the Roman collar. Divine revelation is taught under the rubric "mythology," especially subjects like the Assumption, which, according to Pius XII, has Mary "sitting in splendor at the right hand of her Son."

This kind of "laicism" pervades post-Vatican II Catholicity, especially among priest theologians, who aver without shame that definitions or decrees of the Pope have no standing in the Catholic community anymore – on their own merit – unless they are validated by the learned societies or by the people or by the equivalent of an ecumenical council, whose documents are subject afterwards to broad interpretation. Lay theologians, who now form the majority of the Catholic academe, are beyond censure by priests, it is said, even it they, without sense of sin or guilt, consider a faith declaration of the pope (e.g., his declaration on priestly ordination), as non-binding on their consciences, of no more religious significance than the papal position on the international status of Jerusalem. This imbalance calls for correction.

What happens under the influence of secularism (laicism) to those two neighboring pastorates, mentioned earlier? What if one continues to believe and practice what the Church teaches and commands, while the second believes (because the local pastor does) in women priests, contraception, that the Church should got out of sex-or-marriage business, that general absolution is preferable to the "confessional box," that invalidly married Catholics, even non-Catholics, may receive the Eucharist in good faith because Communion merely symbolizes Christ's presence, that Mary was not a virgin *in perpetuum*, that nothing that a pope says is irreformable really is?

Does not a state of war then exist between priests? And against the pope? That war must be won by bishops.

If the latter parish is a legitimate *status quo* in Catholicity, would not the Catholic condition reflect more than Charles Morris' "organizational pathology" and really represent Christian hypocrisy? Is that *status quo* thinkable in an American Church which once acquired preeminence in the living Body of Christ?

A Final Word

The idea of a "second spring" is as ridiculous to a secularist as the story of Pentecost itself. The present trouble for the Christian is that today's world of the West thinks secularist – even the poor, who were better off with a modicum of Christian faith.

Sooner or later the Catholic Church must cease trying to make unconscionable deals with secularists. They are unlikely converts in the first place, absolute as they are in this-worldism and in the conviction that Catholicity is the opiate of the people.

The Church can no more proselytize a John Dewey-type than a Stalinist. If the Church by chance did reach into the soul of any one of them, it would be the Church of her creeds, not the Church of her unfortunate compromises. Ecclesiastical history is strewn with fallout of misdeals with Henry VIII, Jansenius and his followers, and Alfred Firmin Loisy. Today, Vatican II has been misused to justify divesting religious congregations of their contemplative element, colleges of their commitment to their community's state of grace, academics of their "obedience of faith." Even the Council's calls for better inter-credal cooperation and the reconstruction of the social order are being used by elites to finesse unlawful compromises with articles of the Creed and the Ten Commandments. As if Christ stood idly by while the Scribes and the Pharisees, occasionally one or the other of his Apostles, tried to water down the meaning of his words. As if there are any high Protestant churches left to verify the missionary success of such diluted Catholicity.

Christ is the center of Catholicity. So are the pope and bishops in union with him. Secularized Catholics want the center to be moved their way. In former days, the obstreperous left the Church on their own, while contumacious public offenders were invited to desist or leave. Freedom was properly exercised on both sides of the Catholic spectrum. Today, however, virulent critics of Catholic faith and moral norms insist on holding office in the Church and making bishops bow to them – no matter what this reversal of roles does to the faith or the faithful. Not long ago, when the conduct of unruly college presidents came under public discussion, Denver's young Archbishop Charles Chaput made this comment at a bishops' meeting, saying in essence: "We are worried about them, whereas they should be worried about us." The Holy See made this precise point ten years earlier, chiding American bishops for their over-concern about the feelings of theologians than about their objective wrongdoing.

Restoring order to an unruly community involves profound political wisdom. Civil society rarely handles riots well, and, in the present circumstances, the Church may face one or two such upheavals. The exercise of responsible authority always involves risks. Condemnations and punishments have their place in any society where civilization rules, even if they do not rid all the streets of all evildoers. At times, aroused public opinion, stimulated by competent leaders, does more for public sanity than the force of law. It is amazing what patriotism does for national unity when properly aroused. In the nineteenth century bishops were quite good in stirring up pride in the Catholic faith against Protestant crusaders. Why not against Knight Templars of the Secularist Order?

It the pope is lucky enough to find good opinion-molders on his episcopal slates, he might be doubly blessed with archbishops of superior governing quality, who undertake in his name the oversight of suffragan ordinaries. Once upon a time, archbishops had substantial influence within their region and were not above chiding a suffragan for neglect or malfeasance in office. Today, the spirit of autonomy has so infected some bishops that it would be a hearty archbishop indeed who would challenge misbehavior of a suffragan. Yet, if unused, the archepiscopal structure itself is useless. And what of the apostolic nuncio who is the pope's vicar general?

In times of upheaval, being a bishop or pope is never easy. At the end of the sixth century, Pope St. Gregory, called the Great, laid out the choices facing Catholic hierarchy in crisis: "A spiritual guide should be silent as discretion requires, and speak when words are of service. . . . An imprudent silence may leave in error those who could have been taught. Pastors who lack foresight hesitate to say openly what is right because they fear losing the favor of men. As the voice of truth tells us such leaders are not zealous pastors who protect their flocks, rather they are like mercenaries who flee by taking refuge in silence when the wolf appears."

The battle to keep the American Church a beacon for the Church Universal, fully and faithfully, is far from lost. But it is not going to be won without unusual bishops and a remarkable Peter.

Appendix

Response of the Congregation of the Doctrine of the Faith
to U.S. Bishops on "Doctrinal Responsibilities."
(*Origins*, November 24, 1988)

The text of the observations by Archbishop Alberto Bovone, secretary of
the Vatican Congregation for the Doctrine of the Faith, follows discussing
the proposed text titled "Doctrinal Responsibilities: Approaches to
Promoting Cooperation and Resolving Misunderstandings Between
Bishops and Theologians." (November 10, 1988).

I. General Observations
The proposed document is not without its praiseworthy aspects, particularly in that area where it highlights the specific and different roles of
bishops and theologians, underlining the need for mutual cooperation (pp.
8–18).

We are perplexed, nonetheless, by the realization that the entire third
part of the document, which is dedicated to the formal doctrinal dialogue,
seems to place bishops and theologians on the same level. This lacks
coherence with previous indications regarding the different roles of the
two subjects.

In reality, an attitude which tends to equate bishops and theologians
appears to inspire the whole orientation of the document, since from the
Preface itself (p. 4, line 21) it is stated that "Doctrinal Responsibilities" is
"an instrument for promoting cooperation and for helping to resolve
theological questions between bishops and theologians." On page 5 there

is further clarification of the term "questions" as "unnecessary disputes" (line 11) and "doctrinal disputes between bishops and theologians in dioceses" (line 15). At lines 20–25 it is stated even more explicitly: "The recommended structures . . . for resolving doctrinal disputes draw upon experience already acquired by the church in the United States for building a spirit of collaboration and resolving conflicts. They are designed to address the special problems of disputes of a doctrinal nature.

It is precisely throughout the third part of the document, however, which is titled "A Possibility for Formal Doctrinal Dialogue," that the equalizing attitude emerges most evidently. From the opening lines (p. 31, lines 9 ff.) it is said that between bishops and theologians "there may be difference of opinion, disagreements or questions concerning doctrinal matters." On page 39, line 15 f., it is further stated that "disputes between theologians and members of the ecclesiastical magisterium are usually complex and may involve deep feelings." Even if on page 32, line 1 f., it is said that "each would participate according to his respective role in the church," the two parties in the dialogue are practically placed on the same level, as is clear, above all, from the terminology. In Paragraph B which introduces the "participants" (in the dialogue), at page 33, line 10 ff., it reads: "The theologian or bishop who requests the use of this formal dialogue is termed the 'initiating party.' The other partner who agrees to this formal dialogue is termed the 'second party.'"

One can also see some practical consequences emerging, for example, in the description of the role of other persons involved in the dialogue. On page 34, line 12 f., concerning experts it is said that "if experts are unanimous in agreement, the parties should not reject their opinion without grave reason." Here, above all, the experts come to have a prevalent position even in regard to that of a bishop.

On page 36, line 5 f., regarding the dialogue's format, the possibility of a "contact person" is introduced whose primary function is "to determine whether the request for dialogue is legitimate" (p. 37, line 5 f.). This provision empowers a third person to judge whether, hypothetically, even the request of the bishop is legitimate or not.

II. Particular Observations

On page 16, line 16: "The documents of tradition"; perhaps it would be better to state explicitly the particular value of the documents of the magisterium among the documents of tradition.

On page 24, line 16 f.: "A small committee" is proposed, to which eventual complaints about theologians will eventually be sent and which could evaluate these complaints in first instance. Isn't there a risk that this will create an obstacle to free access to the bishop for every one of the faithful?

On page 25, lines 7–8: "Respecting the legitimate concerns of the American system of higher education." Doesn't this limitation to the imparting of correct doctrine risk being used in terms restrictive of Catholic identity?

Page 27, line 26 f.: Dealing with the "theological consultants" of the bishop, it states: "The competence of theologians who serve in any consultative capacity should be recognized by their peers." Doesn't this limit the freedom of the bishop?

On page 28, line 5 f., it is added that there are advantages in "making public the names of consultants and perhaps even the selection process." Doesn't this too limit the freedom of the bishop?

On page 32, line 5 f.: "If a bishop is to make a final determination of his view of a theologian's teaching, he must present objective grounds for doing so." Doesn't this statement bind too much the autonomy of the bishop?

On page 44, line 17 ff. Here too the role of the church's magisterium is presented. Would it not be helpful in this context to mention explicitly the documents of the Congregation for the Doctrine of the Faith and illustrate their specific value?

III. Concluding Observations

The impression one gets from the quotations cited and from the entire document is that it tends to formulate the problem of the relationship between bishop and theologian principally as a question that concerns the subjective level and, thus, as a problem of the defense of the rights of the persons involved. At the same time the question of the objective level of the content remains on a secondary level. It is on this level of the content that the bishop (especially when one treats of subjects already dealt with by the magisterium) has, for the good of the faithful, an ultimate and specific responsibility.

> *(At a press conference following the session of the 1988 fall bishops' meeting at which the delay of the proposed document on bishops and theologians was discussed, Archbishop Oscar Lipscomb of Mobile, Ala., said he thought there was a "misreading of the intent and content of the paper" by the doctrinal congregation.*

Lipscomb, who guided much of the document's development, is succeeding Bishop Raymond Lessard of Savannah, Ga., as chairman of the. U.S. bishops' Committee on Doctrine. He said that in its objections the doctrinal congregation "misrepresents" the nature of the doctrinal dialogue treated in the guidelines.

In a joint statement the presidents of the Catholic Theological Society of America and the Canon Law Society of America expressed "regret" that the document had been delayed and "surprise" that the Vatican comments "arrived so very late and ... appear to have been done in haste. "

(Father John Boyle, president of the theological society, and Vincentian Father Paul Golden, canon law society president, said their societies would continue to assist the doctrine committee and the bishops' conference "in any way they think appropriate as the consideration of 'Doctrinal Responsibilities' continues.") 11-24-88.

Notes

1. The Catholic Crisis

1. The Chancellor of the Archdiocese of Chicago summarized these declines from 1965 to 1995. Priests from 35,925 to 32,834, brothers from 12,271 to 6,578, sisters from 179,954 to 92,107, seminarians from 48,992 to 5,083. Also, 52,877 fewer adult baptisms. 280,719 fewer infant baptisms, 47,073 fewer Catholic weddings. Annulments grew from 338 in 1968 to 52,000 in 1983. Catholic high schools from 2, 465 in 1965 to 1,350 in 1995, elementary schools from 10,503 in 1965 to 6,911 in 1995 and a loss of enrollment of 2,526,892 students. See Fr. Thomas J. Paprocki, STL, JCD, JD, "Reforming the Reform." *Religious Life* (February 1996). Fr. Paprocki was ordained in 1978.

2. Former Jesuit Peter Hebblethwaite, as early as 1975, coined this phrase for the title of one of his books.

3. A 1995 publication of the National Catholic Educational Association

4. *Origins* (October 26, 1995), pp. 327 ff.

5. See his address to the 30th General Assembly of Bishops in 1957: *The Pope Speaks,* (Spring, 1958).

6. Joseph Becker, S.J., *The Re-Formed Jesuits,* Ignatius Press, 1992.

7. In *What Is a Catholic College?* (America Press, 1956).

8. See the Church's claim to independence from this state in Vatican II's *Dignitatis Humanae* (On Religious Freedom), No. 13.

9. Human Manifestos I and II (Prometheus Books, 1973).

10. Brownson's *Quarterly Review* (October 1845)

11. ·See his *Mere Creatures of the State?* (Crisis Books, 1994)

12. For a brilliant exposition of this unfolding secularist drama, read Paul Mankowski, S.J., in *Church and State in America: Catholic Questions*, ed. by George A. Kelly (St. John's University Edition, 1992), p. 213.

13. *London Tablet* (June 10, 1996).

14. See his *Roman Catholic Modernism* (Stanford University Press, 1970, pp. 66–67).

15. ·Marvin R. O'Connell, *Critics on Trial: An Introduction to the Catholic Modernist Crisis* (Catholic University of America Press, 1994), p. 370.

16. See Harvey Cox, *The Secular City* (Macmillan, 1965); and a Catholic response to post-Vatican II developments within the Church; Donald J. D'Elia and Stephen M. Krason, *We Hold These Truths and More: Further Reflections on the American Proposition* (Franciscan University Press, 1993).

17. *Religious Education* (Spring 1997), p. 15.

2. The Catholic Bishop

1. Cf. Richard Shaw, *Dagger John* (Paulist Press, 1977), pp. 369–70.

2. Dietrich von Hildebrand, *Trojan Horse in the City of God* (Sophia Institute Press, 1993), p. 273.

3. *Dei Verbum*, n. 10.

4. Gerald O'Collins, S.J. (Paulist Press).

5. See Lawrence Cardinal Shehan's treatment of the "nuances" of Raymond E. Brown in *Homiletic and Pastoral Review* (November 1975), pp. 10–23.

3. Catholic Bishops and the Church's Law

1. See his admonition to the *Canon Law Society of Great Britain and Ireland* in *Origins* (June 4, 1992), p. 59.

2. The official language of the *Code* is Latin, whose terminology has acquired precise meaning over centuries. Informed Catholics know today that the Code's English translation is simply an interpretation of the Latin. The wrong English word chosen for the Latin redefines a well-understood concept. Consider, for example, the word "bishop," which derives from the Greek word "episcopos." The latter has Attic roots which means "to oversee" or "to watch over." If one reads the canons carefully, "watchman" is not exactly what a bishop is. Yet, the word "overseer" in American English evokes memories of the straw boss on an antebellum plantation which is hardly what the Church expects of a bishop today, or any day. Therefore, the word "bishop" must be defined

within the context of meanings specified in Canons 378–459 which pertain to the Church's hierarchy.

3. *Origins* (May 24), 1971.

4. Cns 76–78.

5. Cn. 378.

6. *Cf* Cn. 381, where it is called "ordinary, proper, and immediate."

7. *Cf.* Cns. 383–84.

8. Cn. 386.

9. Cf. Cns. 391 and 378.

10. Cf. Cn 394.

11. Cf. Cns. 396–400.

12. Cf. Cns. 436–38.

13. Cf. Cns. 447–60.

14. *Origins* (April 13, 1995).

4. The Present Episcopal Dilemma

1. Cf. Msgr. Francis Weber, *The Life and Times of Francis A. Cardinal McIntyre 1886–1979* (St. Francis Historical Society, 1997), p. 405.

2. Cf. James Hitchcock, "Conservative Bishops, Liberal Results," *Catholic World Report* (May 1996).

3. *American Historical Review* (June 1972), p. 640.

4. *America* (September 1, 1974).

5. *Origins* (April 22, 1993).

6. *Washington Post* Magazine (March 27, 1987).

7. *National Catholic Register* (July 9, 1995).

8. *The Economist* (April 14, 1984

9. *Insight* (July 28, 1986).

10. *First Things* (February 1995).

11. Philip Gleason, *Keepinq the Faith: American Catholicism Past and Present* (University of Notre Dame Press, 1987), pp. 158–59.

12. George Marsden, *The Soul of the American University* (Oxford University Press, 1994), pp. 175–76, 263.

13. This subject is treated by J. Brian Benestad, *The Pursuit of a Just Social Order 1966–1980* (Ethics and Public Policy Center, 1982); and by Michael Warner, *Changing Witness 1917–1994* (Eerdmans, 1995).

5. The Priest – Shepherd or Hired Hand?

1. See Explanatory Note appended to *Lumen Gentium* which makes clear that papal collegiality with bishops is not intended to prevent the pope from acting on his own.

2. *Origins* (October 11, 1984).

3. In 1789 there was one priest for every 1,000 Catholics. By 1939 the ratio was down to 1:600. By 1989 it was back up to 1:1,100, without assessment that large numbers of foreign-born extern priests are now serving American Catholics on a month-by-month basis

4. John Talbot Smith, *The Catholic Church in New York* (Hall and Locke Co., 1905), p. 470.

5. Peter Guilday, *History of the Councils of Baltimore* (Macmillan, 1932), p. 185. Guilday explained the beginnings as follows: "Uniformity of discipline was the principal need of the score of years which followed the (first episcopal) meeting of 1810. It was not easy of attainment for misrule had spread under incompetent leadership in New York, Philadelphia, and New Orleans. The Church here during the period of its infancy was sadly hampered by the presence of priests who knew not how to obey and laity who were interpreting their share of Catholic life by non-Catholic Church systems."

6. Canon 652 of the *New Code* still looks upon "stability" as normative; "The pastor ought to possess stability in office and therefore he is to be named for an indefinite period of time; the diocesan bishop can name him for a certain period of time only if a decree of the Conference of Bishops has permitted this."

7. The doubts and challenges, as well as the factual situations, vary with the personnel and the diocese, priests and religious stonewalling authority more than laity (unless they be academics or teacher representatives), American-born more than foreign-born.

8. Cf. The Ratzinger Report (Ignatius Press, 1985), p. 45.

9. For a simple review of these theories, see Patrick J. Dunn, *Priesthood: A Reexamination of the Roman Catholic Theology of the Presbyterate* (Alba House, 1990), pp. 232 ff.

10. See *Origins* (July 4, 1974).

11. A Religious News Service report Christmas week 1996 has Andrew Greeley still defining the internal schism in these terms. This is precisely how the issues were joined during the "birth control fight."

12. *Origins* (June 16, 1982), p. 119

13. Even the attempt to resist the use of the word "presbyter" for "priest" was rejected to avoid prolonging the overall approval process,

14. See minutes of NCCB's Executive Session, June 22, 1996, Portland, Oregon.

15. *Casti Connubii, No. 27–* .

16. Seven popes, all French, lived in this small town – outside of Italy and Rome from 1309 to1378.

17. See E. L. Mascall, *Theology and the Gospel of Christ: An Essay in Reorientation* (SPCK, 1977).

18. A book reviewer in *America* (February 16, 1974), p. 111.

19. *The Splendor of the Church* (Ignatius Press, 1986), p. 265.

6. The Bishops and the University

1. See Paul Fitzgerald, S.J.'s study, *The Governance of Jesuit Colleges in the United States 1920–1970* (University of Notre Dame Press, 1984), Foreword by Theodore Hesburgh, C.S.C.

2. See a summary of this viewpoint in *Origins* (May 23, 1996), p. 11.

3. Ninety four of the 230 are in five states – California, Illinois, Massachusetts, New York, and Pennsylvania.

4. About fifteen with 10,000 students (none with 20,000 enrollment) twenty teaching 5,000+, forty under 5,000 and 150 under 2,500.

5. "Catholic Identity in Institutional Ministries: A Theological Perspective," an unpublished manuscript of an address for the Conference on the Future of Catholic Institutional Ministries at Fordham University (April 21, 1991), p. 18.

6. "The Soul of the American University," *First Things* (January 1991). He developed this theme in a 462-page book with the same title for Oxford University Press in 1994. In Marsden's view the end result of secularization is the undermining of belief in any particular religion as having a divine origin.

7. Classic to the case: John McGrath's *Catholic Institutions in the U.S.: Canonical and Civil Status* (CUA Press, 1969); *The Sectarian College and Public Purse:* Fordham – *A Case Study,* by Walter Gellhorn and R. Kent Greenawalt (Oceana Publications, 1970). This study prepared the Fordham Board for making application to New York State for so-called "Bundy Money," which required the Jesuit university to declare itself non-denominational. The introduction to this work was written by Timothy S. Healy, S.J.

The positions taken by the above authors are rejected by Adam J. Maida in his Ownership Control and Sponsorship of Catholic Institutions (Pennsylvania Catholic Conference, 1975) and Church Property, Church Finances and Church Related Corporations: A Canon Law Handbook (with Nicholas P. Cadarti and the Catholic Health Association of the United States, 1984). Kenneth D. Whitehead's Catholic Colleges and Federal Funding (Ignatius Press, 1988) takes aim at arguments to the effect that the need for government aid or accreditation precludes a juridical connection with the Church. Whitehead argues that the Federal Law permits Catholic colleges to establish their own accrediting agencies, as Jewish institutions have done.

8. See George A. Kelly, *Catholic Higher Education: In or Out of the Church* (Christendom Press, 1992), pp. 13, 44.

9. For the full observations of the Congregation of the Doctrine of the Faith, forwarded by its Secretary, Archbishop Alberto Bovone, see *Origins* (November 14, 1988).

10. *Catholic New York* (June 27, 1996), p. 7

11. *Origins* (March 15, 1990), pp. 669 ff.

12. Cf. John Langan, S.J. ed., *Catholic Universities in Church and Society: A Dialogue on Ex Cordia Ecclesiae* (Georgetown University Press, 1993), p. 29.

13. *The Ratzinger Report* (Ignatius Press, 1985), p. 26.

14. His address, given April 20, 1991, entitled "The Future Catholic Ministries in the 21st Century," was published in *Origins* (May 23, 1991).

15. The new *Code of Canon Law,* published in 1983, in Canons 807–14, asserts that the Church has the right to supervise any university which bears its name, that faculty members who lack pedagogical suitability, integrity of doctrine, or probity of life are to be removed, and that those who teach theology receive a mandate from competent ecclesial authority.

16. Paul VI's address to Jesuit University Rectors, August 6, 1975; *Origins* (September 4, 1975), pp. 176–177.

17. *First Things* (January 1991), p. 7.

18. See Michael Warner's *Changing Witness: Catholic Bishops and Public Policy* 1917–1994 (Eerdmans, 1995) for examples.

19. For a study of the freedom Catholic colleges have to be Catholic, cf.

Kenneth D. Whitehead, *Catholic Colleges and Federal Funding* (Ignatius Press, 1988).

20. An example at work of "downward negotiation" over Church law is the latest advisory of the USCC Committee on Education, headed by Archbishop Francis B. Schulte. This Committee, in charge of *Ex Corde Ecclesiae* Implementation, announced (March 20, 1997) that it will search "for valued advice, support, and participation" from ACCU, Collegium, CTSA, CTS, CLSA, Men and Women Conferences of Religious – all anti-Roman groups on this issue. No voice favorable to the Roman position is mentioned as deserving of attention. For a full review of the,,results of "downward negotiation," confer Joseph M. Becker, S.J., *The Re-Formed Jesuits*, Vols. I and II (Ignatius Press, 1992 and 1997); and Ann Carey, *Sisters in Crisis* (Our Sunday Visitor Press, 1997).

7. The Catholic Bishops at War

1. *Catholic World Report* (March 1996, p. 52).

2. English *Osservatore Romano* (October 26, 1978).

3. "Conservative Bishops, Liberal Results," *Catholic World Report* (May 1995), pp. 21–27.

4. See *Origins* (February 7, 1980).

5. *Crisis* (June 1998), p. 12.

6. "Here lies Community: Deo Gratias," *America* (August 22, 1970), p. 87.

7. *I Confess* (Ave Maria Press, 1972), p. 53.

8. *Discovery Patterns,* Book I, (Paulist Press, 1969), p. 2.

9. See his *Ministry to Word and Sacraments* (Fortress Press, 1976).

10. *Origins* (April 4, 1974).

11. *Origins* (July 13, 1995).

12. Fort Wayne-South Bend diocesan paper, *Today's Catholic* (April 21, 1996).

13. Fr Dulles in *America* (March 27, 1998), p. 13; Fr. McCormick in *Commonweal* (February 27, 1988), p. 15.

14. In two books, *Archbishop* (Harper and Row, 1990) and *Shephers of the Flock* (Sheed and Ward, 1992).

8. John Paul II and Diocesan Bishops

1. *Origins* (March 10, 1994).

2. *London Tablet* (February 25, 1996).

3. Ladislaus Orsy, S.J. and Francis Sullivan, S.J., in *America* (December 9, 1995), pp. 4–6.

4. *Origins* (April 13, 1995).

5. *Santa Clara Today* (April 1982), pp. 4–5.

6. John Paul II, *Reflections on Humanae Vitae* (St. Paul Editions, 1982), pp. 9–10.

7. An English translation of the letter from the Apostolic Signatura to the bishops of Holland appears in *The Jurist,* (1973), pp. 296–300.

8. *Ibid.*, pp. 299–300. Notre Dame's Robert Vasoli recovered this letter which is cited in his book, *What God Has Joined Together: The Annulment Controversy in American Catholicism* (Oxford University Press, 1998).

9. Documentary cases are almost always civil marriages, and presumptively invalid to begin with. Ordinary cases involve marriages witnessed by a priest and are presumptively indissoluble.

10. See James H. Provost, ed., "Clarification concerning Certain Questions about Tribunals in the United States of America," *The Jurist* (1981), pp. 200–201. Provost also insists that our tribunals are makings use of modern science "as directed by recent popes . . . this must not be mistaken as an anti-dissolubility attitude."

11. *Catholic World Report* (February 1996).

9. The Second Spring

1. Cf. Rosemary Reuther, *Journal of Economic Studies* (Winter 1980), p. 66, and Richard McBrien, *National Catholic Reporter* (October 6, 1991).

2. See Robert Nesbit's *The New Despotism.*

3. John Paul II, *Vita Consecrata*, in *Origins* (April 14, 1996), p. 695.

4. *The Long Island Catholic* (April 8, 1996).

5. English *L'Osservatore Romano* (April 28, 1986), p. 12.

Index